14.95

The *Haustlǫng* of Þjóðólfr of Hvinir

Edited with introduction, translation, commentary and glossary by Richard North

Hisarlik Press
1997

Published by Hisarlik Press, 4 Catisfield Road, Enfield Lock,
Middlesex EN3 6BD, UK. Georgina Clark-Mazo and Dr Jeffrey Alan
Mazo, publishers.

British Library Cataloguing-in-Publication data available.

ISBN 1 874312 20 6

5 4 3 2 1

Printed in Great Britain by Antony Rowe Ltd, Chippenham, Wiltshire

To Miriam Isabel

Foreword

Having worked in the harvest on a farm in Hordaland (Eksingedalen, south of the Sognefjord) about seventeen years ago, I am now glad to offer a critical text and interpretation of *Haustlǫng* ('harvest-long'), a poem which may have been composed at the same time of year for a chieftain of this province. In my view there is a need for a new English-language edition and translation of this poem, despite the manifold semantic problems which *Haustlǫng* presents. Given the dearth of knowledge in what the etyma of some Icelandic words really meant in late ninth-century Norway, it will probably be said or in some quarters that a critical text or edition of this poem should not have been attempted lightly, or even at all. There is the overwhelming number of suppositions rather than facts which is necessary if any work on *Haustlǫng*, let alone this one, is to be completed. Yet the subject cannot remain in stasis, and it seems peculiarly ill-advised not to put forward new arguments about *Haustlǫng* when there is a chance that some of them could be right. It is with this acknowledged weakness that I present a new text, translation and commentary of *Haustlǫng*.

Texts of *Haustlǫng* may be found in editions of *Snorra Edda*, the prose treatise in which this poem survives (for examples, Magnús, pp. vi–vii; see Faulkes, *Gylf*, p. xxxiii). For the English-speaker, Anthony Faulkes' translation of *Snorra Edda* (1987) includes one of *Haustlǫng* and offers thereby a scholarly guide to the meaning and prose context of this poem. Yet apart from the metrically faithful (though impossibly archaized) English translation of *Haustlǫng* by Lee M. Hollander (1945, pp. 38–48, with introduction), little up to now has been written specifically on this poem in English. Outside the context of *Snorra Edda* only Gabriel Turville-Petre's *Scaldic Poetry* (1976) offers both a critical text and English translation of this poem, and then no more than st. 7–10. In other languages the preservation of *Haustlǫng* has fared better. In Swedish Theodor Wisén produced a text (with a glossary in vol. 2) in *Carmina norrœna ex reliquiis vetustionis norrœnœ poësis*, 2 vols. (Lund, 1886–9), pp. 9–11. The standard text of this poem is Finnur Jónsson's, as part of his *Skjaldedigtning* B (1912–15), with an accompanying Danish paraphrase. Finnur's text is syntactically revised in E.A. Kock's *Skaldediktningen* (1946–9), without paraphrase or translation, but with many supporting commentaries to stanzas scattered throughout Kock's earlier *Notationes Norrœnœ* (1921–41). Kock and Rudolf Meissner also offer a text of stanzas (st.) 6–7 in their *Skaldisches Lesebuch* (Halle a.S., 1931), p. 2. Jón Helgason's anthology of Scaldic poetry includes a text of stanzas 14/5–8 and 15, in *Skjaldevers* (Copenhagen, 1968), p. 39. In Norwegian, Anne Holtsmark edited stanzas 1–13 (1949), translating them with a commentary and exegesis in which she used her wide knowledge of philology and folklore to suggest that *Haustlǫng* reflects a ritual drama, with Hœnir representing Óðinn in his role as god of the dead. Also in Norwegian, indeed with a preference for reading words of the *Landsmål* or *Nynorsk* language back into *Haustlǫng*, Vilhelm Kiil (1959) produced an over-emended text with a knowledgeable but mostly far-fetched commentary of this poem. There is a free but alliteratively metrical *Nynorsk* translation in Hallvard Tveiten, *Norrønne Skaldekvad*, II: *Frå Bjarkemål til Noregs Konungatal* (Oslo, 1966), pp. 14–20. And in German, Edith Marold, in her monograph on early Scaldic kennings (1983), has provided a learned commentary to all kennings represented in *Haustlǫng*. Although her study does not claim to be an edition, Marold's work is cautious, thorough and well informed, and without doubt one of the most useful tools for an interpretation of this poem. There are several supporting studies and references, most of these in the Scandinavian languages, one or two in English. The time seems right in this way to open *Haustlǫng*'s doors to English-speaking readers without these other languages.

My source for the prose contexts of *Haustlǫng* is Jón Sigurðsson's edition of *Snorra Edda* (1848; based on R), which is followed here with an emended orthography. Jón's chapter-arrangement for the *Edda* as a whole differs from that of Finnur (1931) and of Magnús (1952), in that it takes account of the heading *Bragarœður* in an earlier edition of *Snorra Edda* by Rasmus Rask (Stockholm, 1818). Jón lists the chapters of *Bragarœður* (*Sermones Bragii*, 'Bragi's tales', *SnE* I, 206–24) as a sequel to those of *Gylfaginning*, thus as *Gylfaginning*, chs. 55–8 (plus an Epilogue, *SnE* I, 224–8). Finnur and Magnús both list Jón's *Bragarœður* as chs. 1–6 of *Skáldskaparmál*.[1] Thus ch. 1 of Jón's *Skáldskaparmál*, in which Ægir raises the topic of poetry (*skáldskapr*) for the first time, is listed as ch. 7 by Finnur and Magnús in their editions of *Skáldskaparmál*. As I shall illustrate in my Introduction below, Snorri quotes *Haustlǫng* 1–13 at a stage further into the composition of *Skáldskaparmál*, although his prose-adaptation of these verses (the story of Iðunn and Þjazi,

---

[1] Jón's ch. 55 = Finnur's ch. 1; Jón's ch. 56 = Finnur's chs. 2-4; Jón's ch. 57 = Finnur's ch. 5 minus three sentences which Finnur places in his ch. 6; and Jón's ch. 58 = Finnur's ch. 6, with these three sentences.

hereinunder section A) occurs separately and falls early within the *Bragarœður*. Since Jón follows Rask in using *Bragarœður* as a section heading, his chapter-arrangement obliges him to label Snorri's prose-adaptation of *Haustlǫng* 1–13 as an epilogue to *Gylfaginning*, although it could be regarded as a prelude to *Skáldskaparmál*. Jón's is an awkward arrangement, but I have followed his prose-text of *Skáldskaparmál* (including *Bragarœður*) because his edition of *Snorra Edda* is held to be the most useful and more accurate than Finnur's (cf. *Gylf*, p. xxxiii). Jón's text of the Prologue and *Gylfaginning* is not followed here, however. For these crucial works, I follow the edition by Anthony Faulkes (Oxford, 1982), which supersedes all other editions of these opening sections of *Snorra Edda*.

It is my usage in this book to set out stanzas of *dróttkvætt* and other metres not by the half-line, as in Finnur's *Skjaldedigtning*, Íslenzk Fornrit and other sources, but by the full line with caesura, on analogy with the line-format in Neckel's edition of the poetic *Edda* (5th ed., rev. Kuhn, 1983). At the same time I number Old Norse-Icelandic stanzas by the half-line, for which my term throughout is 'line', while I use 'full line' to refer to two consecutive half-lines linked by alliteration (in combinations 1–2, 3–4, 5–6 and 7–8). This usage may appear perverse, but is preferable to listing *Haustlǫng* 1/1, for example, as 1/1a, or 1/1–2 as 1/1, or 1/3–4 as 1/2. The other, older, alternative, to set out *dróttkvætt* stanzas into columns of eight half lines (for which the numbering 1/1, 1/1–2 or 1/3–4 was designed), is undesirable for the simple reason that this format encourages non-Icelandic readers to construe the text, rather than to read it, or to treat it like a crossword, rather than to get to know it by heart. With the eight-line format, in short, any engagement with nuance and textual implication becomes harder. Also worth noting is that the italicization of forms in my text of *Haustlǫng* indicates their emendation from forms in RWT. Square brackets indicate substitution of hypothetical forms where there is a textual lacuna common to all manuscripts that cannot be explained as a scribal abbreviation or carelessness. Both my normalized text and and my accompanying textual notes with diplomatic readings (including variants) are based on Finnur's transcription in *Skj* A I, 16–20, checked against the facsimiles of these three principal manuscripts. I am grateful to Professor Anthony Faulkes for having looked through my list of textual notes at an earlier stage; to Mrs Ursula Dronke; to Mr David Ashurst; and to Mr Jon Grove, whose work on *Þórsdrápa* has proved invaluable. Any errors in this book, of course, are mine. I am grateful to Inma, my wife, for sustaining me while I wrote this book.

RN 30. i. 97

Contents

List of Abbreviations

Akv	*Atlakviða*
AM 748 I and II 4to	Arnamagnæan Institute, Copenhagen, and Árnastofnun, Reykjavík (printed in *SnE* II, 397-494 and 573-627)
AM 757 a 4to	Arnamagnæan Institute, Copenhagen (printed in *SnE* II, 501-72)
Am	*Atlamál*
ANF	*Arkiv för nordisk filologi*
AR	J. de Vries, *Altgermanische Religionsgeschichte*, 2nd ed.
Beo	*Beowulf*
Bdr	*Baldrs Draumar*
Fáf	*Fáfnismál*
Fǫl	*Fjǫlsvinnsmál*
Flat	*Flateyjarbók*, ed. Unger; cited by volume and page number
Fritzner	J. Fritzner, *Ordbog over det gamle norske Sprog*; cited by volume and page number
GD	Saxo Grammaticus, *Gesta Danorum*, ed. Olrik and Ræder
Grím	*Grímnismál*
Guð	*Guðrúnarkviða (I, II, III)*
Gylf	*Gylfaginning*, ed. Faulkes
Hárb	*Hárbarðsljóð*
Háv	*Hávamál*
Helreið	*Helreið Brynhildar*
HHj	*Helgakviða Hjǫrvarðssonar*
HHund	*Helgakviða Hundingsbana* (I, II)
Hym	*Hymiskviða*
Hynd	*Hyndlulióð*
ÍF	Íslenzk Fornrit
Lat	Latin
Lok	*Lokasenna*
LP	*Lexicon Poeticum*, ed. Finnur, 2nd ed.
MoM	*Mál og Minne*
MScan	*Medieval Scandinavia*
NN	E.A. Kock, *Notationes Norrœnæ*
NoB	*Namn och bygd*
Oddr	*Oddrúnargrátr*

OE	Old English
OHG	Old High German
OIce	Old Icelandic
OS	Old Saxon
R	GkS 2367 4to, Royal Library, Copenhagen (*Codex Regius of the Younger Edda*, ed. Wessén)
Saga-Book	*Saga-Book of the Viking Society* (formerly *Club*)
Sigsk	*Sigurðarkviða in skamma*
Ska	*Den norsk-isländska skaldediktningen*, ed. Kock.
Skáld	*Skáldskaparmál*
Skí	*Skírnismál*
Skj	*Den norsk-islandske Skjaldedigtning*, ed. Finnur
SnE	*Edda Snorra Sturlusonar*, ed. Jón *et al.*, 3 vols.; cited by page number (slightly normalised)
SSE	*Snorri Sturluson: Edda*, trans. Faulkes
T	MS No. 1374, University Library, Utrecht (*Codex Trajectinus*, ed. Faulkes)
U	DG 11, University Library, Uppsala (*Uppsala-Handskriften*)
Vaf	*Vafþrúðnismál*
Vsp	*Vǫluspá*
Vǫl	*Vǫlundarkviða*
W	AM 242 fol., Arnamagnæan Institute, Copenhagen (*Codex Wormianus*, ed. Sigurður)
Þrym	*Þrymskviða*

Introduction

'Northern pastoral' is my term for the genre of *Haustlǫng*, despite the now standard designation of this work as a 'shield-poem'. This other generic category is inferred from the opening of the poem and from the refrain in stanzas (st.) 13 and 20, in which the poet, Þjóðólfr of Hvinir (*fl. c.* 885 – *c.* 920), sets out to thank or repay a certain Þorleifr for his gift of a shield by describing a number of scenes depicted thereon. Yet Þjóðólfr's new shield, though an important element in our understanding of *Haustlǫng*, is incidental to the question of what kind of poem this is, for the shield represents an occasion, not a genre. To find out the genre of *Haustlǫng*, and to consider the Norwegian world of Þjóðólfr, its late-ninth-century poet, are questions which must wait until due reference has been made to *Snorra Edda*, the thirteenth-century prose work in which *Haustlǫng* has come down to us. So I shall begin with a sketch of *Snorra Edda*, its Icelandic author and the contents of this treatise, before offering an interpretation of the content, style and genre of *Haustlǫng*. Thereafter I shall attempt to outline the poet's life, then to demonstrate two possible routes by which this poem could have been brought to Iceland and thence handed down into the learned pages of *Snorra Edda* in the early thirteenth century. The final part of this introduction consists of my discussion and quotation of those tales of Snorri which accompany scenes from *Haustlǫng* — prose contexts for which the glossary of *Haustlǫng* at the end of this book is also intended.

The *Edda*, a tripartite treatise on Old Norse-Icelandic poetry, is the work for which Snorri Sturluson is now best known. Snorri was a colourful figure in his own day (*c.* 1179–1241), when he was known as a lawspeaker, landowner and political intriguer, as well as a writer.[1] As a school-pupil of antiquarian interests, he may have begun to compile Old Icelandic poetic records already in the last decade of the twelfth century, while he was still fostered with the kindred of Jón Loptsson at Oddi *c.* 1183–97. About a year before the new century, Snorri married into money and settled in Borg (once the home of Egill Skalla-Grímsson; see below). In *c.* 1206 he left his wife and moved to Reykjaholt, which re-

---

[1] For a recent account of Snorri's life and works, see Whaley, *Heimskingla*, pp. 29–40.

mained his home from that day forth. He served the first of two terms as the lawspeaker in 1215–18 (the second was *c.* 1222–31/5), then made the first of two visits to Norway. Having travelled there and also in Sweden for a couple of years, Snorri probably embarked on parts of the *Edda* on his return: first, the *Háttatal* ('list of metres', now known as *Edda* part III), a poem of 102 stanzas exemplifying Scaldic metres and praising the two rulers of Norway, Hákon and his father-in-law and regent Jarl Skúli, with both of whom Snorri had stayed; second, the *Skáldskaparmál* ('Poetics', now *Edda* part II), a discourse with abundant quotation and paraphrase on the many types of 'kennings' or periphrases to be found in Scaldic poetry; and third, *Gylfaginning* ('The Beguiling of Gylfi', now *Edda* part I), a mythography based mostly on quoted and paraphrased Eddic poems in which King Gylfi of Sweden learns of the Norse gods, their creation, adventures and destruction, apparently from three of their descendants; in addition, Snorri or a different author wrote a Prologue to this compilation in which the Norse gods are euhemerized as Trojans who migrated to northern Europe.[2] Snorri wrote the *Edda* in order to encourage young poets in the composition of verse in older Scaldic metres, probably as a reaction to the growing import of French and German romances from Norway. The name *Edda* was later given by mistake to the poems in Codex Regius (GkS 2365 4to, now in the Árni Magnússon Institute in Reykjavík), when this codex was discovered in an Icelandic farmhouse in 1643: hence the distinction between 'prose *Edda*' and 'poetic *Edda*'.[3] Hence, also, the use of the term 'Scaldic' to denote occasional verse of which the poets are usually named; and the use of 'Edd(a)ic' to refer to anonymous balladic mythological and heroic poems which are preserved mostly in Codex Regius. *Edda* is likely to mean 'great-grandmother', the literal meaning of this Icelandic word, the desired implication being that Snorri learnt Eddic and Scaldic poems when he was small and at his great-grandmother's knee. Other interpretations of the name *Edda* have been offered, but they seem arti-

---

[2]See Faulkes, *Gylf*, pp. xii–xxix, and 'The Sources of *Skáldskaparmál*: Snorri's Intellectual Background', in *Snorri Sturluson: Kolloquium anlässlich der 750. Wiederkehr seines Todestages*, ed. A. Wolf (Tübingen, 1993), pp. 59–76; also U. Dronke and P. Dronke, 'The Prologue of the Prose *Edda*: Explorations of a Latin Background', in *Sjötíu Ritgerðir helgaðar Jakob Benediktssyni*, ed. Einar G. Pétursson and Jónas Kristjánsson (Reykjavík, 1977), pp. 153–76 (also published in *Myth and Fiction*, no. III).

[3]Jónas, *Eddas and Sagas*, pp. 25–6.

ficial or figurative by comparison: that *Edda* derives from *óðr* ('poem') and means 'poetics' literally; that it derives from Lat *edo* (on analogy with Faroese *kredda* from Lat *credo*) and means 'edition'; or that it is related to the form of *Oddi*, the estate of Sæmundr *inn fróði* ('the learned') Sigfússon (1056–1133), where it is likely that Snorri learnt much of the native poetry that he quotes and discusses in *Gylfaginning* and *Skáldskaparmál*.[4] The name *Edda* is used to define Snorri's treatise only at the head of the Uppsala-manuscript of *Snorra Edda*, *c.* 1300 (cf. *Gylf*, pp. xiii–iv).

Besides his *Edda*, Snorri wrote a history of the first saint of Scandinavia, King Óláfr *inn digri* ('the fat') Haraldsson (ruled *c.* 1016–30), in two versions, the second of which he augmented with histories of the other kings of Norway from the alleged origin of the Vestfold dynasty to just before the reign of Sverrir (1184–1202), with reference to older historical works.[5] Today this larger compilation is known as *Heimskringla*. In addition, it is believed that Snorri wrote *Egils saga Skalla-Grímssonar*, a biography of a tenth-century Icelandic farmer, warrior and poet, possibly after he had completed *Heimskringla* and following his second visit to Norway in 1237–9.[6] It is the *Edda*, however, which is Snorri's best-known work and also the major source today for any study of Old Norse-Icelandic poetry and mythology. *Haustlǫng* is preserved in this work, in two sections in *Skáldskaparmál*, in the following way:

(A) Prose version of *Haustlǫng* 1–13 (*Gylfaginning*, chs. 55–6)
(B) Prose version, then a quotation, of *Haustlǫng* 14–20 (*Skáld*, ch. 17)
(C) Prose introduction to a quotation of *Haustlǫng* 1–13 (*Skáld*, ch. 22)

Herein the CB sequence of *Haustlǫng* may be justified on two accounts: first, the question in st. 1/1–2 (*Hvé skalk góðs at gjǫldum gunnveggjar brú leggja?*) and the description of the poet gazing on the shield appear to open Þjóðólfr's poem; second, the shield-kenning in st. 13/5–6 (*fjalla Finns ilja brú*) anticipates the story of Hrungnir in the sequence st. 14–20, which must therefore follow 1–13. Since st. 20 ends with no greater final flourish than a copy of the refrain in 13/7–8, it seems probable that Þjóðólfr composed *Haustlǫng* with one or more further sections which

[4]Cf. F. Wagner, 'Que signifie le mot "Edda"?', *Revue belge de philologie et d'histoire* 18 (1939), 962–4; Anthony Faulkes, 'Edda', *Gripla* 2 (1977), 32–9; Sigurður, *Snorri Sturluson*, pp. 22–3.
[5]Jónas, *Eddas and Sagas*, pp. 147–78, esp. 168–78.
[6]*Ibid.*, pp. 265–70, esp. 269; R. West, 'Snorri Sturluson and *Egils Saga*: Statistics of Style', *Scandinavian Studies* 52 (1980), 163–93.

have not survived. Two other, widely dispersed, poems which are known
almost all from *Snorra Edda* and which also claim pictures as their source,
Bragi Boddason's *Ragnarsdrápa* (c. 850, a shield) and Úlfr Uggason's
Húsdrápa (c. 995, carvings on kitchen panels), are also likely to have
come down to us incomplete. With *Haustlǫng*, as with these other poems, it may have been the episodic quality of shield-poems that caused
Þjóðólfr's posterity to drop other section(s) out of recitation by chance,
or by design. In the text of *Haustlǫng* that we have, however, it is possible to see Þjóðólfr as a poet of some character for there is evidence in
this poem of a dynamic sense of imagery, sardonic wit and a distinctly
satirical disposition towards the gods whose cults he must have attended
no less than any other social men and women of his day.

SYNOPSIS OF *HAUSTLǪNG*

The narrative of *Haustlǫng* opens with an image of Þjazi, a giant transformed into an eagle, flying towards three wayfaring Æsir, Óðinn, Loki
and Hœnir, as these gods prepare to roast an ox in an earth-oven cooking-fire (st. 2). Since Þjazi is described as a thief, the wolf who steals a
lady (*snótar ulfr*, 2/2), it appears to be his aim as acknowledged from the
start to rob the gods of Iðunn. This lady is probably to be understood as
an aspect of Freyja, a goddess on whom the gods rely for their youth and
fertility – and in this stanza, it seems, for their meal, since Þjóðólfr
relates the ox to Freyja when he calls it the horse of Gefn who gives the
harvest (*ár-Gefnar mar*, 2/6). Þjazi settles down in a tree nearby and
waits, at first unnoticed by the Æsir.

In st. 3–6 the poet shifts to the scene as viewed from the gods' perspective. Today the Æsir are careless: economizing on trickery, Þjóðólfr
says, although, as defenders of all the gods, they should be vigilant
(*vélsparir varnendr goða*, 4/7–8). The trickery in question is Þjazi's witchcraft, through which the ox-meat stays uncooked and is hard to cut off
the bone (*tormiðlaðr meðal beina*, 3/1–2). Óðinn, in his role as the gods'
educator or informant (*hapta snytrir*, 3/3), is alert enough to say that
something has caused the problem (*hvat því valda*, 3/3–4), but it is not
clear that any of these Æsir see a connection with the eagle, even when
Þjazi begins to speak from the tree. In these stanzas we see Þjazi thus not
with the poet's objectivity – as a vulture with a worn-out coat (*í gemlis
ham gǫmlum*, 2/3) – but through the complacent eyes of individual Æsir,
whose *amour propre* influences the manner in which both they and Þjazi
are described. So, from Óðinn's warlike point of view, the scene is swiftly

tranformed into a field on the eve of battle: as if with his ravens Huginn and Muninn, Óðinn *hjalmfaldinn*, the 'helmeted' war-god (3/4), prepares to augur a solution to the cooking problem from a seagull of the surf of the slaughter-heap (*mǫr valkastar bǫru*, 3/6), a carrion-bird which he spies in the branches of a withered fir-tree (*fornum polli*, 3/8). For his own part, Loki is reluctant to welcome the unexpected eagle (*vasat hǫnum hollr*, 3/7–8), perhaps because he wishes to protect his friend Hœnir. Hœnir is a minor god whose name, not to mention his heroic self-esteem as one who steps like the progeny of mighty Þórr (*fet-Meili*, 4/2) when he faces the eagle, suggests that he is imagined as a cockerel. As a domesticated bird, Hœnir might have reason to fear the wild bird of prey, for it is to Hœnir, not Óðinn, that Þjazi speaks when he asks the puffed-up farmyard fowl to deal him his fill from the holy plate, probably from Hœnir's own diminutive portion (*fyllar sér deila af helgum skutli*, 4/1–3). Loki, presumably under orders from Óðinn the raven-god (*hrafnásar vinr*, 4/4), blows on the fire – this job being as yet the only portion he can hope for – and so adds a new feeling of ill-will to the resentment he harbours towards the eagle for his mockery of little Hœnir. But even Loki fails to realise that the eagle is truly a giant. At the same time, Þjazi's size and ferocity become clear when he sinks down from the tree. While in our view the scene appears to shift to an oceanic world in which Þjazi suddenly takes on the size and menace of a killer whale, a warlike prince of wind-dolphins (*ving-rǫgnir vagna vígfrekr*, 4/5–6), the Æsir are too busy with their own affairs to see the eagle for what he is, a giant and their enemy.

In st. 5 the mood changes, becoming warmer and more secure. There is another shift in figurative scenery to the inside of a crowded hall in which the ebullient Óðinn, lord of the land and handsome among his thegns, orders Loki, now apparently a bad-tempered serving boy fostered into the Æsir's court, to serve his new guest without delay. This meat is carved off an animal which Þjóðólfr describes as a whipped-on whale of spring-times, a plough-ox (*vára þrymseilar hval*, 5/2–4). In the midst of this throng, but at odds with its festive spirit, Loki obeys his master and serves up four sides of beef from the broad table (*af breiðu bjóði*, 5/5). Yet he is sly and even now may be seen preparing a practical joke as a revenge for the slights which he and Hœnir have received. This whole conceit is contained in a stanza in which, at the same time, Þjóðólfr does not allow us to forget the wider implications of Norse mythology. Thus he presents Óðinn also as the husband of the earth (*foldar dróttinn*, 5/1), shows that the ox is roasted in the ground (*bjóð*, 5/5), in an earth-

oven from which Loki serves up the four helpings, and hints that Loki –
probably as a result of the trick that he plays on Þjazi – will become the
enemy of the Æsir one day (*ósvifrandi ása*, 5/7).

This implication of Loki's later hostility to the gods is developed
further in st. 6–8. As the eagle devours his helping of the roasted ox – it
seems ages since he last had a meal – the poet reveals him to be Þjazi, a
giant and thus the hereditary enemy of gods, by referring to him as the
father of Mǫrn (either Skaði, or a mountain torrent in East Agðir, or
both). Loki without warning strikes at this dangerous figure with a pole
just as he stoops to eat off the roots of his tree, now called an oak. As he
strikes the eagle, Loki also appears to curse him as 'the very bold foe of
the field' (*dolg ballastan vallar*, 6/6). Not only the scheming but also
the self-image of deep-counselled Loki (*djúphugaðr*, 6/5) is made bare
in this way. Having seen things through the conceited eyes of Óðinn and
Hœnir, we now see Loki romanticizing himself as the guardian of the
gods' war-booty (*hirði-Týr herfangs*, 6/7–8). This heroic image recalls
the battlefield conceit in which Óðinn first spies Þjazi in the tree, but
proves deluded when Þjazi hoists Loki into the sky and Loki becomes a
piece of booty himself (Þjazi's *fang*, 8/2).

All the gods are mocked in this poem, yet none with such apparent
affection as Loki, whose helpless position is clearly illustrated in st. 7
(and perhaps thus on the shield). The eagle takes off, the pole is stuck by
magic to the eagle, and the hands of Loki the loyal but now desperate
friend of Hœnir (*holls vinar Hœnis hendr*, 7/7–8) to the end of the pole.
At the same time, Loki's fate as the enemy of the Æsir is also acknowledged: in a rare glimpse of the future we see all the gods looking on,
while Loki, the cargo of his wife Sigyn's arms (*farmr Sigynjar arma*, 7/
2), is bound (in retribution for the death of Baldr, by the guts of his son
beneath a serpent's dripping poison under the earth; cf. *Vsp* 33–5). This
scene in *Haustlǫng* is an allusion to the eve of Ragnarǫk, the last war of
the world. Loki wants his link with the eagle to hold, but Þjóðólfr, by
referring to Loki ironically as the father of Fenrir (*ulfs faðir*, 8/4), the
wolf who will one day snap his bonds (cf. *Vsp* 49), makes a second allusion to Ragnarǫk. In this endgame of the Norse poet's mythology, not
only the cosmic Fenrir but also Loki, his father, are destined to break
free from their bonds to lead a monstrous assault against the gods and
their universe. Loki's plight with Þjazi is made to seem a forestalment of
this final episode. It seems thus to have been part of Þjóðólfr's aim in
Haustlǫng to give us an aetiology, an explanation or even an apology for
Loki's role in the final days before Ragnarǫk. The irony of Loki's long

transformation, from being an erstwhile defender of the gods' war-booty to his being an embittered figure who threatens their downfall, is emphasized by Þjóðólfr's juxtaposition of Loki's present and future roles in the conceits and kennings of st. 7–8. Particularly ironic is the use of *Loptr* ('sky', i.e. 'Lofty') as a name for Loki in 8/6 at a point where the meaning of this name can be vividly illustrated to its owner. As he hangs for dear life from Þjazi, Loki achieves a wisdom he did not have before (*með fróðgum tívi*, 8/1), which is to say that he is compelled to accept his life in exchange for that of all the Æsir.

In return for his life, in st. 9, Þjazi asks Loki to bring him the goddess Iðunn. The language of this phrase repeats that of earlier constructions, but for ever higher stakes: first, Þjazi asks Hœnir for a helping off his plate (*bað sér deila fyllar*, st. 4); then Óðinn bids Loki serve Þjazi as he would the others (*bað með þegnum deila*, st. 5); then Loki must beg Þjazi for his life (*varð friðar biðja*, st. 8); finally Þjazi orders Loki to bring him a goddess on whom all gods depend for their survival (*bað sér fœra mey þás ellilyf ása kunni*, st. 9). The gods are thus outplayed by a giant. Þjóðólfr reveals Iðunn's name by slow degrees, just as he revealed Þjazi's cunning plan to get her. First, she is not only a girl, but the girl who knows the old-age medicine of the Æsir (*ibid.*, st. 9). Then Iðunn's name is revealed in st. 10 as a compound split into two elements *ið* and *unnr*. This is probably a clue to a riddle in the stanza before, for Iðunn's name also appears to be present in the otherwise baffling kenning by which Þjóðólfr defines her in st. 9/5–6: *brunnakrs bekkjar dís goða* ('god's lady of the brook of the well-spring's cornfield', hence 'the goddess of the bubbling water's jet', hence 'the goddess eddy's wave', i.e. *iðu unnr*). The effect of these stanzas, of having to pause at *ið* and *unnr* in st. 10 and then go back and use these elements to unlock the riddle in st. 9, mimics the delay with which the Æsir perceive Iðunn's disappearance. Loki has stolen Iðunn without their knowledge, with the guile of his new master Þjazi, having had no choice but to agree to the giant's demand; known for his success as as the thief of Freyja's Brísingamen (*Brísings girðiþjófr*, 9/6–7), Loki brings Iðunn, a manifestation of Freyja, to Þjazi's court, where she may expect to be (sexually) used by this giant as a perpetual source of wealth, on an industrial basis (*í garða grjót-Níðaðar*, 9/7–8). Furthermore, given that Iðunn is pictured as both a cornfield (*akr*, 9/5) and a brook of running water (*brunn- bekkjar*, 9/5–6), it seems that she is also meant to personify the summer. The splitting of Iðunn's name, in addition, around the words *með jǫtnum* ('with the giants') in 10/3–4 may provide an image of water cascading over rocks in the spring thaw. This season now seems to have left the gods and crossed over into the mountains from the south (*nýkomin sunnan*, 10/4). So the success of Þjazi's plan becomes clear. As the sun moves north and the gods' summer turns to winter, the giants enjoy its sunshine hidden in their bright mountain-tops (*bjartra borða*, 10/1–2), whereas all the kin of Ingvi-freyr, the gods (*allar áttir Ing[v]i-freys*, 10/7), grow old and grey (*gamlar ok hárar*, 10/7–8) and begin to die.

The pace of Þjóðólfr's narrative suddenly accelerates in st. 11: despite the apparent corruption of the first *helmingr* or half of this stanza, it seems that the Æsir find out the cause of their ageing from Þjazi, either by seeking him or by meeting him by chance; then bind Loki magically with a wand in order to threaten him into reversing their decline. Loki's cunning and also his subordinate role are apparent in the fact that he abducts Iðunn by leading her off as if her servant (*leiðiþir*, 11/3). The wrathful speaker who makes the threat against Loki (*[v]reiðr mælti svá*, 11/6) is probably to be identified with Ingvi-freyr, Freyja's brother, male counterpart and sexual partner, whose name Þjóðólfr has cited in the previous stanza. As if careful not to name her, Freyr refers to Freyja or Iðunn by periphrasis as the glorious girl who increases the gods' life-joy (*munstærandi mæra mey*, 11/7–8), but he is clear enough about what will happen to Loki if he fails to bring her back: that he will be driven mad and die (*véltr vélum*, 11/5). The demented repetition of rhymes in this stanza as it stands – *sævar hræva, hund fundu, leiði læva, lund bundu* – seems to imitate the metre of *galdralag* in which Norse spells (*galdrar*) were chanted. So Loki is threatened with death for the second time and fulfils the next part of his destiny in st. 12 (sneaking into Þjazi's court while the giant is away). In this stanza, both Loki and Þjazi are suddenly seen airborne once more, although this time Loki is flying as a hawk or falcon with Iðunn (transformed into a nut in his claws). The pace of this stanza is even quicker than that of the last, with the focus on Loki in the first *helmingr* and on Þjazi in the second, in hot pursuit and closing on Loki with seconds to spare. Loki's slim chance of survival puts the courage of Hœnir to the test (*hugreynandi Hœnis*, 12/3): at least one of the Æsir loves him. This epithet, however, serves to highlight Loki's loneliness: in the midst of the second *helmingr*, Loki is portrayed as a fledgling (*ǫglis barn*, 12/7), while Þjazi, in constrast, is loaded with epithets which express his loon-like shrieking (and possibly his reputation for deceit, in *lómhugaðr*, 12/5), the vast and deliberate sweep of his wings (*leikblaðs reginn fjaðrar*, 12/6), the swift rush of air in his eagle's flight (*ern arnsúg*, 12/7–8) and his gigantic size and kin-

dred (*faðir Mǫrnar*, 12/8). With Þjazi moving in for the kill, it is likely
that these images to do with his size and power are meant to arouse our
sympathy for Loki as the unlikely hero of this tale.

Meanwhile, the gods lie in wait in Ásgarðr as if using Loki to entice
Þjazi into a trap of their own (*ginnregin*, 13/2), and there is a flurry of
activity as they shave shafts in order to light a bonfire for Þjazi as he
flies overhead. It must be taken for granted that Loki escapes and that
the Æsir reclaim Iðunn and her *ellilyf*, the means of their eternal youth,
for Þjóðólfr ends this story abruptly with the death of Þjazi, whose wings
seem to be catching fire before his eyes on the shield. Yet before Þjóðólfr
moves into his first shield-refrain in 13/7–8 (a statement to the effect
that he has received his image-painted shield from Þorleifr), he finishes
with a joke about Þjazi's parentage which is contained in a kenning for
Þjazi as the son of Greip's suitor (*sonr biðils Greipar*, 13/3–4). His point
thereby may be to set Þjazi's chances of surviving this encounter with
the Æsir lower than those of his father (Allvaldi or Ǫlvaldi) when he
courted the giantess Greip (presumably Þjazi's mother) in the house of
her psychotic father Geirrøðr. With this parting flourish, not only Iðunn,
but also the bright summer, return home to the world of the gods.

Þjóðólfr alludes to his shield in the second half of st. 13 as the bridge
of the mountain-Lapp's footsoles (*brú ilja Finns fjalla*, 13/5–6), a clear
reference to the tale of Þórr's duel with Hrungnir which can thus be
presumed to have followed *Haustlǫng* 1–13 as st. 14–20 of the complete
poem (see discussion above). This next section of *Haustlǫng* is probably
to be seen as the dramatization of summer in the uplands, for Þórr's duel
with Hrungnir is set in a turbulent landscape in which thunder rolls and
lightning hits mountain peaks. Þjóðólfr now says in st. 14 that on his
shield he sees Þórr visiting or possibly attacking the giant Hrungnir.
This is a scene set *in medias res*, given that Þjóðólfr does not disclose
the causes of the duel. On these causes, Snorri's supplementary story
may help, in which Hrungnir challenges Þórr to a duel after outraging
Óðinn's cunningly contrived hospitality in Ásgarðr, mostly by threaten-
ing to destroy the place and to take both Freyja and Þórr's wife Sif home
with him. On the other hand, Bragi's kenning for a shield in *Ragnarsdrápa*,
as the leaf of the footsoles of the thief of Þórr's lover Þrúðr (*Þrúðar þjófs
ilja blað*, st. 1), seems to imply that Hrungnir, in a version of this tale
even older than *Haustlǫng*, indeed carried out his promise to abduct one
of Þórr's female dependents.

Haustlǫng 14 appears to provide a summary of not only the action,
but also of the illustration painted on Þjóðólfr's shield. As a giant-killer,

Þórr is well enough known to the poem's audience to be introduced as 'giants' dread' (*jǫtna ótti*, 14/1–2), while Hrungnir, already introduced as the 'mountain-Lapp' in st. 13, goes unnamed — unless his name lies concealed in a second (extraordinary) riddle in 14/3–4, in the kenning *hellis bǫr hyrjar haugs grjót[t]úna* ('cavern-tree [giant] of stone-enclosures' [sea's] gravemound's [bed's] fire [golden rings]', hence 'giant of rings', '*hringa*-giant', hence *hrung-nir*). This overfraught kenning, if the name *Hrungnir* is the correct interpretation, appears to blur the person with the phenomenon in such a way that this giant, whom Snorri shows to be made of stone and whose weapon is a whetstone, becomes hard to distinguish from the rocks and boulders that surround him. Although it appears to be Þjóðólfr's tendency to identify Þórr and Hrungnir with natural phenomena in st. 14–16, he gradually allows us to see the personified aspect of these figures in a way which lends them a varied characterization equal in power to that of Óðinn, Loki and Þjazi in st. 1–13. Þórr, now named the son of earth (*Jarðar sunr*, 14/6) and characterized as swelling up with rage (*móðr svall Meila blóða*, 14/7), speeds towards Hrungnir. On his way there, Þórr drives his clattering chariot over the moon's path (*Mána vegr*, 14/8); lets the bucks who draw him kick down hail-storms which lash the ground below; and as a kinsman of the god of brilliance (*Ullar mágr*, 15/1–3), like a jagged streak of lightning, sets fire to the upper atmosphere as he rides by. At the same time Þjóðólfr describes Þórr as a temple-deity (*hofregin*, 15/5), drawn forward in his easy-riding chariot as if in a procession (*hógreiðar fram drógu*, 15/6). The sky, however, is described as the falcons' sanctuary (*ginnunga vé*, 15/4), and the earth, Þórr's mother, as Svǫlnir's (perhaps Óðinn's) widow (*Svǫlnis ekkja*, 15/7). These variously respectful and irreverent turns of phrase afford us a glimpse of Þórr seated in some kind of temple, yet also give him the tearaway aspect of a young man who sets fire to birds' nests or makes a racket sufficient to bring his old mother out of doors. With this varied combination of attitudes towards Þórr, a heathen god, it would be hard to justify st. 15 as the work of a Norwegian or Icelander after the early eleventh century. It is unlikely that a recently converted Christian would have understood the respect, or a later antiquarian the occasional irreverence of a believer towards a living cult. Evidently Þjóðólfr in his own time expressed an affection for Þórr through a mocking sense of humour of which the only limit was set by his respect for the natural power of this god.

Thus, in st. 16, Þjóðólfr refers to Þórr as Baldr's bosom brother (*Baldrs of barmi*, 16/1), presumably in order to hint at Þórr's unwitting part in the missile attacks that lead to Baldr's death (cf. *Gylf,* ch. 49). If Þórr is involved in his brother's death, what hope is there for Hrungnir, a giant and his sworn enemy? The effect of this kenning is not to present Þórr as a blunderer, but rather to caricature Hrungnir as his victim. Þórr's moral reason for fighting the giant also becomes clearer. Given Hrungnir's epithet as the gorged enemy of mankind (*solginn dolgr manna,* 16/2–4), it seems that the rocks with which he is associated are understood as forces of infertility that swallow up men's harvest. A symbolic permutation of this meaning may be found in Snorri's tale of Hrungnir's excess in the hall of the gods. In this part of *Haustlǫng* it is thus Þórr's mission to safeguard mankind. As he draws near to Hrungnir in this stanza, the sky burns and the surrounding peaks begin to crack and shatter. Hrungnir recoils speechlessly from Þórr when he sees him ready for war (*þás vígligan þátti,* 16/7–8). There are no preliminaries, nor any option for Hrungnir to threaten Þórr verbally as it seems he has already done in Ásgarðr. It is possible that Þjóðólfr mocks Hrungnir for verbosity when he portrays this giant as ready to attend a 'meeting' with Þórr (*mót,* 16/5), as a witness for the whales of the dark-bone of the land of Haki (*váttr vagna myrkbeins reinar Haka,* 16/6–8). The mockery implicit in the two kennings for Hrungnir in this stanza amounts to a characterization of him as a glutton and braggart in a prelude to this story now lost to us. Þórr, in contrast, is now presented seriously.

The duel between Þórr and Hrungnir takes place in st. 17–18. An otherwise irrational decision of Hrungnir, to block an attack from below by standing on (the boss of) his shield, is explained by Þjóðólfr as the result of psychic intervention from gods or spirits nearby (*bǫnd,* 17/2; *dísir,* 17/4). The second *helmingr* contains yet more mockery of Hrungnir, whom the poet seems to portray waiting eagerly for the impact of Mjǫllnir, Þórr's hammer, on his giant's snout as if he were expecting a kiss from a hoped-for bride (*varðat hraundrengr lengi tíðr at bíða,* 17/5–8). The force of Mjǫllnir's blow will shatter Hrungnir's skull into many pieces (*hǫggs fjǫllama,* 17/5–8), as if this giant is imagined as a boulder or rock, Þórr as the farmer who breaks it up in his field. Yet the image of a *hólmganga* ('island-duel') is not forgotten, for in the next *helmingr* Þjóðólfr describes Hrungnir as a bear of the refuge of unshallow high sea-swells (*fjalfrs ólágra gjalfra bolm,* 18/2–4), whom Þórr lets drop on the island of his shield-rim (*á randar holmi,* 18/4). That he calls Þórr the spoiler of the lives of Beli's horrific troop (*fjǫrspillir bǫlverðungar Belja,* 18/1–3), reduces the giants to inanimate objects which Þórr breaks up and distributes back to their people like pieces of captured treasure.

Hrungnir is known as the king of the bottom of ravines (*grundar gilja gramr*, 18/5–6), probably because he will end up in one when Þórr, the breaker of the Agðir-men of the mountains, of the giants (*berg-Egða brjótr*, 18/7–8: see note), tips his body over the edge.

First, however, Þórr must shift Hrungnir's leg off his neck, where it has fallen, and afterwards remove a sherd from the giant's whetstone, which has lodged in his skull. In the aftermath of this battle, Þjóðólfr mocks Hrungnir as the housecaller of Vingnir's warrior-woman, probably of Þórr's mistress Þrúðr (*heimþinguðr herju Vingnis*, 19/1–2), on whom the giant is thus shown calling as if he were a pedlar with whetstone, she the housewife whose knives need sharpening. This bathetic image may have been part of the prelude to which Þjóðólfr refers in his account of the duel, or it may be no more than his way of mocking Hrungnir, but it reveals that Þórr has a motive other than the general one, the defence of mankind, for setting out so furiously to despatch this giant. Þjóðólfr takes leave of Þórr by presenting his lineage, as the son of earth (*Grundar sveinn*, 19/4) and of Óðinn (*Óðins burr*, 19/5–6). Þórr's head is the focus of st. 19–20/1–4. In keeping with Þórr's status as the son of gods, his head is now shown in massive close-up as a curving hillside from which blood seeps from the whetstone-sherd like water from a rock in the earth. The sherd will stay embedded, says Þjóðólfr in the last stanza of the surviving poem, until such time as a Gefjun who nurses wounds (*ǫl-Gefjun sára*, 20/2) might chant a spell to remove the red horrific prospect of rust's abode, i.e. the red whetstone (*et rauða ryðs hælibǫl gæli*, 20/3–4). Þjóðólfr also alludes to Þórr's great size by typifying his physician as the goddess Gefjun dragging land out of Sweden to settle it down as an island in the Kattegat (Sjælland). This magnified image of the wound in Þórr's head may allude to a superstition or piety of the poet's day, and it seems likely that Þjóðólfr's reference to a female physician shows that he regarded witches as an integral part of his society. Before the refrain in the last two lines of the extant poem, Þjóðólfr refers to his shield as the fortress of the sea-king Geitir (*Geitis garði*, 20/5–6). If there was more to the poem *Haustlǫng* than the two sections which have survived, it is possible, on analogy with the anticipation of Hrungnir in st. 13/5–8, that the next section of this poem consisted of a story about a sea-battle (such as that between Heðinn and Hǫgni in *Ragnarsdrápa* 8–12) in which men rather than gods were involved.

STYLE AND GENRE OF *HAUSTLǪNG*

This is where our text of *Haustlǫng* ends. Now, before we consider Þjóðólfr's life and times and the possible routes by which *Haustlǫng* came into *Snorra Edda*, let us attempt a speculation about Þjóðólfr's shield and a conclusion about the overall style and genre of his poem. On the shield's presumably wooden or leather surface, if we choose to follow the poet's inference in the opening stanza of *Haustlǫng*, were painted at least three images of scenes from Old Norwegian mythology.[7] The first image is said to be that of three Norse gods and a giant named Þjazi, all on a dangerous journey (*trygglaust far*, st. 1). From what later emerges in the poem (st. 7, 8 and 9/1–4), it is likely that this image shows Óðinn and Hœnir on the ground and Loki in the air, holding on to a pole which dangles from the body of an eagle whom we know to be Þjazi in disguise. An image which may also be painted on the shield, according to Þjóðólfr in st. 13, probably represents a bonfire over which Þjazi, again flying in an eagle's shape, pursues a smaller bird whom we know to be Loki in disguise (and probably carrying the goddess Iðunn with him in the form of a nut). A third image around the shield-boss, adjacent to the bonfire, might be reconstructed as that of the god Þórr and the giant Hrungnir, the latter standing on the boss of both his and Þjóðólfr's shield (cf. st. 13/5–8 and 17–18). Given that Norse shields were mostly round, it is possible that these three images were painted around the iron or gilt boss in the centre of the shield. It may be pointless to speculate further, but it seems probable that the figures on Þjóðólfr's shield were identifiable through defining symbols such as a whetstone in the air and a hammer close to one figure's head, in the case of Þórr and Hrungnir (st. 17/5–8); and through other symbols in the case of the first story, perhaps a helmet for Óðinn (st. 3) and the image of a cockerel to represent Hœnir. That Þjóðólfr's tale of Þjazi and Iðunn (st. 1–13 = 13) is contained in about twice as many stanzas as that of Þórr and Hrungnir (st. 14–20 = 7) may add some weight to the idea that the first

---

[7]No shields of any decent standard of preservation survive from the Viking Age period, but some figures, which may serve as a typology of what could have been painted on Þjóðólfr's shield, are to be found in the Oseberg Ship tapestry-reconstruction, the Tjängsvide, Rasmus Rock and Rök runestone carvings and the Heggen bronze-gilt weathervane: see D. M. Wilson and Ole Klindt-Jensen, *Viking Art*, 2nd ed. (Minneapolis, MN, 1980), figs. xix, xxvi, lix. a.–b. and lxi. a.–b.

tale is proportionately based on two shield-images and the second on one. Since Bragi's shield, if real, probably contained at least four painted scenes on which the episodes of *Ragnarsdrápa* were based (st. 3–6, 8–12, 13 and 14–20), it seems likely that Þjóðólfr's shield contained more than three painted images.

Another consideration concerning the original length of this poem is Þjóðólfr's title *haustlǫng [drápa]*, which seems to mean '[poem composed] the autumn long'. This circumstantial title, *Haustlǫng* rather than **Þorleifsdrápa*, hints that the name was given not by the poet, but by his audience or posterity.[8] This title also implies that Þjóðólfr's admirers knew that the poet had taken about a month over his work (c. 15 September to c. 14 October). It may be a reasonable assumption, therefore, that Þjóðólfr did not send the poem to Þorleifr but composed it while staying as a guest of this chieftain in Hǫrðaland. An apparently self-deprecating reference to Agðir, the poet's home country, in the emended giant-kenning *berg-Egða* in *Haustlǫng* 18/7 might corroborate this tentative conclusion. If it is right to emend this form from *berg-Dana* (all MSS: see note), it appears unlikely that Þjóðólfr could have worked on this kenning in Agðir whether or not he intended to perform the poem there. If Þjóðólfr thus spent about thirty days on his poem in Hǫrðaland where he delivered it in a *haustǫl*-festival on the eve of winter, his poem probably contained more than twenty stanzas. It is unlikely that Þjóðólfr produced less than one stanza a day, or that his poem lasted only the five to ten minutes it requires to speak *Haustlǫng* in its extant form. Also the briskness of the narrative pace of this poem suggests that the poem was composed with more stanzas than the twenty now surviving. Although Margaret Clunies Ross suggests that *Haustlǫng*, 'like a diptych', contains no more than two subjects which are 'thematically complementary', her view seems unduly influenced by her interpretation of Snorri's treatment of this poem in *Skáldskaparmál*.[9] If the poem is considered by its own criteria rather than Snorri's, it is more likely than not that *Haustlǫng* was originally a longer poem.

---

[8]Patrons are usually named: viz. *Ragnarsdrápa* (c. 850), *Hákonardrápa* (c. 960), *Hákonarmál* (c. 960), *Sigurðardrápa* (c. 965), *Gráfeldardrápa* (c. 970), *Hákonardrápa* (c. 985), *Óláfsdrápa* (c. 995) and other poems. Exceptions, however, are *Glymdrápa* (c. 885, for Haraldr hárfagri), *Vellekla* (c. 985, for Hákon Jarl), *Þórsdrápa* (c. 985, apparently for Hákon Jarl) and *Húsdrápa* (c. 995, for Óláfr *pái* Hǫskuldsson).

[9]Clunies Ross, *Prolonged Echoes*, pp. 107–27. esp. 114–15.

For one thing, the style and syntax of *Haustlǫng* are unusually fluent for a work in the *dróttkvætt* metre. Hans Kuhn (pp. 279–81, § 116) draws attention to the almost experimental liberties of Þjóðólfr's metre, which in his view cast some suspicion on the unity of this poem: Þjóðólfr appears to like a fractured syntax, with a high number of short sentences inserted into longer ones, plus an abundance of verbal *of*-particles. Yet this style, far from suggesting a composite authorship, may be the product of an older narrative, or even epic, use of the *dróttkvætt* metre. Þjóðólfr likes epic conventions (*heyrðak svá*, 12/1 and *frák*, 16/5) and his verses are anything but static: Þjazi's pursuit of Loki in st. 12 gives a powerful impression of an eagle gaining on a hawk; and the speed of the next scene, in which the gods light fires below and Þjazi catches fire above, is mostly achieved by blurring two separate constructions in 13/1–2. As if to save time, in this way, Þjóðólfr often appears to use a word, phrase or construction as a key element of two different clauses (*ár-Gefnar* 2/6, *í bǫndum* 7/4, *loddi* 7/5, *goða* 9/6, *vǫru* 10/7–8, *ǫl-Gefnar* 11/2, *skǫpt* 13/1–2, *minni* 13/6, *hyrjar* 14/3, *ímun-* 17/3). There is an economy of diction in these 'double-duty' constructions that goes well with the swift pace of *Haustlǫng*.

To see the style of this poet more clearly, it is worth comparing the relatively deft syntax of *Haustlǫng* with the richer texture of a poem such as *Þórsdrápa* composed by Eilífr Goðrúnarson nearly a hundred years later (in *c.* 985, *Skj* B I, 139–44). Both poems contain stories in which Þórr fights and kills a giant – indeed it is possible that Eilífr (a Norwegian?) knew Þjóðólfr's work – yet whereas Þjóðólfr makes up extra syllables with the *of*-particle twelve times in twenty stanzas (1/6, 3/5, 8/5, 8/6, 9/5, 13/5, 14/1, 14/2, 16/1, 17/7, 19/7, 20/8), a ratio of more than one to two, Eilífr in twenty-one stanzas uses the *of*-particle only four times (2/1, 19/3, 19/7, 20/8), a ratio of just under one to five. Vivid kennings in *Haustlǫng* are chosen to embellish the main figures, not as brilliant epigrams which divert attention from the story into an imaginative *cul-de-sac*, as so often in *Þórsdrápa*, but as elements of poetic conceits which sometimes continue for the length of a *helmingr*, or even a stanza. Thus when Þjóðólfr refers to Hrungnir as *bolmr fjalfrs ólágra gjalfra* ('the bear of the hide-out of the high sea-swells', 18/2–4) whom Þórr fells *á randar holmi* ('on the island of his shield'), he probably means to give us an image of Hrungnir as a bear living in a cave on a coastal island, which Þórr must draw out in order to kill. Eilífr, in contrast, gives a rewarding but variegated image of the younger giants of Geirrøðr's family whom Þórr slaughters next after their father, when he

describes them as *kalfar undirfjalfrs alfheims bliku* ('calves of the underground refuge of the elf-realm's gleam', *Skj* B I, 144). Yet Eilífr's
kenning cannot work as a single conceit, for he switches in mid-kenning
from the image of giants as calves in a stall (an effective conceit for their
deaths as a type of cattle-cull) to another image of elves or demons
fashioning gold underground. This is a relatively straightforward kenning
by the norms of Eilífr's *Þórsdrápa*. It is the tendency of this poet not to
offer us a big conceit, but rather two or more little ones, in such a way
that *Þórsdrápa* becomes a baroque edifice with a myriad number of
ornamentations, each of which functions as a *bon mot* of its own. At
each step of Eilífr's glittering narrative one finds a multiplicity of meanings, some of which – Þórr's 'bun-fight' with his mad host, for example,
with molten ingots for food – are hilarious, others of which have recently appeared dark enough to encourage attempts at psychoanalysis.[10]
Eilífr's rich kennings are typical of the political poetry of Jarl Hákon's
court in the late tenth century, although it is worth noting that his style
of mixed metaphor creates an essentially rhetorical profusion of images
that turns *Þórsdrápa* into a poetic juggernaut. With Þjóðólfr, in contrast,
there is a lightness of touch, an easy pace and a facility for rapid scene-
changes that brings his art closer to vaudeville. In short, whereas Eilífr's
kennings focus attention on their poet's wit rather than on his story,
Þjóðólfr entertains his audience by dramatizing his story with conceits
which exploit the comic potential of his characters.

In *Ynglingatal*, for example, Þjóðólfr perversely characterizes the
dying king Eysteinn as if he were Baldr. Eysteinn is surprised one night
by the Jutes and burned alive in his hall, the seventeenth in Þjóðólfr's list
of kings to die in the extant poem. The merit of this poem consists of its
sardonic treatment of the kings of Uppsala and eastern Norway, each of
whom is portrayed not in the glory of life, but in the unique manner of
his leaving it. In Eysteinn's case:

---

[10]Did Eilífr fear women? See Margaret Clunies Ross, 'An Interpretation of the
Myth of Þórr's Encounter with Geirrøðr and his Daughters', in *Speculum
Norroenum: Norse Studies in Memory of Gabriel Turville-Petre*, ed. Ursula
Dronke, Guðrún P. Helgadóttir, Gerd Wolfgang Weber and Hans Bakker-Nielsen
(Odense, 1983), pp. 370–91, esp. 377–89. Did he love his mother, but wish to
dominate younger women? See John McKinnell, *Both One and Many: Essays
on Change and Variety in Late Norse Heathenism*, with an appendix by Maria
Elena Ruggerini (Rome, 1994), pp. 69–75.

Veitk Eysteins enda folginn
lokins lífs á Lófundi,
ok sikling með Svíum kvǫðu
józka menn inni brenna.

Ok bitsótt í brandnói
hlíðar þangs á hilmi rann,
þás timbrfastr toptar nǫkkvi,
flotna fullr, of fylki brann.

(*Ynglingatal* 23–4)[11]

In this conceit, which he extends over two stanzas, Þjóðólfr appears to satirize the (no doubt common) manner of Eysteinn's end, and perhaps the (even commoner) idiom in which royal poets traditionally recorded the premature exits of their rulers, by phrasing it in the portentous language of Baldr's death.[12] His thread-motif in *enda folginn* invokes the tradition of the fate-spinning Norns and has a later counterpart in *Vǫluspá* (*c*. 1000), whose poet probably relies on the same *topos* for a scene in which a sybil sees the future for Baldr, the bleeding god, as *ørlǫg fólgin* ('the fate concealed', *Vsp* 31).[13] Þjóðólfr takes the Baldr-conceit further, when, with images of seaweed (*þang*), a fire-ship (*brandnór, nǫkkvi*) and doomed sailors (*flotnar*) grouped around the prince (*hilmir, fylkir*) in *Ynglingatal* 24, he pictures Eysteinn's blazing hall as if it were Baldr's funeral ship heading out to sea. The story of Baldr's pyre and funeral ship is preserved in Úlfr Uggason's *Húsdrápa* 7–11 (*c*. 995) and is also known from *Gylf*, ch. 49. There can be little doubt that Þjóðólfr

---

[11]*Heimskringla I*, ed. Bjarni, pp. 60–1 (*Ynglinga saga*, ch. 31): '[23] I know the end of the closed life of Eysteinn [the thread of his life] to have been concealed in Lófund, and that among the Swedes it was said that Jutish men burned the king within [his house]. [24] And the biting sickness of the seaweed of the hillside [forest-fire] coursed onto the prince in his fire-ship, when, filled with sailors, the homestead's firm-timbered prow [hall] burned down upon the chieftain'. See also *Skj* B I, 11, 23–4.

[12]Baldr's death is used as a serious metaphor in Egill's portrayal of his son Bǫðvarr's loss in *Sonatorrek* 17, Eyvindr's of Hákon Aðalsteinsfóstri in *Hákonarmál* 20 and Arnórr Þórðarson's of Þorfinnr Jarl in *Þorfinnsdrápa* 24 (*Skj* B I, 36, 60 and 321).

[13]An even closer parallel to Þjóðólfr's expression occurs in *veit hon Heimdalar hlióð um fólgit* ('she knows the hearing of Heimdallr to be concealed'), in *Vsp* 27.

recalls this theme in *Ynglingatal* 23–4 for an ironic effect of some kind.

Þjóðólfr depicts the world of gods, not men, in the extant *Haustlǫng*, but here, as in *Ynglingatal* 23–4, it appears to be his style to use one world to reflect the other. When Óðinn decides to admit the eagle to the communal meal in *Haustlǫng* 5, Þjóðólfr transplants them suddenly into a crowded hall, in which Óðinn turns into the local lord, Loki into a serving boy and Hœnir and Þjazi into a group of adoring thanes. Their ox-roast has already been interpreted as an expression symbolic of social relationships.[14] With his conceit in st. 5, however, Þjóðólfr seems to mock Óðinn and the other Æsir for an ill-advised decision by comparing them with men. With his (unparalled) kenning for the ox, which he appears to call the 'whale of the cracking rope of spring-times' (*vára þrymseilar hval*, 5/2–4), Þjóðólfr also gives us a vivid image of life on the land outside the hall, from the beginning of the summer to its end, when the ox is slaughtered. The whole conceit is developed over no more than a stanza, yet offers us a window into aristocratic surroundings such as those in which it is possible *Haustlǫng* was first performed. If the point of this conceit is to show the complacency of the gods when faced by an unknown danger, it is interesting that the poet defines their folly in human terms. They are forgetting to be gods — a slip which makes them dearer to their human worshippers. A similar effect is achieved with the portrayal of Þórr as an energetic figure whose wild career rouses the earth, his widowed mother, in st. 15. This motif recalls another young Norwegian in a folktale of a later date, one who recites a tale of riding on a buck on the Gjendin edge to Åse, his widowed mother, in the opening scene of *Peer Gynt*. In *Haustlǫng*, however, the implication of Þórr's wildness is matched with what seems to be an image of his idol sitting in a *hof* ('temple'). Þjóðólfr is as skilled a poet as any when he wishes to allude to his mythology. In his case, however, more than in that of other Scalds, this mythology was down to earth and consisted of the everyday: not only gods and giants, but also lords, thegns and feasting, plough-oxen and spring-fields, witches, temples and the seasonal occupations of Norway in the late ninth century. Though he tells us that his tales happened long ago (*ó- fyr -skǫmmu* 2/4, *fyr lǫngu* 6/2), Þjóðólfr still lets us know that his gods are all around him, and that to him the mundane and sacred are the same.

Haustlǫng, in this way, may be read as a northern work analogous to Vergil's 'Georgics' or Hesiod's 'Works and Days'. There are only two

---

[14]Clunies Ross, *Prolonged Echoes*, pp. 117–18.

episodes which survive, Loki's theft of Iðunn and Þórr's duel with Hrungnir, but each of these contains a story which celebrates occupations in a changing time of year. The first is late autumn, winter and spring; the second, later in the summer. In the case of the first tale, there are three reasons to read *Haustlǫng* as a celebration of spring. First, as we have seen, the Æsir's roasted ox probably reflects the custom of slaughtering excess livestock before winter (*c*. 14 October). With the conceit in st. 5, it is thus likely that Þjóðólfr alludes to a *haustblót*, an 'autumn feast' which marked the culmination of harvest and the end of six months of summer.[15] The ox, which was preferred to the horse as a ploughing-animal, is a subject of kennings which refer to different times of year.[16] Þjóðólfr calls the ox a horse of harvest-Gefn (*ár-Gefnar mar*, 2/6); a reindeer of the dung which was raked out of the cowbyres after winter to spread on the fields (*ta[ð]lhreinn*, 3/2); a whale of the cracking rope of spring-times, or an ox behind which a whip cracks as it ploughs a field (*vára þrymseilar hval*, 5/2–4); and a yoke-bear (*okbjǫrn*, 6/4), an image which embodies his previous three efforts to make a connection between an ox and the plough, between the Æsir's meal and the efforts of men to send it to them. The seasonal occupations thus revealed in these ox-kennings are summer harvest (2/6), winter cattle-feeding in the byre (3/2) and spring dunging and ploughing in the fields (3/2, 5/2–4 and 6/4).[17] Second, when Iðunn arrives in giant-land 'from the south' (*sunnan*, st. 10), both the mountains and their inhabitants become bright with the new sunlight while the valleys below, it may be inferred, begin to suffer the growing darkness of the winter months. Iðunn herself, characterized diffusely throughout this section of *Haustlǫng*, appears to embody various things: female beauty (*snótar ulfr*, 2/2); not only the harvest (*ár-Gefnar...*), but also the beasts which help men to provide it (*...mar*, 2/6); the rejuvenation of gods (*þás ellilyf ása kunni*, 9/3–4) and of men and all living things (*allar áttir Ing[v]ifreys*, 10/5–6); wealth and the creation of treasure (*Brísings goða girðiþjófr í garða grjót-Níðaðar*, 9/6–8); nourishment (*ǫl-Gefnar*, 11/2), the generation of love or life-force (*mæra mun stœrandi mey*, 11/7–8); sexual pleasure (*ása leiku*, 12/2); Iðunn seems to represent the abundance of corn and eddying water in the riddle of her name, in *brunnakrs bekkjar dís goða* (9/5–6); and her name itself, when

[15]Olrik and Ellekilde, *Nordens Gudeverden*, pp. 593–4. See also Hastrup, *Culture and History in Medieval Iceland*, pp. 35–8.

[16]Williams, *Social Scandinavia in the Viking Age*, p. 166.

[17]Cf. Simpson, *Everyday Life in the Viking Age*, pp. 58–61.

split into its elements around *með jǫtnum*, suggests the cascade of melt-water over rocks in springtime Norway. Third, there is the lighting of a fire in order to safeguard Iðunn's return by killing Þjazi. Olrik and Ellekilde show that midsummer bonfires were a standard item on the Norwegian calendar in the eighteenth and nineteenth centuries, as they were throughout Europe.[18] This festival, known as *Jonsvaka* or *Jonsok* ('St John's eve') in Norway, observes both the feast of St John and the summer solstice (21 June), yet had probably been brought forward from the date of a heathen festival celebrated closer to the midpoint of sum-mer in the non-solar calendar (*c.* 14 July).[19] According to *Ágrip* (ch. 19), it was Óláfr Tryggvason (ruled *c.* 995–1000) who first 'abolished sacri-fices and drinking bouts at sacrifices and put in their place as an ap-peasement to the people the ceremonial feasts of Yule and Easter, St John's ale and the autumn ale-feast at Michaelmas'.[20] Another bonfire in Scandinavia, known as the *Majbål* and held in Jutland and Sweden, prob-ably replaced a similar festival which welcomed the beginning of sum-mer earlier in the year (*c.* 14 April).[21] Snorri appears to refer to moun-tain-top beacons when he, but not the authors of either *Ágrip* or *Fagrskinna*, says that King Hákon Haraldsson (died *c.* 960) organized an early-warning system against the invading fleets of the sons of Eiríkr blóðøx and other vikings.[22] This is the only historical reference to Nor-wegian bonfires in early summer (the raiding season). However, although the *Majbål* bonfire-festival is not recorded in most of Norway, Olrik and Ellekilde believe that it goes back to the bronze age.[23] It is possible, therefore, that the Æsir's fire in *Haustlǫng* 13 represents an aetiology for a custom known to Þjóðólfr's contemporaries in Norway, whereby sum-mer's return was symbolized by the burning of a straw of wooden effigy such as that which was recorded in midsummer bonfires in Denmark and Norway in the eighteenth and ninteenth centuries.[24] If winter's end

[18]Olrik and Ellekilde, *Nordens Gudeverden*, p. 668.

[19]*Ibid.*, p. 619.

[20]*Ágrip. Fagrskinna*, ed. Bjarni, p. 22: 'felldi blót ok blótdrykkjur ok lét í stað koma í vild við lýðinn hátíðadrykkjur jól ok páskar, Jóansmessu mungát ok haustǫl at Míkjálsmessu'.

[21]Olrik and Ellekilde, *Nordens Gudeverden*, pp. 618–19.

[22]*Heimskringla I*, ed. Bjarni, p. 176 (*Hákonar saga góða*, ch. 20).

[23]Olrik and Ellekilde, *Nordens Gudeverden*, pp. 619 and 668.

[24]*Ibid.*, p. 671.

was Iðunn's rescue, it is also possible that she was presented as returning to the divine and human world as a nut or seed for planting (cf. Snorri's phrase *í hnotar líki*). Seeding-time in Iceland (*sáðtíð*) fell between the end of April and the end of May.[25]

In the case of the second tale in *Haustlǫng*, Þórr's destruction of Hrungnir reflects the breaking of stones and rocks and their removal from the turf prior to the ploughing of a new field: 'only the best land was cultivated, and even this in the rock-bound Scandinavian peninsular, and to some degrees the remainder of the north, had usually to be cleared of stones before it could be ploughed'.[26] This was a job for the summer, presumably after the ploughing of existing fields. The giant Hrungnir, possibly concealed in the kenning *hellis bǫr hyrjar haugs grjót[t]úna* in st. 14, is characterized not only as an enemy of the gods, but particularly as a 'gorged enemy of men' (*solginn dolgr manna*, 16/2–4), i.e. as a rock which devours men's harvest by keeping their ploughland infertile. This episode is soon over, but on the level of natural phenomena, it is likely that it expresses both the play of thunder and lightning over the mountain-tops and an aetiology for a summer occupation, the clearing of new land. There are about three months between this physical labour and the autumn month of mid-September to mid-October in which it is supposed that Þjóðólfr composed his poem in exchange for a shield. So there may be one or more other similar aetiological stories in *Haustlǫng* which have fallen out of this poem in its transmission. It seems clear that Þjóðólfr delivered this poem at a *haustǫl*, and that his method of connecting his shield with the bounty of Þorleifr, its bestower, was to elaborate on the three or more images on the shield with oblique reference to the farming year which led up to this occasion. It is for these reasons that his genre might be called 'northern pastoral'.

ÞJÓÐÓLFR OF HVINIR: LIFE AND TIMES

Little is known about Þjóðólfr, apart from what he tells us in his own poems. Finnur, who edited his poems, described him as 'an honourable, cheerful, humorous and considered man who believed in destiny (cf. *Ynglingatal* 7/17) and in the gods, although he seems not to have been

[25]Williams, *Social Scandinavia in the Viking Age*, p. 165; Hastrup, *Culture and History in Medieval Iceland*, pp. 32–3.

[26]Williams, *Social Scandinavia in the Viking Age*, p. 165.

religious in the deeper meaning of the word'.[27] Six poems, or fragments of poems, are variously ascribed to Þjóðólfr, of which only four survive; of these four, only two, *Ynglingatal* and *Haustlǫng*, are likely to be his. In *Haustlǫng*, as we have seen, there is the implication of the title, *haustlǫng [drápa]* ('harvest-long [poem]'), that the poet composed his work throughout the autumn (thus from *c.* 15 September to *c.* 14 October), as payment for a shield presented to him by a man named *Þorleifr* who is likely to have been Þorleifr *inn spaki* ('the wise') Hǫrðu-Kárason. Since, according to *Skáldatal*, Þjóðólfr made 'a poem about Þorleifr inn spaki' (*kvæði um Þorleif hinn spaka*), Finnur was probably right to identify this man with the Þorleifr cited in *Haustlǫng* (st. 1, 13 and 20).[28] The other poem, *Ynglingatal* ('list of the Ynglingar'), is ascribed to Þjóðólfr by Snorri as he quotes it at intervals throughout *Ynglinga saga*, which is the poem's only surviving context.[29] At the end of *Ynglingatal*, Þjóðólfr appears to refer to a royal patron:

> Þat veitk bazt   und blǫum himni
> kenninafn,   svát konungr eigi,
> es Rǫgnvaldr,   reiðar stjóri,
> heiðumhárr   of heitinn es.

> (*Ynglingatal* 37)[30]

Snorri tells us that Rǫgnvaldr, as the son of Óláfr *Geirstaðaálfr* ('demon of Geirstaðir') who was the brother of Hálfdanr *svarti* ('the black'), was a cousin of Haraldr *hárfagri* ('fair-hair'). In the *Þáttr af Upplendinga konungum*, a thirteenth-century work, it is said that Rǫgnvaldr ruled Grenland, the next kingdom south from Haraldr's home province of Vestfold.[31]

---

[27]Finnur Jónsson, *Den oldnorske og oldislandske Litteraturs Historie*, 2nd ed., 3 vols. (Copenhagen, 1920–4) I, 432–42, esp. 439: 'en retsindig, frejdig og humant, tænkende mand, der troede på skæbnen (Yng. 7.17) og på guderne, skønt han ikke synes at have været religiøs i dybere forstand'.

[28]*Ibid.* I, 439. Cf. *SnE* III, 397–404, esp. 401.

[29]*Heimskringla I*, ed. Bjarni, pp. 26, 27, 29, 31, 32, 33, 36, 38, 40, 41, 46, 49, 52, 54, 58, 60, 61, 64, 71, 74, 76, 77, 79, 80, 82 and 83.

[30]Text based on *Heimskringla I*, ed. Bjarni, p. 83: 'The best distinguishing name that I know beneath the blue sky, such as a king may possess, is the name whereby Rǫgnvaldr, steersman of the waggon, is called Heath-Grey'. Also based on *Skj* B I, 14.

[31]*Heimskringla I*, ed. Bjarni, p. xxxiv. Cf. Map, p. iv.

The ninth-century authenticity of *Ynglingatal* seems probable on grounds of its high number of semantic difficulties relative to that of overtly Christian poems, but this date has never been taken for granted. Most recently Claus Krag proposes that *Ynglingatal* is not Þjóðólfr's poem, but was rather abstracted from a now-lost prose chronicle in the twelfth century. Krag, though he shows little interest in the semantics of this poem, suggests that the first four stanzas of *Ynglingatal* were contrived to represent the four elements, earth, water, air and fire, and cites as further evidence for this scholastic input the kennings for natural elements 'fire' (*sævar niðr*, 'sea's kinsman', st. 4; and *sonr Fornjóts*, 'Fornjótr's son', st. 23) and 'water' (*Loga dís*, 'fire's ?sister', st. 9).[32] Yet there is no reason why these and other kennings in *Ynglingatal* are not derived from folktale motifs which Þjóðólfr considered to be a part of his mythology. Edith Marold, on the evidence of a style of conceit or verbal metaphor common to both poems, shows that *Ynglingatal* was probably composed by the same author as *Haustlǫng*; no-one has yet claimed that the battered, obscure and no doubt incomplete poem *Haustlǫng* is a twelfth-century forgery.[33] Thus it is likely that *Ynglingatal* is largely what Snorri says it is, the work of Þjóðólfr of Hvinir.

The other works attributed to Þjóðólfr may be cited as they come up in his story, which unfolds essentially through deductions from the twelfth- and thirteenth-century histories of Norway and Iceland. Þjóðólfr seems to have belonged to an established family, for his variant epithet *hvinverski* ('of the family of Hvinir') seems to imply a Norwegian kindred named the *Hvinverjar* (analogous to the Icelandic *Oddaverjar* of the eleventh and twelfth centuries). Þjóðólfr lived in the reign of King Haraldr hárfagri (ruled *c.* 880–*c.* 930). The ideology of this king, if we consider his epithet ('fair-hair') in combination with the later sources, claims that he refused to cut or comb his hair until he had mastered Norway: according to these sources, Haraldr conquered region after region, showed mercy to those who joined him and cruelty to those who resisted, and eventually bent all Norway to his will, making erstwhile kings now his tenants over previously their land of which he now made himself the owner of

[32]Claus Krag, *Ynglingatal og Ynglingesaga: en studie i historiske kilder*, Studia Humaniora 2 (Kristiansand, 1991), 47–59 and 182–200.

[33]Marold, *Kenningkunst*, pp. 153–210.

every square foot.³⁴ The defining moment in Haraldr's ascendancy was
later presented as the sea-battle in Hafrsfjǫrðr (*c.* 885), a sheltered inlet
to the south-west of Stavanger, in which Haraldr routed the last of his
opponents and forced many of them to flee first to Orkney, Shetland, the
Hebrides and Ireland, and then to Iceland. In his prologue to *Ynglinga
saga*, Snorri states unequivocally that 'Þjóðólfr of Hvinir was the court
poet of Haraldr Fairhair; he composed a poem for King Rǫgnvaldr Higher-
than-the-Heath which is called List of Ynglingar'.³⁵ Þjóðólfr is named as
the court poet of King Haraldr in the *Skáldatal* (a 'list of poets' found in
the U-text (*c.* 1300) of *Snorra Edda* and yet probably drawn up in the
twelfth century), in which it is also said that Þjóðólfr composed a work
for Þorleifr inn spaki.³⁶ The author of *Egils saga*, ch. 8, does not mention
Þjóðólfr alongside Þorbjǫrn *hornklofi* ('horn-claw') and some other poets of Haraldr's court. This omission, however, may be explained if we
accept Jónas' argument that Snorri wrote *Egils saga* after the
Heimskringla-compilation, and following his second visit to Norway in
1237–9. It is possible that Snorri chose not to associate Þjóðólfr with
Haraldr because he had now conceived of this king, on the basis of his
young enemy King Hákon Hákonarson, as the worst kind of tyrant.³⁷

    The fact that Þjóðólfr describes Rǫgnvaldr as a *konungr* ('king') in
Ynglingatal 37, may imply two things: first, that he lived in the court in
Grenland before Haraldr had accomplished at least the greater part of

---

³⁴For example: *Ágrip. Fagrskinna*, ed. Bjarni, pp. 4–5 (*Ágrip*, ch. 2), 58–71
(*Fagrskinna*, chs. 2–3); *Heimskringla I*, ed. Bjarni, pp. 94–118 (*Haralds saga
ins hárfagra*, chs. 1–20); and *Egils saga*, ed. Sigurður, pp. 7–15 (chs. 3–6), esp.
11–12. See also G. Turville-Petre, 'The Cult of Óðinn in Iceland', *Nine Norse
Studies*, Viking Society for Northern Research: Text Series 5 (London, 1972),
1–19, esp. 15–16; originally published as 'Um Óðinsdýrkun á Íslandi', *Studia
Islandica* 17 (1958), 5–25; and Hastrup, *Culture and History in Medieval Iceland*, pp. 190–1.

³⁵*Heimskringla I*, ed. Bjarni, p. 4 (prol.): 'Þjóðólfr ór Hvini var skáld Haralds
konungs ins hárfagra. Hann orti kvæði um Rǫgnvald konung heiðumhæra, þat
er kallat Ynglingatal'.

³⁶*SnE* III, 253, 261 and 273. On the date of *Skáldatal*, see Turville-Petre, *Scaldic
Poetry*, p. xxi.

³⁷Jónas, p. 269. This argument is a revision of Sigurður's (*Egils saga*, ed., p. liii–
xcv, §§ 5–6, and *Snorri Sturluson*, pp. 28–30), in which Snorri's authorship of
Egils saga is postulated as being after he moved away from Borg in *c.* 1206 and
before his trip to Norway in 1237.

his mission, to conquer Norway; and second, that he achieved a position as one of Haraldr's court-poets on the strength of his work for Haraldr's cousin Rǫgnvaldr — possibly through *Ynglingatal*. The true extent of Haraldr's conquests has been questioned, but it seems plausible that Haraldr made himself the overlord of at least the south-eastern and central regions of Norway.[38] The chronology of Þjóðólfr's movements must remain uncertain, however. What can be suggested is that this court-poet travelled widely at least in the southern half of Norway, since he is thought to have composed works for Rǫgnvaldr of Grenland, Þorleifr Hǫrðu-Kárason of Hǫrðaland, and King Haraldr of Vestfold and other southern and central provinces. Þjóðólfr is known not by his father's name, which is lost, but by the name of his home estate (*ór Hvini* or *hvinverski*). This epithet also shows that Þjóðólfr must have been known in kingdoms and provinces outside Agðir, his homeland (modern west Agder, where Kvinesdal is situated).

No genuine work by Þjóðólfr in honour of Haraldr has survived, although he is said to have composed a poem about Haraldr in the *Skáldatal*.[39] This tradition is probably related to a passage in *Fagrskinna*, ch. 3 (*c*. 1220), in which five stanzas of another poem elsewhere attributed to Þorbjǫrn hornklofi are ascribed to *Þjóðólfr ór Hvini*. These stanzas are now classified as st. 7–12 of a poem of twenty-three stanzas which Finnur treats as Þorbjǫrn's and which scholars have named *Hrafnsmál* or *Haraldskvæði* (*Skj* B I, 23). Snorri read *Fagrskinna*, and in *Gylf*, ch. 2 (p. 7), Snorri quotes the first half-stanza of *Hrafnsmál* 11 similarly with reference to Þjóðólfr *inn hvinverski*; although in *Haralds saga ins hárfagra*, ch. 18, he gives st. 7–11 of this poem to Haraldr's poet Þorbjǫrn, whose only surviving poem is likely to be *Glymdrápa*, a lay of nine extant stanzas which hails Haraldr's victories against Norwegians, Gautar and Scots or Irishmen (*Skj* B I, 20–1). *Hrafnsmál*, though Finnur classifies it as Þorbjǫrn's work, is an untitled and uneven piece of work. Like *Glymdrápa*, *Hrafnsmál* glorifies Haraldr's victories and in particular Hafrsfjǫrðr, and is most likely to have been composed in the eleventh or twelfth century at the earliest. St. 7–11 focus on Hafrsfjǫrðr and on the ignominious flight of Haraldr's last-remaining enemies, principally Kjǫtvi *inn auðgi* ('the wealthy') and his son Þórir *haklangr* ('long-chin'). That Þjóðólfr was held to be the author of these stanzas by the compiler

---

[38]See Claus Krag, 'Norge som odel i Harald Hårfagres ætt', *Historisk Tidsskrift* [Norwegian] 68 (1989), 288–302.

[39]*SnE* III, 397–404, esp. 400.

of *Fagrskinna*, or in the tradition on which this compiler relied, is probably to be explained by a use of place-names which could be taken to imply a local knowledge of the south-west coast of Norway: between Hafrsfjǫrðr and *Útsteinn* in the north (an island to the north of Stavanger, in Rogaland, in st. 9) and Listafjorden in the south (along the coast of *Jaðarr*, modern Jæren, in st. 11).[40] The poet whose name linked him with this region was naturally Þjóðólfr, since his home county Hvinir (Kvinesdal) lies not far from the southern coast along which the losers of this battle fled. Snorri may have had his first attribution of these stanzas to Þjóðólfr corrected when he stayed with Skúli Jarl on his first trip to Norway in 1218–20. There is little doubt that the later Icelanders took a greater interest in Þjóðólfr than in Þorbjǫrn, probably because of the political opportunities provided by the genealogy within his poem *Ynglingatal*.

According to *Skáldatal*, Þjóðólfr also composed a 'poem' (*kvæði*) in honour of Hákon Jarl Grjótgarðsson of Hlaðir, who, in *Fagrskinna*, is said to have been the northern ally of Haraldr and to have died in action in Stafanessvágr against one of the king's enemies, shortly before the climactic battle of Hafrsfjǫrðr.[41] No work of this description survives, but if the attribution in *Skáldatal* is based on fact, then it is possible that Þjóðólfr composed this poem as a memorial lay in *c.* 885, before or when he became a poet in Haraldr's court.

Haraldr took many women as concubines during his long reign. In *Haralds saga*, Snorri names twenty-two children begotten by Haraldr with women along his route, and these were only prominent women; Snorri also tells a story in which Haraldr began his conquest of Norway because a certain Gyða refused to go with him until he had first made himself a king like those of Denmark and Sweden.[42] In one story, which Snorri probably read in chs. 3–4 of *Ágrip* (a Norwegian work *c.* 1190, now preserved in an Icelandic manuscript), King Haraldr hárfagri fell in love with a Lappish woman named Snjófríðr, whose native magic had bewitched him. In Snorri's version of this tale, *Haralds saga hárfagra*

[40]Berg and Berg, *NAF Veibok*, pp. 6, B3, and 2–3, D3. Cf. Map, p. iv.

[41]*SnE* III, 401. *Ágrip. Fagrskinna*, ed. Bjarni, pp. 65–6 (ch. 3).

[42]*Heimskringla I*, ed. Bjarni, p. 96 (*Haralds saga hárfagra*, ch. 3): herein Haraldr's named children are Álǫf, Hrœrekr, Sigtryggr, Fróði, Þorgils (by Gyða); Guthormr, Hálfdanr svarti, Hálfdanr hvíti, Sigurðr (by Ása); Eiríkr blóðøx (by Ragnhildr); Óláfr Geirstaðaálfr, Bjǫrn, Ragnarr (by Svanhildr); Dagr, Hringr, Guðrøðr skíri, Ingigerðr (by Áshildr); Sigurðr hrísi, Hálfdanr háleggr, Guðrøðr ljómi, Rǫgnvaldr réttilbeini (by Snæfríðr).

(ch. 25), Haraldr made *Snæfríðr* his consort and had four sons by her. Snorri says that these boys were named Sigurðr *hrísi* ('brushwood'), Hálfdanr *háleggr* ('high-leg'), Guðrøðr *ljómi* ('gleam') and Rǫgnvaldr *réttilbeini* ('straight-bone').[43] When Snæfríðr died after the birth of Rǫgnvaldr, Haraldr went mad, forgot his kingdom and stared at her lifeless body, which, due to Lappish magic, remained in a lifelike state. Þorleifr inn spaki arrived, a resourceful royal adviser who succeeded in bringing the king to his senses by asking him to move Snæfríðr's corpse. Yet in the the aftermath of his madness, Haraldr rejected his four sons by this woman. Snorri then says that one of them, Guðrøðr, 'went to see Þjóðólfr of Hvinir, his foster-father, and asked him to accompany him to the king, because Þjóðólfr was the king's close friend'.[44] Þjóðólfr and Guðrøðr go to the king in Upplǫnd and conceal themselves on the bench furthest out from the king; later that evening, when the party is in full swing, Haraldr declaims a question to his guests in verse, asking why there seem to be too many drinkers in his retinue with grey hair. Þjóðólfr answers in the same metre:

> Hǫfðum vér í hǫfði   hǫgg at eggja leiki
> með vellbrota vitrum.   Vǫruma þá til margir.[45]

This poem is not likely to be Þjóðólfr's true work, but its statement may be true, that Þjóðólfr supported Haraldr in his first bid to conquer Norway. In the story, Þjóðólfr takes down his hood, Haraldr recognises him and Þjóðólfr asks him not to spurn his sons, 'for they would have been glad to have a better mothering if you had got that for them' (*því at fúsir væri þeir at eiga betra móðerni, ef þú hefðir þeim þat fengit*). With this daring ridicule, Þjóðólfr, a man evidently associated with a sense of humour, succeeded in restoring the sons to their father.

Although Haraldr gave in to Þjóðólfr, he 'asked him to take Guðrøðr to live with him at home just as he had before, but Sigurðr and Hálfdanr he asked to go to Hringaríki, and Rǫgnvaldr to Haðaland'.[46] Snorri may thus imply that Þjóðólfr had previously fostered all four of the boys. Towards the end of Haraldr's life, according to Snorri, the king's fa-

[43]*Heimskringla I*, ed. Bjarni, p. 126.
[44]*Ibid.*, p. 127 (ch. 26): 'fór á fund Þjóðólfs ins hvinverska, fóstrfǫður síns, ok bað hann fara með sér til konungs, því at Þjóðólfr var ástvinr konungs'.
[45]*Ibid.*, p. 128: 'We had blows on our heads in the play of blades with the wise gold-breaker. We weren't too many then.'
[46]*Ibid.*, p. 128: 'bað hann hafa Guðrøð heim með sér, svá sem hann hafði fyrr verit, en Sigurð ok Hálfdan bað hann fara á Hringaríki, en Rǫgnvald á Haðaland'.

voured son Eiríkr *blóðøx* ('blood-axe'), son of Gunnhildr, took a force of men to Haðaland, surrounded Rǫgnvaldr réttilbeini along with eighty male witches in their house, and burned them inside – apparently with Haraldr's approval – on the grounds of *seiðr* ('perversity').[47] There is a poem in this story in defence of *seiðr* which Snorri attributes to Rǫgnvaldr, although it is likely that Haraldr's charge of moral depravity was quoted after the deed in order to cloak the pressing need of his son, Eiríkr, to eliminate his rivals for the succession. Among these rivals would have been the sons of Snæfríðr. Eiríkr's unbridled *realpolitik* may be implicit in Snorri's narrative, for in the next sentence we see Guðrøðr ljómi, Rǫgnvaldr's brother, interrupting a winter stay with his foster-father Þjóðólfr *í Hvini* ('in Hvinir'). In a hurry to leave, though at the wrong time of year, Guðrøðr 'had a skiff fully manned and wanted to sail north to Rogaland' (*hafði skútu alskipaða, ok vildi hann fara norðr á Rogaland*). There are gales, Þjóðólfr knows the winds, 'and yet Guðrøðr was impatient to go on his journey and took the delay badly' (*en Guðrøði var títt um ferð sína, ok lét hann illa um dvǫlina*). At this moment, Snorri quotes one stanza of *dróttkvætt* which he attributes to Þjóðólfr:

> Fariða ér, áðr fleyja   flatvǫllr heðan batnar,
> verpr Geitis vegr grjóti,   Guðrøðr, um sjá stóran.
> Vindbýsna skaltu, vísi   víðfrægr, heðan bíða.
> Vesið með oss, unz verði   veðr. Nú's brim fyr Jaðri.[48]

When Guðrøðr ignores Þjóðólfr's advice and drowns with all his men in a storm before Jaðarr, the pathos of this verse become clear. But it is unlikely that this *ad hoc* piece of work is Þjóðólfr's, if only because the speaker, with the 2nd pl. imperative in *fariða*, uses a courtly form of address which did not come into use until the twelfth century at the earliest.[49] The forger of this verse may have had his eye on Þjóðólfr's more established canon, for his use of *Geitir* as a sea-king's name seems to emulate that in Þjóðólfr's shield-kenning *Geitis garðr* ('fortress of Geitir') in *Haustlǫng* 20/5–6. As I shall attempt to show a little later,

---

[47]*Ibid.*, pp. 138–9 (*Haralds saga ins hárfagra*, ch. 34).

[48]Text after *ibid.*, p. 139: 'Do not sail out of here, Guðrøðr, over the great sea, before the flat-land of cutters [sea] begins to improve; the road of Geitir [sea] roars on the shingle. From here, widely famed prince, you must sit out the wind's portents. Stay with us until the good weather comes. There are breakers now before Jæren'. See also *Skj* B I, 19.

[49]See Einar Haugen, *The Scandinavian Languages: An Introduction to their History* (London, 1976), pp. 303–4.

verses of this kind may have been created for the reading of sagas about Haraldr, Þjóðólfr and Þorleifr in Oddi in the early twelfth century.

In Snorri's account of the life and times of King Haraldr hárfagri, both Þjóðólfr and Þorleifr inn spaki have a role to play at court in relation to the Lappish witch Snæfríðr and her sons. In keeping with the allusion in *Skáldatal*, the same Þorleifr inn spaki is probably the name of the benefactor whom Þjóðólfr rewards with a poem in *Haustlǫng*. Þorleifr inn spaki figures in two stories preserved in the later prose sources. In one, in *Fagrskinna*, ch. 1, Þorleifr advises Haraldr's father King Hálfdanr *svarti* ('the black'), who never dreams, to see the future by sleeping in a pigsty; Hálfdanr dreams that he is naked and yet covered in long locks of his own hair, some of which drop down to the earth, some to his knees or middle, some no further than to his neck and some just little tufts; these locks come in all colours, some ugly, some fair. Þorleifr interprets the locks of hair as different lineages, one of which is later known to be that of Óláfr Haraldsson, the first saint of Scandinavia.[50] Snorri repeats this tale, in some places almost word for word, in *Hálfdanar saga svarta*, ch. 7.[51] In the other story, as we have seen, Þorleifr is the adviser who succeeds in tricking Haraldr Hálfdanarson out of a bout of insanity after this king dotes on the dead body of Snæfríðr, his Lappish consort, for three years. Þorleifr asks the king to show Snæfríðr and thereby himself more honour after such a long period, by changing her clothes; when she is moved, her body rapidly decays and Haraldr comes to his senses. This story is first recorded in ch. 4 of *Ágrip*, which appears to be a Norwegian work, probably by a Þrándheimr cleric *c.* 1190, yet preserved in an Icelandic manuscript.[52] The author of *Fagrskinna*, who knew *Ágrip*, seems to have left this story out because it showed Haraldr in an unheroic light.[53] Yet Snorri, who used both sources, thought enough of this story to repeat it in *Haralds saga hárfagra*, ch. 25, this time with the sequel in ch. 26 in which Þjóðólfr of Hvinir saves the boys.[54] If Snorri may be taken as a guide, it seems that Þorleifr and Þjóðólfr were linked in respect of Snæfríðr and her sons. Þjóðólfr's apparent familiarity with Lappish and Norwegian witchcraft seems to be reflected in both *Ynglingatal* (*vitta véttr*, 3/3 and 21/3) and *Haustlǫng*

[50]*Ágrip. Fagrskinna*, ed. Bjarni, pp. 57–8.

[51]*Heimskringla I*, ed. Bjarni, pp. 90–1.

[52]*Ágrip. Fagrskinna*, ed. Bjarni, p. 6.

[53]*Ibid.*, pp. lxxviii–ix.

[54]*Haralds saga ins hárfagra*, ed. Bjarni, *Heimskringla I*, pp. 126–7.

(*Hildar vetts*, 1/8 (see note); *véltr vélum* in 11/5 and in the content and rhymes of st. 11; the noun *Finnr*, 13/6; and *ǫl-Gefjun sára gœli*, 20/2–4). His representation on behalf of Snæfríðr's boys would have occurred about a generation before the deaths of Rǫgnvaldr and Guðrøðr as grown men, which, if we are to believe Snorri again, occurred a few years before the death of Haraldr hárfagri. Given that Haraldr is thought to have died *c.* 930, it appears that Þorleifr and Þjóðólfr would have been known in his court at the same time, and thus on conversant terms with each other, in *c.* 900. If these deductions are accepted, it is possible to date the composition of *Haustlǫng* tentatively at about this time.

Finally, there is a reference in *Skáldatal* to a poem which Þjóðólfr is said to have composed for Strút-Haraldr Jarl of Skáney (Skåne), whose son Sigvaldi Jarl held a feast in memory of him in Jómsborg in c. 985 (one which led to an attempted invasion of Norway).[55] As Skáney was a Danish province in the tenth century, it is likely that Strút-Haraldr was a Dane. No poem of this description survives, but if the attribution is correct, Strút-Haraldr could have received a poem from Þjóðólfr when he was a young earl in the first half of the tenth century, perhaps as early as *c.* 930–40. In this case, the poem for Strút-Haraldr Jarl would have been the last major work of the poet Þjóðólfr before his death, the date of which is unknown. Given that Þjóðólfr was associated with Haraldr's sons by Snæfríðr, it is possible that he, too, was eventually forced to leave Hvinir when Eiríkr consolidated his power in southern Norway in *c.* 930–3, and that this poem for Strút-Haraldr, if genuine, was thereafter composed by Þjóðólfr in exile. The author of *Ágrip* portrays Eiríkr as fratricidal, an easy prey to the influence of Gunnhildr, his scheming wife, and otherwise 'so susceptible to cruelty and to all kinds of oppression against the people that it was heavy to bear'.[56]

In short, the outline of Þjóðólfr's life may be surmised as follows. Born of a landed family in Hvinir in West Agðir (perhaps in *c.* 860–70), Þjóðólfr became the court-poet of King Rǫgnvaldr of Grenland. It is possible that he took part in some of the fighting which led to the alleged supremacy of Rǫgnvaldr's powerful cousin, King Haraldr hárfagri of Vestfold. Before *c.* 884, he may have composed a memorial lay in honour

---

[55]*SnE* III, 401. A certain Sveinn *Jarl*, said to be the poet's patron in the Uppsala MS, may be Strút-Haraldr's older kinsman (*ibid.*, p. 268). *Ágrip. Fagrskinna*, ed. Bjarni, pp. 122–4 (*Fagrskinna*, chs. 19–20).

[56]*Ágrip. Fagrskinna*, ed. Bjarni, p. 7 (ch. 5): 'svá áhlýðinn til grimmleiks ok til allskyns áþjánar við lýðinn, at þungt var at bera'.

of Hákon Jarl Grjótgarðsson, who had fallen in battle against an enemy of Haraldr before the crucial battle of Hafrsfjǫrðr. Perhaps subsequently, after having secured his reputation in Grenland and Vestfold with *Ynglingatal*, Þjóðólfr became a courtier of King Haraldr in *c.* 890. After some more years, it seems that Þjóðólfr received or inherited land in Hvinir, for he became close enough to the king to foster Guðrøðr ljómi Haraldsson in his home, if not also the other sons of Haraldr by the king's reputedly Lappish consort Snæfríðr. Þjóðólfr represented the interests of Snæfríðr's sons in court when this lady died, and he succeeded in keeping Guðrøðr with him and perhaps even in saving these boys from the malign attention of rival consorts or half-brothers. By the same token, it seems that Þjóðólfr was no longer at court; it may have been at about this time, perhaps in *c.* 900, that he stayed in the court of another friend of the Snæfríðr-faction, the chieftain Þorleifr inn spaki Hǫrðu-Kárason, when he received a shield from Þorleifr and notoriously (hence the title *haustlǫng [drápa]*) spent a month from *c.* 15 September to *c.* 14 October composing a poem of thanks which he delivered at a *haustǫl*-festival in Hǫrðaland before the onset of winter. As the years went by and Þjóðólfr grew older, he appears to have lived on his estate in Hvinir. Towards the end of Haraldr's reign, when Eiríkr blóðøx began to take over parts of Norway not long before *c.* 930, Þjóðólfr in Hvinir suffered the loss by drowning of his foster-son Guðrøðr Haraldsson, who is implied to have been staying with him there. Perhaps before *c.* 940, it is possible that Þjóðólfr composed a poem in honour of Strút-Haraldr Jarl of Skáney, in whose court he may have spent the last years of his life as an exile.

TRANSMISSION OF *HAUSTLǪNG*

Haustlǫng was first passed down by word of mouth, across an interval of two hundred years, to scholars and antiquarians in Iceland who could have taken more deliberate steps as early as the early twelfth century to ensure the survival of this poem. Up to this point, which was probably the library in Oddi, two routes of transmission emerge as the main possibilities: one, from Þorleifr inn spaki to the law-reformer Úlfljótr and thence to his kinsmen in northern Iceland in *c.* 930; the other, more plausible, from Þjóðólfr to King Haraldr and thence to the poetic tradition of the Norwegian royal family, from where *Haustlǫng* could have travelled to Iceland at any time, in company with *Ynglingatal*, *Ragnarsdrápa* and other kings' poems.

In the first instance, once *Haustlǫng* was performed publicly for
Þorleifr inn spaki, it is fair to say that this poem would have been regarded as his property. The first (extant) line of *Haustlǫng* indicates
Þjóðólfr's wish to compose a poem *góð at gjǫldum gunnveggjar* ('in
payment for a good battle-wall [shield]'), and a refrain surviving in st.
13/ and 20/7–8 reiterates Þorleifr's name as Þjóðólfr's benefactor. There
is an earlier example of the same *topos* in the first two stanzas of
Ragnarsdrápa (*c.* 850), where the poet Bragi asks a certain Hrafnketill
if he wishes to hear how he intends to praise the king [Ragnarr]:

> Nema svát góð ens gjalla   gjǫld baugnafaðs vildi
> meyjar hjóls enn mæri   mǫgr Sigurðar Hǫgna.

(*Ragnarsdrápa* 2)[57]

Although Bragi pretends that his poem is not 'good payment' (*góð gjǫld*)
for the shield, his modest words reveal an assumption that poets had to
pay for their shields with verses. Þjóðólfr appears to refer to his benefactor in similar words in *Haustlǫng*, in which he and presumably his audience consider the poem, when performed, to be Þorleifr's *gjǫld* for the
shield. A story in the thirteenth-century *Egils saga* throws some more
light on the ritual involved in giving and receiving ornamental shields.
In this story, the young poet Einarr *skálaglamm* ('cup-clatter') Helgason
comes back from Norway with a shield which Hákon Jarl (ruled *c.* 975–
995) has given him in return for his poem *Vellekla* ('gold-shortage'), a
eulogy of Hákon Jarl (title notwithstanding). Full of admiration for Egill
Skalla-Grímsson, his mentor in this fine tale, Einarr calls by at his house
in Borg intending to give him the shield. Egill is out on a tour of some
northern districts, but Einarr waits. After three days and no Egill, Einarr
makes ready to leave, hangs up the shield in Egill's bed-chamber and
rides off. Egill, arriving shortly thereafter, is not amused to find the
shield waiting for him along with a message from his servants that Einarr
skálaglamm had left it there: 'Let him be the poorest of all bene-
factors! Does he think I should stay awake over his shield in there
making up a poem about it?'.[58] Egill first thinks of killing Einarr, then
gives up the idea and speaks a verse, instead, about composing a poem

---

[57]*Skj* B I, 1: 'unless it is that the famed son of Sigurðr [Ragnarr] would like a
good payment for the ring-?painted resounding wheel of Hǫgni's girl [Hildr's
wheel: shield]'.

[58]*Egils saga*, ed. Sigurður, p. 272 (ch. 78): 'Gefi hann allra manna armastr!
Ætlar hann, at ek skyla þar vaka yfir ok yrkja um skjǫld hans?'.

in thanks for the shield: *Mál es lofs at lýsa ljósgarð, es þák barða* ('It's time to glorify the ship's light-wall that I have received'). Although this story and its poor accompanying verse are likely to have been made up after Egill's lifetime, perhaps as late as the thirteenth century, it remains clear from these sources that the gift of a shield was synonymous with the composition of a poem in exchange. Thus Þjóðólfr's poem could have become the property of Þorleifr Hǫrðu-Kárason in *c.* 900.

Þorleifr seems to have been gifted with an exceptional memory, even by the standards of his preliterate day. Although there are two other tales about his resourcefulness (Hálfdanr's pigsty-dream and the Snæfríðr-affair), it is possible that Þorleifr was first named *inn spaki* ('the wise') because he was known to have memorized the codes of his local Norwegian law. In his *Íslendingabók* (*c.* 1122–33), Ari Þorgilsson says that his foster-father Teitr Ísleifsson told him that Úlfljótr, a *maðr austrœnn* (probably 'man from Norway'), brought to Iceland a new constitution based on Norwegian laws, 'and these were mostly based on the laws of the Gulaþing or on what the counsels of Þorleifr the wise, son of Hǫrðaland-Kári, were at that time, where additions or deletions should be made or the text should be altered'.[59] This constitutional reform seems to have happened a few years before *c.* 930, while Úlfljótr was still the Icelandic lawspeaker.[60] Teitr, one of Ari's most learned informants (*þess manns es ek kunna spakastan,* ch. 1), was probably born in the 1040s, not long after or before before his brother Gizurr (*c.* 1042), who became bishop after their father Ísleifr Gizurarson; Jakob thinks it likely that Teitr (d. 1110) had shared some of Gizurr's travels, and it is possible that Teitr had learnt of Þorleifr's connection with the basis of the Icelandic *Úlfljótslǫg* ('laws of Úlfljótr') from a visit to Norway.[61]

If Úlfljótr was the father of Icelandic law, Þorleifr could thus be said to be its godfather, and the link between him and Úlfljótr was strengthened further by Icelanders who wrote about a century after Ari. Styrmir *inn fróði* ('the learned') Kárason (1170s–1245), lawspeaker in 1210–14 and 1232–5 and a friend and probably scribe of Snorri Sturluson, is thought to have drafted one of the earliest versions of *Landnámabók*

---

[59] *Íslendingabók. Landnámabók*, ed. Jakob, p. 7 (ch. 2): 'en þau váru flest sett at því sem þá váru Golaþingslǫg eða ráð Þorleifs ens spaka Hǫrðu-Kárasonar váru til, hvar við skyldi auka eða af nema eða annan veg setja'.

[60] Ari says that Hrafn Hœngsson took up this office *nœstr Ulfljóti* ('next after Úlfljótr'), See *ibid.*, pp. xxxviii–ix and 9 (ch. 3).

[61] *Ibid.*, pp. vii–viii.

('book of settlers').[62] In a genealogy now contained in ch. 268 of the *Hauksbók*-recension of *Landnámabók*, but one which can be identified as having originated with Styrmir, it is said that a settler named Þórðr skeggi sold his lands in Lón in Iceland to Úlfljótr 'son of Þóra the daughter of Ketill Hǫrðaland-Kári' (*syni Þóru, dóttur Ketils Hǫrðu-Kára*); and that Úlfljótr, when he was sixty years old, stayed for three winters in Norway, where 'he and Þorleifr the wise, his mother's brother, established those laws which were later called the laws of Úlfljótr'.[63] Þorleifr is also given as the mother's brother of Úlfljótr in *Hauksbók*, ch. 11.[64] The relationship between a man and his sister's son is traditional in Germanic societies.[65] Two other texts in which Úlfljótr is Þorleifr's nephew, and which Jón Jóhannesson has established to be even closer than *Hauksbók* to Styrmir's draft of *Landnámabók*, are *Þorsteins þáttr uxafóts* (ch. 1, the closest, yet with an altered sequence of passages); and *Brót af Þórðar sǫgu hreðu* (ch. 1, less close).[66] Common to all three versions of Styrmir's text is his or a family predecessor's supplement to Ari's record to the effect that Úlfljótr was an Icelander of the same blood as Þorleifr Hǫrðu-Kárason.

Three names, *Kári*, *Ketill* and *Þóra*, are common both to Styrmir's family in Iceland and the kindred of Þorleifr inn spaki in Norway. Although Styrmir's lineage is uncertain, it is thought that his father Kári was the grandson of Ketill Þorsteinsson (1075–1145), who became bishop of Hólar in 1122. Ketill was one of the men who advised Ari to revise his

[62]On Styrmir, see Jón, *Gerðir Landnámabókar*, pp. 137–40. On Styrmir's (now lost) text and its history through the vicissitudes of different transcribers and editors, see *ibid.*, pp. 140–74; *Íslendingabók. Landnámabók*, ed. Jakob, pp. l–liv (§ 8) and xcvi–cvix (§§ 13–14); and Turville-Petre, *Origins of Icelandic Literature*, pp. 102–3.

[63]Cf. *Íslendingabók. Landnámabók*, ed. Jakob, p. 313: 'settu þeir Þorleifr inn spaki móðurbróðir hans lǫg þau, er síðan váru kǫlluð Úlfljótslǫg'. Two other recensions, *Skarðsárbók* and *Þórðarbók*, give Þorleifr to be Úlfljótr's maternal grandfather's brother, but this is probably a later extension. See *ibid.*, p. 312, n. 5.

[64]*Ibid.*, p. 49.

[65]See Rolf Bremmer, 'The Importance of Kinship: Uncle and Nephew in "Beowulf"', *Amsterdamer Beiträge zur älteren Germanistik* 15 (1980), 21–38.

[66]Jón, *Gerðir Landnámabókar*, pp. 161–2. See also *Þorsteins þáttr uxafóts*, ed. Þórhallur Vilmundarson and Bjarni Vilhjálmsson, ÍF 13 (Reykjavík, repr. 1991), pp. 341–2; and *Brót af Þórðar sögu hreðu*, ed. Jóhannes Halldórsson, ÍF 14 (Reykjavík, 1959), pp. 230–1 (ch. 1).

first draft of *Íslendingabók* (*c.* 1122–33); in his *ættartala*, which is probably Ari's postscript to *Íslendingabók* and preserves material excised from
the first draft of that work, Ketill's lineage is recorded as far back as
Helgi *inn magri* ('the lean').[67] It can thereby be established with a reasonable degree of certainty that Helga, a daughter of Helgi, was the
great-grandmother of Guðmundr *ríki* ('the powerful'), whose own great-
grandson was Bishop Ketill.[68] In *Landnámabók*, Úlfljótr's son Gunnarr
is said to have married another daughter of Helgi whose name was Þóra,
a sister of Helga.[69] So it is possible that Ketill, or another member of his
family, wished to connect his Helgi-lineage by marriage to the kindred
of Hǫrðu-Kári, a Norwegian chieftain, by making Úlfljótr into Hǫrðu-
Kári's grandson through an otherwise unknown woman named Þóra.
Styrmir's thoughts about the importance of lineage are preserved in the
epilogue to *Þórðarbók*, a relatively late recension of *Landnámabók*:

> Many people say that writing a record of settlement is an irrel-
> evant kind of scholarship. Yet we think we can sooner answer
> foreigners when they take us for being descended from slaves or
> criminals, just as we can those men who want to know old learn-
> ing or how to trace their ancestry, if we know precisely how to
> trace the true origins of our families back to the beginning rather
> than be cut off in the middle, in that all peoples are sufficiently
> wise to know the beginning of the settlements in their land or
> how which settlements began or what their kindred was.[70]

It is reasonable to suppose that these thoughts reflect the thinking of
Bishop Ketill, Styrmir's great-grandfather, on the matter of his family
tradition.

The alleged blood-kinship between Úlfljótr and Þorleifr in

---

[67]*Íslendingabók. Landnámabók*, ed. Jakob, pp. 3 (prol.) and 27. On the authenticity of the postscript, see *ibid.*, pp. 26–7; and Joan Turville-Petre, 'The Gene-
alogist and History: Ari to Snorri', *Saga-Book* 20 (1978–9), 7–23, esp. 9–10.

[68]*Íslendingabók. Landnámabók*, ed. Jakob, fig. XVIIb.

[69]*Ibid.*, p. 266 (*Hauksbók*, ch. 197 and *Sturlubók*, ch. 231).

[70]Quoted in *ibid.*, pp. cii–ciii (§ 13): 'Þat er margra manna mál, at þat sé óskyldr
fróðleikr at rita landnám. En vér þykjumsk heldr svara kunna útlendum mǫnnum,
þá er þeir bregða oss því at vér séim komnir af þrælum eða illmennum, ef vér
vitum víst várar kynferðir sannar, svá ok þeim mǫnnum, er vita vilja forn frœði
eða rekja ættartǫlur, at taka heldr at upphafi til en hǫggvask í mitt mál, enda eru
svá allar vitrar þjóðir, at vita upphaf sinna landsbyggða eða hvers[u] hvergi til
hefjask eða kynslóðir'.

Landnámabók and related sources, which may have been accomplished by Bishop Ketill, seems to have pushed Þorleifr's lifetime further into the tenth century. A sentence in *Ágrip* shows that Þorleifr Hǫrðu-Kárason was probably dead when Eiríkr fled to England and the young King Hákon Haraldsson Aðalsteinsfóstri (ruled *c.* 947–60), presumably in *c.* 950, revised the *Golaþingslǫg* 'according to the approved text of Þorleifr the wise, which had been in use formerly'.[71] This sentence seems to indicate that Þorleifr's laws were memorized after his death, but it is ambiguous enough to be read as a statement that he was still alive when Hákon reached that part of Norway. Thus Þorleifr, if we believe *Fagrskinna* (a work written after *Ágrip* in Norway *c.* 1220, yet probably by an Icelander), was still alive when Hákon 'established laws across all of Norway with the counsels of Þorleifr the wise and of other men of wisdom'.[72] Likewise, in *Hákonar saga góða*, Snorri says that Hákon 'established the laws of the Gulaþing with the counsels of Þorleifr the wise', although he qualifies the extent of Þorleifr's influence by adding that Hákon established the laws of the Frostaþing with the advice of Sigurðar Jarl (son of Hákon Jarl Grjótgarðsson and father of Hákon Jarl *inn ríki*, 'the powerful') and of other wise men of the Þrándheimr region.[73] In a context one generation after Þorleifr inn spaki, the author of *Fagrskinna* alludes to Klyppr Þórðarson, a brother's son of Þorleifr, as being alive in the reign of Hákon Haraldsson's successor, Haraldr *gráfeldr* ('grey-cloak') Eiríksson (ruled *c.* 960–75).[74] Finally, in *Óláfs saga Tryggvasonar*, ch. 54, Snorri cites Þorleifr inn spaki among four sons of Hǫrðu-Kári, one of whom, Ǫlmóðr *inn gamli* ('the old') is still alive to parley with King Óláfr when he arrives to convert the men of Hǫrðaland to Christianity, presumably in *c.* 995.[75] On the basis of these references, Sophus Bugge assumed that both Þorleifr and *Haustlǫng*, a poem dedicated to Þorleifr, and consequently Þjóðólfr himself, all lived in the mid-tenth century.[76]

---

[71]*Ágrip. Fagrskinna*, ed. Bjarni, p. 9 (ch. 5): 'eptir ráðagørð Þorleifs spaka, er verit hafði forðum'.

[72]*Ibid.*, p. 80 (ch. 9): 'setti lǫg um allan Nóreg með ráði Þorleifs ins spaka ok annarra vitra manna'.

[73]*Heimskringla I*, ed. Bjarni, p. 163 (ch. 11): 'setti Gulaþingslǫg með ráði Þorleifs spaka'.

[74]*Ágrip. Fagrskinna*, ed. Bjarni, p. 102 (ch. 14).

[75]*Heimskringla I*, ed. Bjarni, p. 304 (cf. pp. 306–7).

[76]Sophus Bugge, 'Iduns Æbler', *ANF* 5 (1889), 1–45, esp. 1–4.

Bjarni Aðalbjarnarson suggests that Óláfr Tryggvason's reign (*c.* 995–1000) is the correct context for Qlmóðr Hǫrðu-Kárason, Þorleifr's brother.[77] But these views are questionable in that they favour Snorri's accuracy over that of earlier sources, particularly that of Ari Þorgilsson a century before him.[78] Snorri also mentions a certain Þorgrímr *ór Hvini* ('from Hvinir'), a son of Þjóðólfr, implying that he fought amidships on Tryggvason's longship in the battle of Svǫlð (*c.* 1000).[79] Since Þjóðólfr can be dated by his own reference in *Ynglingatal* 37 to King Rǫgnvaldr, who died in *c.* 920, it is unlikely that this Þorgrímr from Hvinir, if he existed, was the son of the poet Þjóðólfr. In these ways, it seems more likely that Þorleifr and the other sons of Hǫrðu-Kári lived around the beginning rather than at the end of the tenth century, and that Þorleifr, in particular, was truly associated with Þjóðólfr and the kings Hálfdanr (died *c.* 880) and Haraldr hárfagri (ruled *c.* 880–*c.* 930).

A second possible route for the transmission of *Haustlǫng* would have been through the court-poets themselves. If only to prove their lineage, it is likely that kings expected their poets to have memorized the poems composed in honour of their ancestors. There is no record of a Norse poetic cadre comparable to the Irish *filid* of the pre-Norman period, who preserved royal and monastic tradition in oral and then literary form.[80] On the other hand, it is reasonably clear that Bragi's *Ragnarsdrápa*, presumed to be composed in honour of the Danish king Ragnarr *loðbrók* ('shaggy-breeches') Sigurðarson (thus *c.* 850), was preserved orally in the court of Haraldr hárfagri, whose Danish mother Ragnhildr is said to have been Ragnarr's granddaughter.[81] Thus, although a royal poet's works became the property of their honorands, they would rapidly have become known among other royal poets. When together in royal courts, Norse and Icelandic poets imitated their predecessors no less than poets anywhere else in the world. The last Norwegian poet to be named before the Christianization of Norway (*c.* 1030), Eyvindr Finnsson (*fl. c.* 960–85), was named *skáldaspillir* ('plunderer or poets'), probably because

---

[77]*Heimskringla I*, ed. Bjarni, p. 304, n. 2.

[78]On Snorri's factual accuracy in this regard, see Whaley, *Heimskingla*, pp. 115–16.

[79]*Heimskringla I*, ed. Bjarni, p. 345 (ch. 94).

[80]On the *filid*, see Kim McCone, *Pagan Past and Christian Present in Early Irish Literature*, Maynooth Monographs 3 (Maynooth, 1990), 24–8.

[81]*Ágrip. Fagrskinna*, ed. Bjarni, p. 57 (*Fagrskinna*, ch. 1); *Heimskringla I*, ed. Bjarni, pp. 88–9 (*Hálfdanar saga svarta*, ch. 5).

the extent of his borrowings was considered to go too far. It is now accepted that Eyvindr lifted *Hákonarmál* 21/1–2 (*c.* 960) from a stanza in *Hávamál* (76 or 77);[82] and that he later modelled *Háleygjatal*, his celebration of the dynasty of Hákon Jarl in *c.* 985, on Þjóðólfr's *Ynglingatal*. In the light of this second borrowing, in particular, it seems likely that Eyvindr knew also *Haustlǫng* and perhaps other poems by Þjóðólfr. Given the number of intervening wars and usurpations and the tenuous link between Haraldr's family and Jarl Hákon's, it might be thought surprising that a poem from Grenland or Vestfold such as *Ynglingatal* could be passed down to a poet who worked nearly a hundred years later for another dynasty in Þrándheimr on the other side of Norway. Yet Eyvindr was Haraldr's great-grandson, and *Háleygjatal* shows that this transmission of *Ynglingatal* appears to have taken place; and it is most plausibly from the home-coming Icelandic court-poets of Hákon Jarl, Eyvindr's colleagues, that Snorri Sturluson ultimately derived his texts not only of such works as Eyvindr's poems, Einarr's *Vellekla*, Eilífr Goðrúnarson's *Þórsdrápa* and Hallfreðr Óttarsson's *Hákonardrápa*, but also of late-ninth- and early-tenth-century works such as Bragi's *Ragnarsdrápa*, Þorbjǫrn's *Glymdrápa* and Þjóðólfr's *Ynglingatal* and *Haustlǫng*.

Some poets from the courts of Hákon Jarl and his successor Óláfr Tryggvason settled down in Iceland: Einarr skálaglamm, whose friendship with Egill is fondly imagined in *Egils saga*, was the father's brother of Guðrún Ósvífrsdóttir, whose wide-rangeing family is celebrated in *Laxdœla saga*; and both Tindr Hallkelsson, who composed a *Hákonardrápa* of his own (*c.* 985), and Hallfreðr vandræðaskáld also came home to Iceland, where Hallfreðr's adultery inspired a killing and then eventually a saga (*Hallfreðar saga*); Þorleifr *jarlsskáld* ('earl's poet') Ásgeirsson, who fled Norway from the wrath of Hákon after causing him itching-sickness, and who is said to have been killed by a demon sent from the pagan earl, was probably another court-poet, although no likely genuine work of his survives and he is not named in any recension of *Landnámabók*.[83] Any or none of these poets may have brought older and contemporary poems to Iceland from Norway. Although there is little evidence in this regard, the best candidate from among these men

---

[82]See *Hávamál*, ed. D. A. H. Evans, Viking Society for Northern Research, Text Series 7 (London, 1986), 13–14; and North, *Pagan Words*, pp. 128–9.

[83]*Íslendingabók. Landnámabók*, ed. Jakob, fig. II; fig. III; and p. 224. Cf. also *Eyfirðinga sǫgur*, ed. Jónas Kristjánsson, ÍF 9 (Reykjavík, 1956), pp. 226–7 (*Þorleifs þáttr Jarlsskálds*).

is the competitive Einarr skálaglamm. The author of *Egils saga* (probably Snorri) says that Einarr 'began to compose poetry even when he was young, and was a man who was *eager to learn*'; and that he and Egill 'discussed poetry'.[84] In a verse attributed to him while he was in Norway, Einarr complains that Hákon pays no heed to his work, although 'I have bravely made the drink of Swing-father [Óðinn's drink: poetry] while other men slept'.[85] Einarr only needs to have 'discussed poetry' with Eyvindr, the *éminence grise* of praise-poetry in the court of Hákon Jarl in *c.* 980 – *c.* 995, to have learnt by heart *Ynglingatal*, and presumably *Haustlǫng* as well. Back in Iceland, therefore, it is possible that these and other poems memorized in Norway were transmitted orally from Einarr to his niece Guðrún, and later from her to her great-grandson, Ari Þorgilsson.[86]

Ari's genealogy in the postscript to *Íslendingabók* shows not only that he knew or knew of Þjóðólfr's poem *Ynglingatal*, but that this poem had been in his family long enough for his older kinsmen to reconstruct a lineage connecting them with the prestigious Ynglingar of Uppsala. Ari on his father's death was brought up at Helgafell by his grandfather Gellir, then by Hallr Þórarinsson from the age of seven to twenty-one, whereafter little more is known of his career apart from his consecration as a priest (probably by Bishop Gizurr Ísleifsson).[87] *Íslendingabók* is the only work by Ari that survives, although there has been much discussion of other books that he may or may not have written (such as a separate *konunga ævi* and *ættartala*).[88] Ari says that his book was the revision of a first draft which had been read by Sæmundr *inn fróði* ('the learned') Sigfússon (1056–1133), Bishop Þorlákr of Skálholt (1086–1133) and Bishop Ketill of Hólar.[89] In the postscript the lineages of Þorlákr and Ketill come before Ari's and after those of the bishops Gizurr and Jón. Here Ari derives his own paternal line from Rǫgnvaldr's ancestor King Ólafr trételgja of Vestfold. Ari's list of forefathers follows the names of

---

[84]*Egils saga*, ed. Sigurður, p. 268 (ch. 78): 'hann tók at yrkja, þegar er hann var ungr, ok var maðr *námgjarn*'; 'rœddu um skáldskap'.

[85]*Ibid.*, p. 270 (vs. 52): 'Gerðak veig (...) meðan aðrir, ǫrr Váfaðar, sváfu'.

[86]*Íslendingabók. Landnámabók*, ed. Jakob, fig. IXb.

[87]*Ibid.*, pp. v–vi; Turville-Petre, *Origins of Icelandic Literature*, pp. 88–90.

[88]*Íslendingabók. Landnámabók*, ed. Jakob, pp. viii–xvii (§ 2); Turville-Petre, *Origins of Icelandic Literature*, pp. 91–108.

[89]*Íslendingabók. Landnámabók*, ed. Jakob, p. 3 (ch. 1).

Ynglingatal as far as Guðrøðr, before going a separate way; and also follows Þjóðólfr's order up to this point (barring the sequence *XI. Dagr. XII. Alrekr. XIII. Agni*, where *Ynglingatal* puts Agni before Alrekr).[90] Ari's genealogy extends back further than King Rǫgnvaldr's within the extant *Ynglingatal*, where it runs *I. Yngvi Tyrkjakonungr. II. Njǫrðr Svíakonungr. III. Freyr. IIII. Fjǫlnir* ('I. Yngvi king of the Turks. II. Njǫrðr king of the Swedes. III. Freyr. IV. Fjǫlnir'). These names were apparently copied by the anonymous author of *Historia Norvegiae* (*c.* 1220), who omits Ari's reference to the Turks.[91] Ari's allusion to Turkey was part of his contemporary learning, a *topos* used by Geoffrey of Monmouth in *c.* 1135 and probably inherited from Fredegar in the sixth century, who was apparently the first, since Vergil with Aeneas, to trace his people back to Troy.[92] That Ari's lineage goes back as far as the Turks reveals not only his but perhaps also his family's genealogical ambition, and may show the ultimate use to which this family put its knowledge of *Ynglingatal* in the late eleventh or early twelfth century.

It seems probable that a form of *Haustlǫng* was known alongside *Ynglingatal*, if not by Ari, then by his kinsmen, although his adult contact with them is not clear until the end of his life, when he seems to have moved back west to Snæfellsnes.[93] The *fróði*-epithet of Ari and of Sæmundr Sigfússon, his older contemporary, shows that both men were learned in the native Old Norse-Icelandic as well as in the European Latinate traditions.[94] Given that Ari submitted his first draft of *Íslendingabók* to Sæmundr, probably in *c.* 1120, it is possible that both *Ynglingatal* and *Haustlǫng* formed part of their common knowledge. In relation to Þorleifr inn spaki and to the first possible route of *Haustlǫng*'s transmission, is worth noting that Sæmundr (through his mother, Þórey, a sister of Þorsteinn) was a cousin of Bishop Ketill Þorsteinsson who also collaborated with Ari, and that both Sæmundr and Ketill were thus

---

[90]*Ibid.*, p. 27, n. 3.

[91]*Historia Norvegiae*, ed. Gustav Storm, Monumenta Historia Norvegiae (Christiania [Oslo], 1880), p. 97: 'Rex itaque Ingui, quem primum Swethiae monarchium rexisse plurimi astruunt, genuit Neorth, qui vero genuit Froy; hos ambos tota illorum posteritas per longa saecula ut deos venerati sunt'. For the date of this work, cf. *Heimskringla I*, ed. Bjarni, p. xv.

[92]Faulkes, 'Descent from the Gods', pp. 110–24.

[93]*Íslendingabók. Landnámabók*, ed. Jakob, p. vi.

[94]Turville-Petre, *Origins of Icelandic Literature*, p. 82.

descended through a common grandfather (Eyjólfr halti) from Helga, sister of the Þóra who had married Gunnarr Úlfljótsson.[95]

Before the end of the eleventh century, Sæmundr founded not only a church (of St Nikulás) but also a school in his family seat in Oddi, at which native learning (i.e. lawcodes, genealogies and royal praise-poems such as *Ynglingatal*) could be taught to young noblemen as a corollary to the ecclesiastical learning of their day. Thereafter it is likely that the diffusion of this native learning became more widespread than before. There is a well-known passage in the early thirteenth-century *Þorgils saga ok Hafliða* (in *Sturlunga saga*), in which it is said that games were played, dances performed and wrestling carried out, sagas read out and verses recited at a party held in Reykjahólar each year to celebrate the feast of St Óláfr. In one such party, in 1119 (two years after Icelanders had begun to transcribe their laws in *Grágás* for the first time), it is said that Hrólfr of Skálmarnes told a story of Hrómundr Gripsson, which King Sverrir (1184–1202) had also heard 'and he called such lying stories the most entertaining of all. And yet there were some people who could trace their ancestry back to Hrómundr Gripsson'.[96] Hrómundr was the great-grandfather of Ingólfr Árnason, to whom Ari (though not the *Landnámabók*-recensions) attributes the first sighting as well as the settlement of Iceland. The author of *Þorgils saga* alludes to this early twelfth-century interest in genealogy in order to counterbalance Sverrir's remark that this saga was fiction, as part of his wider discussion about truth and falsehood. But thereby he also reveals that the study of family lineage must have provided Icelanders with a strong incentive for the compilation and performance of sagas and verses in the early twelfth century.

Styrmir Kárason, a kinsman of Sæmundr, also links sagas and ancestry, as we have seen, when he describes antiquarians as 'those men who want to know old learning or how to trace their ancestry';[97] and Snorri Sturluson, after discussing Ari and before citing Þjóðólfr of Hvinir and

---

[95]*Íslendingabók. Landnámabók*, ed. Jakob, fig. XVIIb.

[96]*Þorgils saga ok Hafliða*, ed. Ursula Brown [Dronke] (Oxford, 1952), p. 18 (ch. 10): 'ok kallaði hann slíkar lygisǫgur skemtiligastar. Ok þó kunnu menn at telja ættir sínar til Hrómundar Gripssonar'. Brown suggests that Hrólfr's *saga* 'probably resembled in form the Helgi lays of the *Edda*: i.e. it consisted of verses set in a simple narrative framework of prose' (*ibid.*, p. 75, n.). Also discussed in Sigurður, *Snorri Sturluson*, pp. 106–9.

[97]*Íslendingabók. Landnámabók*, ed. Jakob, p. ciii (§ 13): 'þeim mǫnnum, er vita vilja forn frœði eða rekja ættartǫlur'.

Ynglingatal, divides his sources into genealogy and narrative when he
says that some of his material is found 'in a list of forefathers whereby
kings or other men of great family have traced their ancestry, and some
is written according to old poems or songs of narrative which men have
had for their entertainment'.[98] It is in gatherings in Oddi, such as St
Óláfr's feast in Reykjahólar in 1119, that not only the poems *Ynglingatal*
and *Haustlǫng*, but also apocryphal stories and verses about Þjóðólfr,
Þorleifr and Haraldr, could have been read out by people who would
thereby prove their descent from one or more of these figures: either by
Ari from the records of his own family, or by Sæmundr from those of his
and Ketill's family, or by both men together, or by other learned people.
Oddi is thus the place where a form of *Haustlǫng* could have been transcribed for the first time, perhaps as a companion-piece to *Ynglingatal*.

It seems that *Ynglingatal* was no less important to Sæmundr's family
than it was to Ari's. When Sæmundr's grandson, Jón Loptsson (d. 1197),
became a powerful *goði* in the later twelfth century, it was discovered (as
it were) that his mother Þóra was the illegitimate daughter of King Magnús
berfœttr ('bareleg') of Norway.[99] *Nóregs konungatal* ('list of the kings of
Norway') is the name of a genealogical poem which was composed in
Jón's honour in *c*. 1190. This poem owes a debt to Eyvindr's *Háleygjatal*
(*c*. 985), in that both poems were structured with twenty-seven genera-
tions (a number apparently taken by Eyvindr from his probably incomplete version of *Ynglingatal*).[100] Stylistically, too, *Nóregs konungatal* is
also close to *Ynglingatal*, and there are frequent attempts to capture not
only the metre but also the spare diction of both Þjóðólfr and Eyvindr as
they report the entrances and exits of their kings.[101] A now-lost Latin
history of Norwegian kings written by Sæmundr was probably consulted
by the poet of *Nóregs konungatal*, who alludes to Sæmundr as his source
in st. 40.[102] Yet another branch of Sæmundr's learning may have been
invoked in two stanzas, shortly after, which reveal the eulogist's attempt

[98]*Heimskringla I*, ed. Bjarni, p. 3 (prol.): 'í langfeðgatali, þar er konungar eða
aðrir stórættaðir menn hafa rakit kyn sitt, en sumt er ritat eptir fornum kvæðum
eða sǫguljóðum, er menn hafa haft til skemmtanar sér'.

[99]Turville-Petre, *Origins of Icelandic Literature*, pp. 84–5.

[100]See Anthony Faulkes, 'The Genealogies and Regnal Lists in a Manuscript in
Resen's Library', in *Sjötíu Ritgerðir helgaðar Jakob Benediktssyni* (Reykjavík,
1977), pp. 188–9; and 'Descent from the Gods', p. 99.

[101]Particularly in st. 4–5, 9–10, 16–17, 19, etc: cf. *Skj* B I, 575–90.

[102]*Ibid*. B I, 582; cf. *Heimskringla I*, ed. Bjarni, p. x.

to bypass the genealogical uncertainty surrounding St Óláfr Haraldsson (ruled *c.* 1016–30). As holy as Óláfr was:

Þats mér sagt,   at Sigurðr hrísi
Haralds sonr   héti forðum;
vas Hálfdan   Hrísa arfi,
en Sigurðr sýr   sonr Hálfdanar.

Þá gat son   Sigurðr ok Ásta
þanns Haralds   heiti átti...

(*Nóregs konungatal* 42–43/1–4)[103]

In other words, Jón Loptsson traced himself back to Haraldr hárfagri through Sigurðr hrísi, one of Haraldr's sons by Snæfríðr and therefore also the brother of Guðrøðr ljómi, whom Snorri held to have been fostered out to Þjóðólfr of Hvinir (*Haralds saga*, chs. 25–6). In Jón's case, it is hard to see whence his understanding of King Haraldr's court could have come, unless from his grandfather Sæmundr, who may have helped to communicate it, through memorized and transcribed law-codes, genealogies, poems and verses, to his pupils at the school in Oddi.

Oddi is where Snorri Sturluson (*c.* 1179–1241) was educated as the young foster-son of Jón Loptsson in 1183–97.[104] There is little doubt that Snorri accumulated the bulk of his knowledge of northern genealogy and history from the library to which Sæmundr and Ari had helped contribute nearly a century earlier.[105] Likewise, Snorri may have derived from Oddi, as well as from Jón himself, at least part of that immense body of Eddic and Scaldic material in his *Edda* which includes *Haustlǫng*.[106]

---

[103]*Skj* B I, 582: '[42] It was said to me that Sigurðr brushwood was once the name of Haraldr [Fairhair]'s son; Hálfdanr was the descendant of Brushwood, and yet Sigurðr Sow was the son of Hálfdanr. [43/1–4] Then Sigurðr [Sow] and Ásta got a son who had the name of Haraldr [the cruel]'.

[104]Sigurður, *Snorri Sturluson*, pp. 12–13; *Heimskringla I*, ed. Bjarni, pp. xix–xxiii.

[105]Sigurður, *Snorri Sturluson*, pp. 23–8 and 49–53; Turville-Petre, *Origins of Icelandic Literature*, pp. 220–2.

[106]On the *Edda* as a reflection of Snorri's education and beliefs, see Sigurðr, *Snorri Sturluson*, pp. 73–102.

TREATMENT OF *HAUSTLǪNG* IN *SNORRA EDDA*

Not one of the surviving manuscripts of *Snorra Edda* was written during Snorri's lifetime. For this reason, the use of Snorri's name as an authority for the treatment and prose adaptations of *Haustlǫng* is acknowledged to be a useful convention, not a fact. Nor is the precise history and relationship of these manuscripts as yet a question which can be answered. The four principal and oldest manuscripts of *Snorra Edda* are U (*c.* 1300, with a text briefer than that of other MSS and in a different order), R (*c.* 1325, copied from a now-lost exemplar of *c.* 1250–1300), W (*c.* 1340–50, with the text of *Skáldskaparmál* altered and curtailed) and T (*c.* 1600, copied from a now-lost exemplar of *c.* 1250–1300).[107] In addition, three fragments of *Snorra Edda* which contain parts of *Haustlǫng* are AM 748 I 4to (*c.* 1300–25), AM 757 a 4to (*c.* 1375–1400) and AM 748 II 4to (*c.* 1400, similar to R).[108] Of all these manuscripts, only RWT contain *Haustlǫng* 14–20 and st. 1–13 in two sequences, although W lacks st. 11/6–13/8 and T lacks st. 4. All three *helmingar* quoted in other chapters of *Skáldskaparmál* (st. 14/5–8 in ch. 23; 3/1–4 in ch. 55; and st. 2/1–4 in ch. 60) are found in URWT. In addition, st. 14/5–8 is found in AM 757 a 4to; 3/1–4 in AM 748 I 4to and II 4to; and st. 2/1–4 in all three fragments. Leaving U and these fragments aside, I follow Finnur in generally preferring the readings of WT to those of R.

We owe the preservation of *Haustlǫng* to Snorri, but it is most unlikely, given the above facts and the interval of time between the thirteenth century and the early tenth, that what we take to be his text of this poem renders the work quite as Þjóðólfr composed it. There were clearly attempts in its transmission to alter or clarify this difficult Scaldic poem. The clearest sign of such an interference may be found in st. 7/1–2 (see note), which was written down as part of st. 1–13 in *Skáld,* ch. 22: on this line the R-scribe appears to have written a form *sigyniar* (so WT) as *signyiar*, thus revealing that he was paying little attention to the meaning of his exemplar and thought that he recognized one line as a reference to the tale of Signý and the Vǫlsungar ('then the cargo of Signý's arms became a fast friend of his foster-son', i.e. then Sigmundr became friends with Sinfjǫtli). Snorri tells a version of the Vǫlsung-tale later in *Skáldskaparmál*, in chs. 40–2, in which he names Sigmundr once in association with Sinfjǫtli, his son (ch. 42, *SnE* I, 370). Other

---

[107]Cf. *Gylf,* pp. xxix–xxxiii.

[108]*Ibid.*, p. xxx.

rationalizations of *Haustlǫng* appear to be older, in that they are found in all relevant manuscripts. These are a subject for conjecture, since the emended forms obviously have no manuscript support and depend entirely on arguments based on the demands of *dróttkvætt* metre and on parallel idioms in Eddic or Scaldic poems. One example of a rationalization of this kind appears to be RWT *gǫrðusk* in st. 10/5–6 (see note): it seems clear that *gǫrðusk* was written for (Finnur's reconstructed) *gættusk* in the line *gǫrðusk allar áttir Ing[v]i-freys at þingi* in order to provide the adjectives *hárar* and *gamlar* (10/7–8) with a verbal complement linking them more intelligibly with *áttir*. Since Snorri quotes most of this line verbatim in his prose adaptation of *Haustlǫng* 1–13, it is possible that it was he who rationalized st. 10/5–8 in this way in the 1230s. A third change may have been made earlier than Snorri by any of the Icelanders who helped to preserve this poem or otherwise to transmit it from Norway to Iceland: it seems plausible that a topographical reference to the giants as *berg-Danir* ('mountain-Danes') in st. 18/7 (see note), was created in a new era of national awareness to replace the metrically more suitable *berg-Agðir* ('mountain-Agðir-men'), which would have had little value once Þjóðólfr's poem had been circulated out of its context in regional Norway. Thus, in my critical text, I have emended both *gǫrðusk* and *berg-Danir* accordingly. These cases, however, may represent only a few of many oral and scribal changes which it is no longer possible to identify.

Snorri's manner of quotation may show that he treats Þjóðólfr's *dróttkvætt* poem as a text with which he and his society were quite familiar. Twice naming this poem as *Haustlǫng*, he quotes (some of) it in two sections which are five chapters apart, in reverse order. Snorri evidently wished to safeguard the techniques of older poetry in a new era of ballads and romances, but it appears that his chief means of doing so in *Skáldskaparmál*, as we see from his contingent quotations, was to focus on isolated kennings and related figures of speech. Snorri thus shows an inclination to anthologize, not to protect, older poems such as *Haustlǫng*: elsewhere he quotes Bragi's *drápa (...) um Ragnar loðbrók* in individual stanzas scattered throughout the treatise as the need arises, and gives a limited sequence of stanzas only in one chapter (ch. 42, *SnE* I, 370–4); Úlfr Uggason's *Húsdrápa*, for instance, is named but not quoted in ch. 8 (*SnE* I, 266), then apparently quoted in single stanzas at intervals throughout. With this piecemeal approach to some of the great works, Snorri gives the unfortunate impression that he regarded these poems as common knowledge, perhaps as 'classics', and took their survival for granted.

Snorri thus chooses the tale but not the verses of Iðunn and Þjazi
(*Haustlǫng* 1–13) for the opening section of Bragi's dialogues with Ægir
(*Gylfaginning*, chs. 55–6: A). Then, after the myth of Óðinn's theft of
Óðrerir (the Mead of Poetry), an epilogue blending the native myth of
Ragnarǫk (the end of the world) with the fall of Troy and the illustration
by cited verses of kennings for Óðinn, poetry and twelve other male
Æsir, Snorri proceeds to tell the story of Þórr's duel with Hrungnir (*Skáld*,
ch. 17: B) and to exemplify this tale with the quotation of *Haustlǫng* 14–
20. Still on the theme of Þórr and the giants, Snorri now tells us the story
of Þórr's visit to the giant Geirrøðr, of the obstacles he faces *en route*
and of his final duel with the giant in his cavernous home; then Snorri
quotes the title, plus all nineteen extant stanzas, of the *Þórsdrápa* of
Eilífr Goðrúnarson. Abruptly after this poem, indeed as if nothing had
happened since he listed kennings for Loki, Snorri picks up the thread of
gods and their kennings and continues with Frigg, Freyja, Sif and Iðunn.
Only in his chapter on Iðunn, and then apparently as an afterthought
(*Skáld*, ch. 22: C), does Snorri quote *Haustlǫng* 1–13 in order to illustrate the theft of Iðunn and her apples. This quotation marks the end of
Snorri's section on the kennings for gods and goddesses.

As regards the myths contained in *Haustlǫng* and other poems, Snorri
embarked on the writing of *Gylfaginning* probably at a stage later than
Skáldskaparmál; and with Ægir, here cast as a magician visiting the
Æsir, we may have a prototype of Gylfi as he calls on a more mysterious
race of beings who turn out to be descended from the Æsir now imagined as a group of historical figures. Earlier, when he was writing
Skáldskaparmál, Snorri abandoned his question-and-answer scheme with
Ægir and Bragi just after Bragi tells Ægir the story of the Mead of Poetry: hence the editorial title *Bragarœður* for four chapters and an epilogue which are closer in style and content to *Gylfaginning*. Since Snorri
does not begin to quote Scaldic verses in *Skáldskaparmál* until he discusses kennings for Óðinn and poetry, it could be argued that this section of his *Edda* does not properly begin until after his tale of Þjazi and
the theft of Iðunn. In this light, Snorri may have made a false start with
his prose adaptation of *Haustlǫng* 1–13 (and with the aftermath involving Skaði and Loki). Yet Margaret Clunies Ross has argued that Snorri
intended his prose tale of Þjazi and Iðunn to complement the tale that
follows it, the myth of the Mead of Poetry.[109] Both tales culminate in a
similar way: in the first, a god (Loki) in disguise as a hawk rescues a

[109]Clunies Ross, *Prolonged Echoes*, pp. 115–17.

goddess from the giants and is pursued by one of them disguised as an eagle (Þjazi); in the second, another god (Óðinn) disguised as an eagle steals from the giants three draughts including Óðrerir (the Mead of Poetry) within his stomach while being pursued by one of them in disguise also as an eagle (Suttungr); at the end of each tale the pursuing eagle is destroyed by the Æsir in their own compound. This is a plausible view of a narrative sequence which Snorri could have planned at the outset of his composition of *Skáldskaparmál*. The pattern of this sequence, a diptych, provides an aetiology of the warfare between gods and giants: first in the giants' attempt to rob the gods of their lives, then in Óðinn's successful revenge for this attempt in stealing Óðrerir from the giants, thereby enriching mankind with the gift of poetry. Later in *Skáldskaparmál*, when Snorri got as far as Iðunn (following the tale of Óðrerir and a list of kennings for fourteen Æsir and three Ásynjur), he seems to have felt excused the need to write an explanatory prose preface for *Haustlǫng* 1–13, thanks to the tale of Þjazi which he had already told in the opening section of *Skáldskaparmál*. After his chapter on Iðunn, Snorri proceeds to a new category of kennings (beginning with sky, earth and sea) and nowhere quotes verses which can be identified as another part of *Haustlǫng*. Whether or not Snorri knew other now lost sections of this poem, no-one knows. However, since none of his other quoted stanzas or *helmingar* can be identified as part of a greater *Haustlǫng*, it seems likely that Snorri quoted all the *Haustlǫng* which he knew.

Snorri's prose versions of *Haustlǫng* 1–13 and 14–20 are a helpful guide to this poem, written in a style which also succeeds in rendering some of the poet's humour, albeit in a less dark form. His additions and changes may be described as follows. At the start of the poet's first tale, the Æsir's adventure with Þjazi, Snorri says that they run out of food on their travels and take the ox from a herd which they find in a valley. This 'oxen of the sun' motif adds a moral dimension to the story as Þjóðólfr tells it, for it imputes blame: if the ox belongs to the giants, then the gods have provoked Þjazi by slaughtering it. The ox fails to roast; like Þjóðólfr, Snorri shows the Æsir unable to divine the cause. One hour later, after their second attempt to roast the ox, Snorri says that the gods hear an eagle freely admitting his part in their failure from the tree directly over their heads. Snorri's eagle then asks the gods in general, not Hœnir in particular, for some of the ox. His word *fylli* appears to derive from *Haustlǫng* 4/1, and to be taken literally, for Snorri shows the eagle devouring most of the meat without waiting for Loki to serve him one of four portions. Thus the hall-conceit of st. 5 is gone — understandably, since this is an essentially poetic device. Also gone, however, is any attempt to characterize Hœnir. Loki in Snorri's tale becomes angry only through the eagle's lack of table-manners, not because his friend is threatened or insulted. When he strikes the eagle and is hoisted into the sky, Loki's hands stick to the pole apparently with the same magic as the pole to the eagle, although in Þjóðólfr's poem (st. 7) it is possible that the choice of jumping is left to Loki, whose hands stay fixed to his end of the pole through fear, not magic. When the deal is made to save Loki's life, naturally without any of the poet's circumlocutions, Þjazi simply asks for Iðunn and her 'apples' (*epli sín*) as part of the deal as if these apples were widely known to be the goddess' property. In Þjóðólfr's poem there are no apples and Iðunn is presented as a prize on her own account, with or without the 'old-age medicine' that she knows (*ellilyf*, 9/3). Snorri turns the apples to advantage in staging a comedy of conspiracy and kidnapping to which the poet barely alludes at all. Thus, when Loki at an agreed time lures Iðunn to the woods with a promise of more special 'apples', Þjazi appears and abducts her to the land of the giants. Only Þjóðólfr's kenning *leiðiþírr* ('leading-servant', 11/3) appears to hint at the means by which Loki tricks the goddess out of Ásgarðr without the gods' (and her) knowledge. Snorri now makes his second borrowing from his text of the poem (st. 10/5 all MSS *gǫrðusk*: see note) and 10/7–8) when he says that the gods *gerðusk brátt hárir ok gamlir* ('soon became greyhaired and old') and summoned a *þing* ('meeting'). Here he seems to simplify the poet's version of events, such as this can be deduced from the first half of st. 11. Snorri's Æsir do not learn the reason for Iðunn's disappearance from Þjazi, as I have argued in the poem, but deduce that Loki is to blame for losing her and then set about extracting the whole story from Loki, though without using magic. Then, as if in compensation for the absence of Ingvi-freyr, Snorri says that Loki asks Freyja for the loan of a 'falcon's shape' which she owns (*valshamr*). This detail and also the narrative up to Loki's flight from giant-land are not found in *Haustlǫng* and are added by Snorri, in whose version Loki turns Iðunn into a nut which may be held in his falcon's claws. As there is no indication or even apparent interest in the poem in what form Iðunn is rescued, it is possible that a nut was what Þjóðólfr had in mind, although Iðunn's epithet *ása leika* ('playmate of the Æsir', 12/2) could imply that she comes back to Ásgarðr as a corn-dolly or as another apt symbol for the summer. Loki enters Þjazi's home and finds the goddess inside; while he does so, Snorri pictures the giant in a boat out at sea, as if living in a peaceful domestic occupation in Snæfellsnes or another Icelandic peninsular. So

Loki gets a head start, for in Snorri's story Þjazi must first return, find Iðunn gone and only then take up his eagle-shape. The excitement of the poet's eagle-pursuit is much reduced in Snorri's prose. Here, however, Snorri makes his third borrowing from the poem when he says, as if declaring his debt to Þjóðólfr, that Þjazi *dró arnsúg í flugnum* ('moved with an eagle-soughing in his flight'). Snorri also makes up for his relatively unhurried account of Þjazi's pursuit by giving a clearer picture of the movements in the final minutes before the walls of Ásgarðr: Loki ducks and the eagle flies into the flames, whereupon he falls burning into the citadel and is killed by the Æsir within their gates. In this picture of the gods working in concert to trap the giant, Snorri seems to follow the implication of *ginna* ('to beguile') in *ginnregin*, which is Þjóðólfr's term for the gods as they light the fires in st. 13/2. Snorri's next story, his epilogue concerning Skaði, Þjazi's daughter, is not in the poem, but its inclusion as a sequel shows Snorri's (never fully realized) tendency to build Old Norse-Icelandic myths into a coherent mythography of his own. Although Snorri probably had no other source on which to base his story of Þjazi, his remark before he quotes st. 1–13 later in *Skáld*, ch. 22 (C), to the effect that Þjóðólfr composed *Haustlǫng* according to the story which Snorri has earlier presented (*eptir þeirri sǫgu*), gives a misleading impression that the Icelander knew more about this story than the Norwegian, his source.

Before the start of Þjóðólfr's second tale, Snorri adds a prologue of his own. This story, in which Óðinn rides out on Sleipnir one day and challenges Hrungnir to a horse race, is not contained in any form in *Haustlǫng*, but in Snorri's case seems to derive from a poem. When Hrungnir asks *hvat manna sá er með gullhjálminn er ríðr lopt ok lǫg* ('what man is that with the golden helmet who rides over sky and sea?'), Snorri reveals a poem probably in *ljóðaháttr*, with a half-stanza that might be reconstructed thus (with Snorri's words italicized):

Hvat er þat gumna   er í gullhjálmi *ferr*
    ok *ríðr lopt ok lǫg?*[110]

Whether or not this hypothetical reconstuction is close to the original poem, there can be little doubt that Snorri based his prologue to the tale of Þórr and Hrungnir on a lost *Hrungnismál*, or on a poem similar to

---

[110]For '*Hvat er* þat gumna', cf. *Vaf* 7/1 (*hvat er þat manna*) and *Ski* 17/1 (*hvat er þat manna*); for 'er í *gullhjálm*i ferr', cf. *Akv* 16/2 (*at þú í brynio fœrir*); for '*ríðr lopt ok lǫg*', cf. *Ski* 6/6 (*alt lopt oc lǫg*).

Vafþrúðnismál, in which Óðinn visits a giant in order to trick him. The next movement in this prologue, once Hrungnir has accepted the challenge and ridden on his horse Gullfaxi right after Óðinn into Ásgarðr, appears to be a flyting which takes place between the giant and Þórr. Snorri prepares for the flyting by showing Hrungnir to be drunken, boastful and out of control. He drinks out of Þórr's cups and in the WU-recension only Sif and Freyja dare to serve him. When he threatens to take these goddesses home with him, Snorri forgoes a reference to Bragi's Hrungnir-kenning *Þrúðar þjóf* ('thief of Þrúðr', *Ragnarsdrápa* 1) or to Þjóðólfr's reference to Hrungnir as *heimþinguðr herju Vingnis* ('the home-caller of Vingnir's warrior-woman', *Haustlǫng* 19). Snorri in this way appears to have his attention fixed entirely on this poetic source.

When Þórr enters, Snorri again reveals his source to be a poem, this time more clearly: Þórr asks *hverr því rœðr er jǫtnar hundvísir skulu þar drekka, eða hverr seldi Hrungni grið at vera í Valhǫll* ('who decides that dog-clever giants should drink there and who was it who gave Hrungnir sanctuary in Valhǫll'). There is also the intrusion of the name *Valhǫll* in a place which Snorri has named Ásgarðr. A hypothetical reconstruction of the stanza which it may be assumed underlay Snorri's prose words might go as follows (with the prose words italicized):

> *Hverr því rœðr*   er hundvíss jǫtunn
> *drekkr* með dróttmǫgo,
> *eða hverr* um *grið*   Hrungni seldi
> *í valhǫll vera?*[111]

Hrungnir makes the challenge and in Snorri's story Þórr goes off to prepare for their duel without a word. *Lokasenna* also ends with the prospect of Þórr and the gods settling scores with Loki, and there is no indication in Snorri's ensuing prose that his source-poem about Hrungnir continued any further.

The chief difference between Þjóðólfr's and Snorri's stories of the duel represented in *Haustlǫng* 14–20 is in Snorri's addition of extras to the cast: Þórr brings his human servant Þjálfi, while the giants, fearful if Hrungnir loses, build their champion an assistant out of mud or clay,

---

[111]For '*Hverr því rœðr*', cf. *Lok* 28/4 (ec *því rœð*); for '*er hundvíss jǫtunn*', cf. *Hym* 5/3 (*hundvíss Hymir*) and *HHj* 25/4 (*hundvíss jǫtunn*); for '*drekkr* með dróttmǫgo', cf. *Akv* 2/1 (*drukko þar dróttmegir*); for '*í valhǫll vera*', cf. *Akv* 2/3 (vín *í valhǫllo*) and *Hákonarmál* 1/6 (oc í *Valhǫll vesa*, *Skj* B I, 57) and 9/7 (*til Valhallar vega*).

whom they name 'Muck-calf' (*Mǫkkurkálfi*). There is no reference to either figure in the poem, although at least one scholar has strained credibility by attempting to identify Mǫkkurkálfi in a kenning for Þórr in st. 17/5–8 (see note). Hrungnir's ostensibly irrational decision to expose himself to Þórr's hammer by standing on his shield, which Þjóðólfr imputes to the intervention of supernatural *bǫnd* and *dísir* (st. 17), becomes in Snorri's version of this tale a stratagem conceived by Þjálfi, Þórr's helper, which he recommends to Hrungnir on the grounds that Þórr will attack him from below. When Þórr's hammer smashes Hrungnir's head into fragments, the giant falls with his leg over Þórr, who finds himself unable to push it off. Þjóðólfr appears to picture Þórr as he begins to do so but mentions no helpers. Þjálfi in the meantime cuts down Mǫkkurkálfi, who falls with little glory. Also only in Snorri's tale, Þórr is soon joined by his son Magni, the only member of the Æsir who proves strong enough to shift the giant's leg. The sequels follow: first, Þórr awarding Gullfaxi, Hrungnir's horse, to his son for lifting off the leg, with Óðinn begrudging this gift because Magni's mother, Járnsaxa, is a giantess and he had wanted the horse for himself; and second, a tale in which the nurse imagined in the act of healing Þórr's head-wound in *Haustlǫng* 20 is named as a *vǫlva* ('sibyl') named Gróa, whose efforts to loosen a whetstone-sherd in the head are almost successful, until, inexplicably, Þórr tells her a story about her husband Aurvandill, hidden in Þórr's basket on his way home, whose frozen toe Þórr broke off and turned into a star; Aurvandill will soon be home, Þórr says; so glad is Gróa that she forgets to sing the remaining chants to loosen the stone and it stays where it is. With his own aetiology, Snorri has already said that all whetstones come from Hrungnir's whetstone; now he appears to say that it is 'recommended as a precaution' (*boðit til varnanar*) to throw a (new) whetstone across the floor, for then the sherd in Þórr's head will stir.[112]

With the exception of the word *Grjótúnagarðar*, which he treats as a proper noun, Snorri on this occasion seems not to use words or phrases from *Haustlǫng* to illustrate his prose adaptation of this tale. *Grjótúnagarðar* appears to be based on an *ofljós* kenning involving the compound *grjót[t]únir* in *Haustlǫng* 14 (one which I suggest conceals the giant's name *Hrungnir*). Yet it may not be Snorri who adapted *Grjótúnagarðar* from this kenning and otherwise he seems almost care-

---

[112] Faulkes (*SSE*, p. 80) takes this phrase another way: 'something that is taboo, throwing whetstones across a room, for then the whetstone in Thor's head stirs'.

ful to avoid expressions from the poem. For example, his description of Hrungnir's fatal manoeuvre is written as if on the basis of a duel between agile saga-heroes (*skaut Hrungnir skildinum undir fœtr sér, ok stóð á*), whereas Þjóðólfr's expression is naturally a circumlocution in which the shield seems to move on its own (*brátt fló ímunfǫlr randar íss und iljar*, st. 17). Although Snorri keeps clear of *Haustlǫng's* language here, nonetheless it is worth noting that he writes a more detailed version of this story than he does of the longer tale of Þjazi and Iðunn. Not only are there extra *dramatis personae*, with a prologue and two sequels, but when the duel starts Snorri begins to present information of which before we had no inkling: Hrungnir is the strongest of the giants (*þeirra sterkastr*); his heart is made of stone and with three points, like a runic symbol since named after him (*hǫrðum steini ok tindótt, með þrimr hornum, svá sem síðan er gert ristubragð þat er Hrungnishjarta heitir*); his head and shield are also of stone and complement his whetstone, which he swings over his shoulder; he throws it with both hands. Mǫkkurkálfi is also a finely developed figure, not only with a name, but also in his size: thirty-six miles high and twelve from shoulder to shoulder, with a mare's heart implanted in his breast. It seems improbable that Snorri invented these details, when he could so easily have introduced some of them into the story when we first meet Hrungnir. Mǫkkurkálfi in this way, wetting himself when he sees Þórr, is unlikely to have reached *Snorra Edda* in a poem. He and the other minor figures are more likely to be the product of a lively folktale tradition, whose narrators reshaped the story of *Haustlǫng* 14–20 for an audience of Christian Icelandic farmers. Their image of Þórr was not tangible, like Þjóðólfr's idol (*hofregin*, st. 15), but confined instead to the literary ideal of a strongarm hero whose opponents, the giants, were no longer a vivid threat to mankind, but rather his convenient foil. To find a source for Mǫkkurkálfi is no easy task: the name may identify him with the *kalfar undirfjalfrs bliku alfheims* ('calves of the underground refuge of the elf-realm's gleam'), whereby Eilífr *c*. 985 refers to young giants in *Þórsdrápa* 20 (*Skj* B I, 144); there is a wooden man (*trémaðr*), a demon named Þorgarðr, whom Hákon Jarl is said to have made in order to assassinate an Icelander in a story in the fifteenth-century *Flateyjarbók*;[113] but an even closer analogue is to be found in the late sixteenth-century folktale of the Golem of Prague, a clay giant created by the persecuted Jews of this town to

[113]*Eyfirðingasǫgur*, ed. Jónas Kristjánsson, ÍF 9 (Reykjavík, 1956), pp. 226–7 (*Þorleifs þáttr jarlsskálds*).

defend them from the casual violence of gentiles.[114] There could be no better insight into the scapegoat's role which the giants have now adopted, nor into the origin of Mǫkkurkálfi, a figure who reveals the diversity of Snorri's sources most clearly of all.

To sum up, Snorri appears to anthologize the two sections of *Haustlǫng* which he quotes. His prose adaptation of st. 1–13 (A) introduces his poetic treatise. He retells their stories fluently and with some humour and aetiology of his own, which reinforces that of the poem. In place of Þjóðólfr's conceits and fond characterization of Loki and Þórr, Snorri portrays the Æsir collectively and presents their dealings with the giants as part of a larger conflict involving men and the forces of evil. The diversity of giants and their qualities in *Haustlǫng* (hunger, ancient cunning, infertility and the vastness of landscape) becomes simplified in Snorri's text into a general posture of enmity and morose jealousy against gods and men. Snorri finishes by quoting *Haustlǫng* 14–20 (B), but not until he gives his own story also here a greater authenticity than that of Þjóðólfr, whose *Haustlǫng*, he says, is composed 'on the basis of this story' (*eptir þessi sǫgu*). Five chapters later (C), Snorri quotes *Haustlǫng* 1–13, perhaps as an afterthought, in order to illustrate terms for Iðunn. For those who wish to read Snorri's treatment of this poem at nearer hand, the relevant passages from *Skáldskaparmál* are quoted below.

CONTEXTUAL PROSE PASSAGES

A. Þjazi and Iðunn: prose version of *Haustlǫng* 1–13 (ch. 56)

Gylfaginning, ch. 56 (*Bragarœður, SnE* I, 208–14)[115]

Hann hóf þar frásǫgn at þrír Æsir fóru heiman, Óðinn ok Loki ok Hœnir, ok fóru um fjǫll ok eyðimerkr ok var illt til matar. En er þeir koma ofan í dal nǫkkurn, sjá þeir øxna flokk ok taka einn uxann ok snúa til seyðis. En er þeir hyggja at soðit mun vera, raufa þeir seyðinn ok var ekki soðit. Ok í annat sinn er þeir raufa seyðinn, þá er stund var liðin, ok var ekki soðit. Mæla þeir þá sín á milli hverju þetta mun gegna.

Þá heyra þeir mál í eikina upp yfir sik, at sá, er þar sat, kvazk ráða

---

[114]See Isaac Bashevis Singer, *The Golem*, with illustrations by Uri Shulevitz (New York, 1982).

[115]My normalizing policy is to add single inverted commas for dialogue; *œ* for *æ*; *ǫ* or *ø* for *ö* or *au* in *aung*; *-sk* for *-st*; *-zk* for *-ðst* or *-zt*; *é* for *è*; *á* for *â*; *-it* for *-ið*; *-s* for *-ss*; and *-ing* for *-íng*.

því, er eigi soðnaði á seyðinum. Þeir litu til ok sat þar ǫrn ok eigi lítill. Þá mælti ǫrninn, 'Vilið þér gefa mér fylli mína af oxanum, þá mun soðna á seyðinum.' Þeir játa því. Þá lætr hann sígask ór trénu ok sezk á seyðinn ok leggr upp þegar it fyrsta lær oxans tvau ok báða bógana. Þá varð Loki reiðr, ok greip upp mikla stǫng ok reiðir af ǫllu afli ok rekr á kroppinn erninum. Ǫrninn bregzk við hǫggit ok flýgr upp; þá var fǫst stǫngin við kropp arnarins, ok hendr Loka við annan enda. Ǫrninn flýgr hátt svá, at fœtr taka niðr grjótit ok urðir ok viðu; hendr hans hyggr hann at slitna munu ór ǫxlum. Hann kallar ok biðr allþarfliga ǫrninn friðar, en hann segir, at Loki skal aldri lauss verða, nema hann veiti honum svardaga at koma Iðunni út of Ásgarð með epli sín. En Loki vill þat; verðr hann þá lauss ok ferr til lagsmanna sinna, ok er eigi at sinni sǫgð fleiri tíðindi um þeirra ferð, áðr þeir koma heim. En at ákveðinni stundu teygir Loki Iðunni út um Ásgarð í skóg nǫkkurn ok segir at hann hefir fundit epli þau, er henni munu gripir í þykkja, ok bað at hon skal hafa með sér sín epli, ok bera saman ok hin. Þá kemr þar Þjazi jǫtunn í arnarham ok tekr Iðunni ok flýgr braut með ok í Þrymheim til bús síns. En Æsir urðu illa við hvarf Iðunnar ok gerðusk þeir brátt hárir ok gamlir. Þá áttu þeir Æsir þing ok spyrr hverr annan hvat síðarst vissi til Iðunnar; en þat var sét síðarst, at hon gekk út ór Ásgarði með Loka. Þá var Loki tekinn ok fœrðr á þingit, ok var honum heitit bana eða píslum; en er hann varð hræddr, þá kvazk hann mundu sœkja eptir Iðunni í Jǫtunheima, ef Freyja vill ljá honum valshams, er hon á. Ok er hann fær valshaminn, flýgr hann norðr í Jǫtunheima ok kemr einn dag til Þjaza jǫtuns; var hann róinn á sæ, en Iðunn var ein heima. Brá Loki henni í hnotar líki ok hafði í klóm sér ok flýgr sem mest. En er Þjazi kom heim ok saknar Iðunnar, tekr hann arnarhaminn ok flýgr eptir Loka ok dró arnsúg í flugnum. En er Æsirnir sá er valrinn flaug með hnotina ok hvar ǫrninn flaug, þá gengu þeir út undir Ásgarð ok báru þannig byrðar af lokarspánum. Ok er valrinn flaug inn of borgina, lét hann fallask niðr við borgarvegginn. Þá slógu Æsirnir eldi í lokarspánu, en ǫrninn mátti eigi stǫðva er hann misti valsins; laust þá eldinum í fiðri arnarins ok tók þá af fluginn. Þá váru Æsirnir nær ok drápu Þjaza jǫtun fyrir innan Ásgrindr, ok er þat víg allfrægt.

En Skaði, dóttir Þjaza jǫtuns, tók hjálm ok brynju ok ǫll hervápn ok ferr til Ásgarðs at hefna fǫður síns; en Æsir buðu henni sætt ok yfirbœtr, ok hit fyrsta at hon skal kjósa sér mann af Ásum ok kjósa at fótum ok sjá ekki fleira af. Þá sá hon eins manns fœtr forkunnar fagra ok mælti, 'Þenna kýs ek, fátt mun ljótt á Baldri.' En þat var Njǫrðr ór Nóatúnum.

Þat hafði hon í sættargjǫrð sinni, at Æsir skyldu þat gera, er hon hugði at þeir skyldu eigi mega, at hlæja hana. Þá gerði Loki þat at hann batt um skegg geitar nǫkkurrar ok ǫðrum enda um hreðjar sér ok létu þau ýmsi eptir ok skrækti hvártveggja við hátt. Þá lét Loki fallask í kné Skaða ok þá hló hon; var þá gjǫr sætt af Ásanna hendi við hana. Svá er sagt, at Óðinn gerði þat til yfirbóta við hana at hann tók augu Þjaza ok kastaði upp á himin ok gerði af stjǫrnur tvær.

B. Þórr's duel with Hrungnir: prose version, then quotation, of *Haustlǫng* 14–20

Skáld, ch. 17 (*SnE* I, 270–8)

Nú skal enn segja dœmi af hverju þær kenningar eru, er nú váru ritaðar, er áðr váru eigi dœmi til sǫgð, svá sem Bragi sagði Ægi, at Þórr var farinn í Austrvega at berja trǫll, en Óðinn reið Sleipni í Jǫtunheima ok kom til þess jǫtuns er Hrungnir hét.

Þá spyrr Hrungnir, hvat manna sá er með gullhjálminn er ríðr lopt ok lǫg, ok segir at hann á furðu góðan hest. Óðinn sagði, at þar vill hann veðja fyrir hǫfði sínu at engi hestr skal vera jafngóðr í Jǫtunheimum. Hrungnir segir, at sá er góðr hestr, en hafa lézk hann mundu miklu stórfetaðra hest; sá heitir Gullfaxi. Hrungnir varð reiðr ok hleypr upp á hest sinn ok hleypir eptir honum ok hyggr at launa honum ofrmæli. Óðinn hleypti svá mikit at hann var á ǫðru leiti fyrir, en Hrungnir var í svá miklum jǫtunmóð at hann fann eigi fyrr en hann sótti inn of Ásgrind.

Ok er hann kom at hallardurum, buðu Æsir honum til drykkju; hann gekk í hǫllina ok bað fá sér drykkju. Váru þá teknar þær skálir er Þórr var vanr at drekka ór, ok snerti Hrungnir ór hverri. En er hann gerðisk drukkinn, þá skorti eigi stór orð. Hann lézk skyldu taka upp Valhǫll ok fœra í Jǫtunheima en søkkva Ásgarði en drepa goð ǫll nema Freyju ok Sif vill hann heim fœra með sér. En Freyja fór þá at skenkja honum[116], ok drekka lézk hann munu allt ásǫl.

En er Ásum leiddisk ofrefli hans, þá nefna þeir Þór – því næst kom Þórr í hǫllina ok hafði uppi á lopti hamarinn ok var allreiðr, ok spyrr hverr því ræðr er jǫtnar hundvísir skulu þar drekka, eða hverr seldi Hrungni grið at vera í Valhǫll, eða hví Freyja skal skenkja honum sem at gildi Ása.

---

[116] WU-texts of *Snorra Edda* here read *ok Fræyja ein þorir þá at skenkja honum* (cf. *SnE* I, 272), a reading which both Magnús (p. 119) and Faulkes (p. 77) adopt, making this phrase into a parenthesis within a larger sentence which begins with *Hann lézk* and ends with *allt ásǫl*.

Þá svarar Hrungnir ok sér ekki vinaraugum til Þórs, sagði, at Óðinn bauð honum til drykkju ok hann var á hans griðum. Þá mælti Þórr, at þess boðs skal Hrungnir iðrask áðr hann komi út. Hrungnir segir, at Ása-Þór er þat lítill frami at drepa hann vápnlausan; hitt er meiri hugraun, ef hann þorir at berjask við hann at landamæri á Grjótúnagǫrðum, 'ok hefir þat verit mikit fólskuverk,' sagði hann, 'er ek lét eptir heima skjǫld minn ok hein. En ef ek hefða hér vápn mín, þá skyldu vit nú reyna hólmgǫnguna, en at ǫðrum kosti legg ek þér við níðingskap, ef þú vill drepa mik vápnlausan.'

Þórr vill fyrir engan mun bila at koma til einvígis, er honum var hólmr skoraðr, því at engi hefir honum þat fyrr veitt. Fór þá Hrungnir braut leið sína ok hleypti ákafliga þar til er hann kom í Jǫtunheima, ok var fǫr hans allfræg með jǫtnum, ok þat at stefnulag var komit á með þeim Þór.

Þóttusk jǫtnar hafa mikit í ábyrgð, hvárr sigr fengi; þeim var ills ván at Þór ef Hrungnir létisk, fyrir því at hann var þeirra sterkastr. Þá gerðu jǫtnar mann á Grjótúnagǫrðum af leiri, ok var hann níu rasta hár en þriggja breiðr undir hǫnd, en ekki fengu þeir hjarta svá mikit at honum sómði, fyrr en þeir tóku ór meri nǫkkurri, ok varð honum þat eigi stǫðugt, þá er Þórr kom. Hrungnir átti hjarta þat er frægt er, af hǫrðum steini ok tindótt, með þrimr hornum, svá sem síðan er gert ristubragð þat er Hrungnishjarta heitir; af steini var hǫfuð hans, skjǫldr var ok steinn, víðr ok þjǫkkr, ok hafði hann skjǫldinn fyrir sér, er hann stóð á Grjótúnagǫrðum ok beið Þórs, en hein hafði hann fyrir vápn ok reiddi of ǫxl ok var ekki dæligr. Á aðra hlið honum stóð leirjǫtunninn er nefndr er Mǫkkurkálfi, ok var hann allhræddr: svá er sagt, at hann meig, er hann sá Þór.

Þórr fór til hólmstefnu ok með honum Þjálfi. Þá rann Þjálfi fram at þar er Hrungnir stóð, ok mælti til hans, 'Þú stendr óvarliga, jǫtunn! Hefir skjǫldinn fyrir þér, en Þórr hefir sét þik ok ferr hann it neðra í jǫrðu ok mun hann koma neðan at þér.' Þá skaut Hrungnir skildinum undir fœtr sér, ok stóð á, en tvíhendi heinina. Því næst sá hann eldingar ok heyrði þrumur stórar; sá hann þá Þór í ásmóði. Fór hann ákafliga ok reiddi hamarinn ok kastaði um langa leið at Hrungni. Hrungnir fœrir upp heinina báðum hǫndum, kastar í mót, mœtir hón hamrinum á flugi ok brotnar sundr heinin; fellr annarr hlutr á jǫrð (ok eru þar af orðin ǫll heinberg), annarr hlutr brast í hǫfði Þór, svá at hann fell fram á jǫrð. En hamarinn Mjǫllnir kom í mitt hǫfuð Hrungni ok lamði hausinn í smá mola ok fell hann fram yfir Þór, svá at fótr hans lá um háls Þór. En Þjálfi vá at Mǫkkurkálfa, ok fell hann við lítinn orðstír.

Þá gekk Þjálfi til Þórs ok skyldi taka fót Hrungnis af honum ok gat hvergi valdit. Þá gengu til Æsir allir, er þeir spurðu at Þórr var fallinn, ok skyldu taka fótinn af honum ok fengu hvergi komit. Þá kom til Magni, sonr Þórs ok Járnsǫxu, hann var þá þrévetr; hann kastaði fœti Hrungnis af Þór ok mælti: 'Sé þar ljótan harm, faðir, er ek kom svá síð, ek hygg at jǫtun þenna munda ek hafa lostit í hel með hnefa mér, ef ek hefða fundit hann.' Þá stóð Þórr upp ok fagnaði vel syni sínum ok sagði hann mundu verða mikinn fyrir sér, 'ok vil ek,' sagði hann, 'gefa þér hestinn Gullfaxa, er Hrungnir hafði átt.' Þá mælti Óðinn ok sagði at Þórr gerði rangt, er hann gaf hinn góða hest gýgjarsyni, en eigi fǫður sínum.

Þórr fór heim til Þrúðvanga, ok stóð heinin í hǫfði honum. Þá kom til vǫlva sú, er Gróa hét, kona Aurvandils ins frœkna; hon gól galdra sína yfir Þór, til þess er heinin losnaði. En er Þórr fann þat ok þótti þá ván at braut mundi ná heininni, þá vildi hann launa Gró lækninguna ok gera hana fegna, sagði henni þau tíðindi, at hann hafði vaðit norðan yfir Élivága ok hafði borit í meis á baki sér Aurvandil norðan ór Jǫtunheimum, ok þat til jartegna, at ein tá hans hafði staðit ór meisinum ok var sú frørin, svá at Þórr braut af ok kastaði upp á himin ok gerði af stjǫrnu þá, er heitir Aurvandilstá. Þórr sagði, at eigi mundi langt til at Aurvandill mundi heim koma, en Gróa varð svá fegin at hon mundi enga galdra, ok varð heinin eigi lausari ok stendr enn í hǫfði Þór. Ok er þat boðit til varnanar at kasta hein of gólf þvert, því at þá hrœrisk heinin í hǫfði Þór. Eptir þessi sǫgu hefir ort Þjóðólfr hvinverski í Haustlǫng. Svá segir þar:

[14.] Eðr of sér es jǫtna   ótti lét of sóttan
(to end of st. 20)

C. How to refer to Iðunn: prose introduction to *Haustlǫng* 1–13

Skáld, ch. 22 (*SnE* I, 304)

Hvernig skal kenna Iðunni? Kalla hana konu Braga, ok gætandi eplanna, en eplin ellilyf Ásanna; hon er ok ránfengr Þjaza jǫtuns, svá sem fyrr er sagt, at hann tók hana braut frá Ásum. Eptir þeirri sǫgu orti Þjóðólfr inn hvinverski í Haustlǫng:

[1.] Hvé skalk góðs at gjǫldum   gunnveggjar brú leggja?
(to end of st. 13)

I

Text, Translation and

Textual Notes

Haustlǫng

1. Hvé skalk góðs at gjǫldum   gunnveggjar brú leggja?
   *** *** ***   naddkleif at Þorleifi.
   Týframra sék tíva   trygglaust *of* far þriggja
   á hreingǫru hlýri   Hildar vetts ok Þjaza.

2. Segjǫndum fló sagna   snótar ulfr at móti
   í gemlis ham gǫmlum   glamma ó- fyr -skǫmmu;
   settisk ǫrn, þars æsir   (ár-Gefnar) mar bǫru
   (vasa byrgi-Týr bjarga   bleyði vændr) á seyði.

3. Tormiðlaðr vas tívum   ta[ð]lhreinn meðal beina,
   hvat, kvað hapta snytrir   hjalmfaldinn, því valda.
   Margspakr of nam mæla   mǫr valkastar bǫru
   (vasat Hœnis vinr hónum   hollr) af fornum þolli.

4. Fjallgylðir bað fyllar   fet-Meila sér deila
   (hlaut) af helgum skutli   (hrafnásar vinr blása);
   ving-rǫgnir lét -vǫgna   vígfrekr ofan sígask,
   þars vélsparir vóru   varnendr goða farnir.

1/1–8 R, W, T. **1/1** æc gott (at) R; goðs at W; ec got at T. **1/2** veɢiar R *(unclear)*; veigar T. b... R; bru leggia W, T. **1/3** *missing* R, W, T *(space left open* W). **1/4** ...at þo... R; raddkleif *(r damaged)* at þorleifi W; naddkleif at þorleifi T. **1/5** framra R, W; framma T. tifa R, T; tiva W. **1/6** oc RTW: *emend.* of. fia... R; far W; fiar T. þriggia W, T; *missing* R. **1/7** ...ro hlyri R; a hreíngoro hlyrí W; a hleingòru hlyrí T. **1/8** hild.. R; hílldar W; hildar T. vez R, W, T.

2/1–8 R (: R¹), W, T (: T¹); 2/1–4 *elsewhere* R (: R²), T (: T²), U, 748 I, 757, 748 II. **2/1** Seggiondvm R¹, R², W; segiondom U, T¹, T², 748, 757, 748 II. **2/2** sn....oti R¹; snotar ylgr at moti R²; snotar vlfr at moti W, U, T. **2/3** ha.. R¹; ..m W; ham *all others*. **2/4** glamma: lam *(damaged)* W. á *all other mss.* á fyrir U; ofyr T; ofra T²; ófyrs 748 I; æigi firi 757; vlfr fyr 748 II. **2/5** æs.. R; æsir W, T. **2/6** gnæfar R; gefnar W, T. mat R, ma W *(with a final letter erased)*; mar T. **2/7** vara R, W; naca T. **2/8** vǫndr R; vendr W, T. seðe R; seiði W; seydi T.

Translation

1. How shall I build a bridge in payment for a good battle-wall [shield]?
*** *** *** rivet-cliff [shield] from Þorleifr. On the polished
finely-wrought cheek of Hildr's drum [shield] I see the unsafe journey of three divinely prominent deities and Þjazi.

2. Not a short time ago did the wolf of the gentlewoman [Þjazi] fly
with a clatter towards the tellers of tales in a vulture's worn-out shape;
the eagle settled down where the Æsir were bearing harvest-Gefn's
horse [an ox] (the Týr who would imprison harvest-Gefn within rocks
was not accused of cowardice!) to the cooking fire.

3. Between its bones the dung-reindeer [ox] was divided with difficulty
by the gods; something is the cause of this, said the wisdom-teacher of
the divine powers encased in his helmet [Óðinn]; the much-prophetic
seagull of the surf of the slaughter-heap (Hœnir's friend [Loki] was not
gracious to him) began to speak from the ancient fir-tree.

4. The wolf of the fells [Þjazi] (it fell to the portion of the raven-god's
friend [Loki] to blow) bade the stepping-Meili [Hœnir] deal him his
fill from the holy trencher (/ harpoon); the combat-fierce prince of
wind-dolphins let himself sink down to where the trick-sparing defenders of the gods had come.

3/1–8 R (:R¹), W, T (: T¹); **3/1–4** *elsewhere* R (: R²), U, T (: T²), 748 I, 748 II. **3/1** -miðlaðar
R¹; -mildaðr R²; -miðlaðr W, T¹, T², U, 748 I, 748 II. tifom R¹, T; tivi R², 748 I, 748 II; tifum
W, U; tauu T². **3/2** tal[l]- *emend. Holtsmark.* hrein R¹; hreinn W, T, R², T², 748 II. **3/3** kvað
emend.: qvoþo R¹; q'þu R²; kvaðv W; kvað þv U; kveðv 748 I; kvat þv 748 II; kveðu T¹, T².
hapta R¹: hapt W *(perh. with a final letter erased);* spacra T. snytrir R¹, T: snyrtir W, R². **3/4**
hialm R¹: hialms T. **3/5** mola T. **3/6** baro R: bara T. **3/7** vara R: varat W; var at T. henis
(unclear) R; hænis W; hònis T. vior R; vinr W; ..nr T.

4 *lacking* T. **4/1** gylþir R; gylðer W. fvllan R; fyllar W. **4/2** fet mela R; fetmeila W. sér deila:
sier deila W; *missing* R. **4/3** hlvt R; hlavt W. helgo R; helgv W; helgvm *emend.* **4/4** asar R;
asa W. vin R; vin *or* vm W. blasa R; lᶻsa W. **4/5** ravngnir R; rognir W. vagna W; *missing in*
R.

5. Fljótt bað foldar dróttinn   Fárbauta mǫg vára
 þekkiligr með þegnum   þrymseilar hval deila,
 en af breiðu bjóði   bragðvíss at þat lagði
 ósvífrandi ása   upp þjórhluti fjóra.

6. Ok slíðrliga síðan   svangr (vas þat fyr lǫngu)
 át af eikirótum   okbjǫrn faðir Mǫrna[r],
 áðr djúphugaðr dræpi   dolg ballastan vallar
 hirði-Týr meðal herða   herfangs ofan stǫngu.

7. Þá varð fastr við fóstra   farmr Sigynjar arma,
 sás ǫll regin eygja,   ǫndurgoðs, í bǫndum;
 loddi rǫ́ við ramman   reimuð Jǫtunheima,
 en holls vinar Hœnis   hendr við stangar enda.

8. Fló með fróðgum tívi   fangsæll of veg langan
 sveita nagr, svát slitna   sundr ulfs faðir mundi;
 þá varð Þórs of rúni   (þungr vas Loptr of sprunginn)
 mǫ́lunaut, hvats mátti,   miðjungs friðar biðja.

5/2 far R, T; faar- W. mǫg R; ..g W. vǫro R; vara W; ..ra T. 5/6 at R; a(?) W. 5/7 osvifrande] osviptandi W. 5/8 þior R; þor W; þiorir T. hlifi ora R; hluti fiora W, T.

6/1 -liga] loga W. 6/2 firir R, *runic* F W, firi T. 6/3 át R; let W. -rot.. R *(final letters illegible)*; rotu W; rotum T. 6/4 oc R; z W. morna R; niorna T. 6/6 ballastan R, T; balladan W. 6/7 hirð.. R *(final letters illegible)*; hirði W, T. 6/8 -fangs ofangs ofan R; -fang ofan W; -fangs ofan T.

7/2 farmr R *(first r altered from* |t*)*. signyiar R; sigyniar W, T. 7/3 sa er R, T; þa er W. eygia R, T; æygia W. 7/4 bavndom R; hondvm W. 7/7 hænis RW, hònis T.

8/1 fróðgom R; ...vm W. tifi R; tifa W. 8/4 vlfs R: v *resembles* a). favðor R; faðir W, T. 8/5 þors R; þor T. rvnni R; rvni W, T. 8/6 þvngrs R; þvngs W, T. 8/7 navtr R; nautz T. 8/8 mildings R; miðivngs W, T. friðar R: a *altered from* r.

5. Swiftly the handsome lord of the land [Óðinn] bade Fárbauti's boy
   [Loki] deal out the whale of the cracking rope of spring-times [whale
   of the whip: ox] among the thanes, and after that the Æsir's prank-
   wise disobliger [Loki] served up four bull-portions from the broad
   table.

6. And hungry then (that was long ago) Mǫrn's father [Þjazi] ferociously ate the yoke-bear off the oak-tree's roots, before the deep-
   counselled Týr who was watching over the war-booty [Loki] struck
   the very bold foe of the field down between the shoulders with a
   pole.

7. Then set fast was the cargo of Sigyn's arms, whom all the divine
   powers glare at in his bonds, to the foster-father of the ski-goddess
   [father of Skaði: Þjazi]; the sailyard stuck to the mighty spectre of
   the giants' world [Þjazi], and the hands of Hœnir's loyal friend [Loki]
   to the end of the pole.

8. With a wise deity now the blood-?woodpecker flew happy in his
   booty over such a long way that the wolf's father [Loki] was ready to
   tear asunder; then Þórr's confidant ('Lofty' [Loki] was heavy and
   near dead with exhaustion) was obliged to beg the giant's meal-companion for whatever deal he could get.

6   *Haustlǫng*

9. Sér bað sagna hrœri   sorgœra[n] mey fœra,
þás ellilyf ása,   áttrunnr Hymis, kunni;
brunnakrs of kom bekkjar   Brísings goða dísi
girðiþjófr í garða   grjót-Níðaðar síðan.

10. Urðut bjartra borða   byggvendr at þat hryggvir;
þá vas Ið- með jǫtnum   -unnr nýkomin sunnan;
gœttusk allar áttir   Ing[v]i-freys at þingi
(vǫru heldr) ok hárar   (hamljót regin) gamlar,

11. unz hrynsævar hræva   hund ǫl-Gefnar fundu
leiðiþír ok læva   lundar geiri bundu;
'Þú skalt véltr nema vélum,'   [v]reiðr mælti svá, 'leiðir
munstœrandi mœra   mey aptr, Loki, [hapta].'

12. Heyrðak svá, þat síðan   sveik ept ása leiku
hugreynandi Hœnis   hauks flugbjalfa aukinn,
ok lómhugaðr lagði,   leikblaðs reginn fjaðrar,
ern at ǫglis barni   arnsúg faðir Mǫrnar.

9/2 eyra R, eura T. 9/5 brvN R; brvn W; brun T. akrs] akr W. keckiar R; beckiar W, T. 9/6 goða R: ð *altered from* g. 9/8 niþ- R; uid- T.

10/1 biartra R, T; brattra W. borþa R. 10/2 byGvendr R; byggendr W, T. hryGvir R; hryggir W, T. 10/4 vðr R, T; vǫr *glossed by a later hand to* vnnr W. 10/5 gorðoz R, W; gerðoz T. 10/6 at R, T; .. W.

11/1–8 R, T; 11/1–5 W. 11/1 hrvn sævar R (r *seems erased*). 11/2 hrvnd R; hund W, T. 11/3 þiR R; þir W, T; þjóf *emend.* Holtsmark. oc læv R; ok leva T; at leva W. 11/4 lvnd avlgefnar bvndo R, W, T. 11/5 velltr R; vellt W *(a prick over the* t *apparently by later hand).* vælom R; velom T; vel.. W: *hereafter space left open for the rest of this extract to end of stanza 13.* 11/6 reiðr R, T. mællti R; myil T. leiðar R, T. 11/7 mora R, mòra T. 11/8 hapta: *omitted in* R, T; *Finnur Jónsson:* hapta; *Sveinbjörn Egilsson:* deyia.

9. The kin-branch of Hymir [Þjazi the giant] bade the rouser of tales, who was mad with pain, to bring him a girl, the one who knew the old-age medicine of the Æsir; the thief of the gods' Brísing-girdle [Loki] later got the gods' lady of the brook of the well-spring's corn-field [wave of the eddy: *ið[u]-unnar*] into the courtyards of the rock-Níðuðr [Þjazi].

10. Those who dwell in the bright mountain-tops [giants] did not become downcast after that; this was when Eddy-Wave [*Iðu-unnr*] had newly arrived from the south among the giants; all the kin of Ingvi-freyr (the divine rulers were looking rather ugly) deliberated in the assembly, grey-haired and old,

11. until they met the hound of of the falling sea of corpses of the nourishing-Gefn [wolf: robber of the goddess: Þjazi] and bound the servant who had led her *with a spear of* the tree of venoms [with a magic wand]; 'you shall be tricked out of your mind', angry, he [Ingvi-freyr] spoke, 'with trickery, unless also with trickery, Loki, you lead the glorious joy-increasing girl of the gods [Iðunn] back here.'

12. I heard this, that afterwards, he who was putting Hœnir's courage to the test [Loki], increased by a hawk's flying-fur, betrayed the playmate of the Æsir [Iðunn] back and that the ruler-deity of the feather's swinging leafblade, the loon-minded father of Mǫrn [Þjazi], laid an eagle's vigorous wing-draft right onto the child of the bird of prey.

12/1 Heyrðat R. 12/2 ept R; ept T. leikom R; leiko T. 12/3 -reyn- R; -rǫn- T. hænis RW, hǫnis T. 12/4 havðs R; haucs T. flvg R, T; fló *emend. Finnur Jónsson.* bialba R. 12/6 fiadran T.

13. Hófu skjótt en skófu   skǫpt ginnregin brinna,
     en sonr biðils sviðnar   (sveipr varð í fǫr) Greipar.
     Þats of fátt á fjalla   Finns ilja brú minni:
     baugs þá bifum fáða   bifkleif at Þorleifi.

14. Eðr of sér es jǫtna   ótti lét of sóttan
     hellis bǫr á hyrjar   haugs grjót[t]úna baugi;
     ók at ísarnleiki   Jarðar sunr, en dunði
     (móðr svall Meila blóða)   Mána vegr und hǫnum.

15. Knǫttu ǫll (en Ullar   endilǫg fyr mági
     grund vas grápi hrundin)   ginnunga vé brinna,
     þás hofregin hafrar   hógreiðar fram drógu
     (seðr gekk Svǫlnis ekkja   sundr) at Hrungnis fundi.

16. Þyrmðit Baldrs of barmi   (berg-) solgnum þar -dolgi
     (hristusk bjǫrg ok brustu,   brann upphiminn) manna;
     mjǫk frák móti hrøkkva,   myrkbeins Haka reinar
     þás vígligan vǫgna   váttr sinn bana þátti.

13/2 gin- R. **13/3** biðiss R; bidils suidnar T. **13/7** bavgs R; þa] þa er T; omitted in R. **13/8** bifcleifi R; bifkleifT.

14/1–8 R, W, T; **14/5–8** elsewhere in R, W, U, T, 757. **14/1** sér all mss.; lítk Finnur Jónsson. er R; of W. **14/2** let R, T. sottvm R; sottan W, T. **14/3** biaur R; baur W (worn); maur T. a h- R scraped off in W. **14/4** havg R; haugs W. **14/5** oc R¹, T. isarn-: jsíarns 757. **14/6** iarðr R; iarðar all other mss. (T² jardar crossed out, ardar). en R¹; ok R²; hinn 757. dvndi: dvlþi U; diarfe 757. **14/7** moþvr R¹, R²; moðr all other mss. except T¹: miodr. Meila: meide 757. broþvr R¹, T¹; bloþa R¹, W², T²; bloþi U; blóde 757.

15/1–8 R, W, T. **15/2** firir R; firi W; f' T. **15/4** ginnivnga R; ginnvnga W; ginuga T. hriɴa R; brinna W; brinra T. **15/5** hafrir R; hofǫv W; hafdi T. **15/6** -reiþar R; reidir T. **15/7** seðr R; seiðr W; seidi T.

13. Quickly the shafts while the enticer-gods shaved them started to burn, and the son of the suitor (there was a flurry in his journey) of Greip [Þjazi] singes. A memorial of that is painted on my bridge of the foot-soles of the Lapp of the fells [Hrungnir's bridge: shield]. I have received the coloured cliff of the shield-rim, painted with tales, from Þorleifr.

14. And yet one may see on the ring of fire [shield] where giants' dread [Þórr] paid a call on the cavern-tree [giant] of the fire of the grave-mound of stone-enclosures [?: of sea-bed's gold: of rings: *hringa*-giant: *Hrungnir*]; Earth's son drove towards the play of iron, while Moon's path [sky] (the passion of Meili's blood-kinsman [Þórr] swelled) clattered beneath him.

15. All the sanctuaries of falcons (/ of the abyss) did burn, while down below, thanks to Ullr's father-in-law [Þórr], the ground was kicked with hail, when the bucks drew the temple-deity of the easy-riding-chariot forward (at the same time Svǫlnir's widow [Óðinn's widow: Earth] split asunder) to meet Hrungnir.

16. Baldr's bosom-brother [Þórr] did not show mercy in that place (mountains shook and cliffs shattered, heaven burned above) to the gorged mountain-foe of men [giant]; hugely, I have learned, did he shrink back from the meeting, when the witness for the whales of the dark-bone of Haki's land [witness for rock-whales, for the giants: Hrungnir] knew his killer [Þórr] to be ready for war.

16/1–8 R, W, T. **16/1** þverriðit W; þyrmdit T. of R, T; af W. **16/4** vpp R; raan W. maNa R; mana W. **16/5** moti R; mæti W; mòti T. **16/6** myrk hreins R; myrkbeins W; meinþorns T. baka R; haka W, T. **16/7** vaugna R, T; vogna W. **16/8** vátr R; vatt W, T. þatri R.

17. Brátt fló bjarga gæti   (bǫnd ollu því) randa
    ímun-fǫlr und iljar   íss (vildu svá -dísir);
    varðat hǫggs frá hǫrðu[m]   hraundrengr þaðan lengi
    trjónu trolls of rúna   tíðr fjǫllama at bíða.

18. Fjǫrspillir lét falla   fjalfrs ólágra gjalfra
    bǫlverðungar Belja   bolm á randar holmi;
    þar hné grundar gilja   gramr fyr skǫrpum hamri,
    en berg-*Egða* bægði   brjótr við jǫrmunþrjóti.

19. Ok harðbrotin herju   heimþingaðar Vingnis
    hvein í hj*arn*a mœni   hein at Grundar sveini,
    þar svát, eðr í Óðins   ólaus burar hausi,
    stála vikr of stokkin   stóð Einriða blóði,

20. áðr ór hneigihlíðum   hárs ǫl-Gefjun sára
    reiði-Týs et rauða   ryðs hælibǫl gœli.
    Gǫrla lítk á Geitis   garði þær of ferðir.
    Baugs þák bifum fáða   bifkleif at Þórleifi.

17/1–8 R, W, T. 17/3 ok R; vnd W, T. 17/5 var þat W. horþv R (W, T). 17/6 drengs R; drengr W, T. 17/8 fiǫll lama W. bidia T.

18/1–8 R, W, T. 18/6 gramm W; gnir T. firir R; firi W. 18/7 bægði T. 18/8 iormvn R; jorman T; iormunþrioti W.

19/1–8 R, W, T. 19/1 brotiɴ R; brotinn W; brotin T. 19/2 þingoþar R; þíngaðar W; þuingadar T. 19/3 hjarna] hinka R, T; hina W *(no sign of abbreviation).* 19/5 svá at T. 19/7 virtr R; vikr W, T. of R, T; vm W. stǫkkvi W. 19/8 eind- R; ein- T; æin- W.

20/1–8 R, W, T. 20/1 hnegi- T. 20/3 tyrs R; tyss W, T. it R, T; hið W. 20/4 heyli R, T; heili W. 20/6 þeir R; þr W; þeyr T. 20/7 baugs baugs R. þa er R; þa ek W. bifð R; bífa W; bifom T. 20/8 bif- R; bi- W.

17. Quickly the battle-pale [gleaming] ice of shield-rims [shield-boss] flew (the powers caused this) beneath the soles of the keeper of the cliffs [Hrungnir] (the battle-spirits wanted it so); after that the eager gallant of the rubble-field [Hrungnir] did not have to wait long for a many-times-mutilating blow from the hard confidant of the troll's snout [Mjǫllnir].

18. The life-spoiler of Beli's horrific troop [Þórr] let fall the bear of the hide-out of high sea-swells [Hrungnir] on the island of his shield [shield-boss]; there sank the king of the bottom of ravines [Hrungnir] before the sharp hammer, and the breaker of the Agðir-men of mountains [giant-breaker, Þórr] pushed against the titanic boor [Hrungnir].

19. And the hard-broken hone of the home-caller of Vingnir's warrior-woman [Hrungnir's whetstone] whizzed into the ridge of the brains of Ground's lad [Þórr], so that there to this day, rigid in the skull of Óðinn's boy [Þórr], the pumice-stone of steel blades [whetstone] has been standing soaked in the blood of Einriði [Þórr],

20. until such time as a nursing-Gefjun of the wounds [Gróa] of the chariot-Týr [Þórr] might chant the red horror of rust's boasting [red whetstone] out of his hair's sloping hillsides. I behold these expeditions clearly on the fortress of Geitir [shield]. I have received the coloured cliff of the shield-rim, painted with tales, from Þórleifr.

II

Commentary

1.How shall I build a bridge in payment for a good battle-
wall? *** *** *** rivet-cliff from Þorleifr. On the polished
finely-wrought cheek of Hildr's drum I see the unsafe
journey of three divinely prominent deities and Þjazi.

1/1 *góðs*] 'good.' Kock emends W *goðs* (1/1) to *gilds*, in order to make a rhyme
with *gjǫldum*, (*NN* § 2985 D and *Ska* 9). This emendation is unnecessary, despite the metrical anomaly. Kock substitutes the extant 1/3–4 with a refrain
based on 13/7–8 and 20/7–8: *Baugs þák bifum fáða bifkleif at Þórleifi* (*NN* §
3036 and *Ska* 9).

1/2 *brú leggja*] 'build a bridge.' Kock emends WT *bru leggia* to *orð leggja* on
the basis of OIce *orðalag* ('way of speaking'), to give 'how shall I arrange my
words in thanks for the good shield?' (*NN* § 157, 'Hur skal jag lägga mina ord
till tack för goda skölden?'); then emends to *hróðr leggja* ('compose [a poem
of] glory', *NN* § 2985 D and *Ska* 9). The word *brú* occurs as a baseword for
'shield' in 13/6, but nowhere else for 'poem'. Holtsmark, accordingly, emends
brú to *brag*, 'the poem' ('kvadet', p. 9). This emendation seems unnecessary,
however, for it is possible to retain *brú* as 'bridge' as part of a metaphor for
poetry, if we compare this word with similar expressions at the end of Eyvindr
skáldaspillir Finnsson's poetic genealogy of the Háleygir, the dynasty of his
patron Hákon Jarl:

> Jólna sumbl   enn vér gǫtum,
> stillis lof,   sem *steinabrú*.
> (*Háleygjatal* 16 c. 985);[1]

and at the end of Egill Skalla-Grímsson's eulogy of Arinbjǫrn, his oldest friend:

> Hlóðk *lofkǫst*,   þanns lengi stendr
> óbrotgjarn   í bragar túni.
> (*Arinbjarnarkviða* 25/5–8, c. 960);[2]

---

[1]*Skj* B I, 62: 'a banquet of the gods [poem] we have now achieved, the prince's
praise, like a *bridge of stone*'.

[2]*Ibid.* B I, 4: 'I have loaded the *cairn of praise* that will long stand, uneager to
shatter, in the garden of poetry'.

In each case, the implication seems to be that a poem works as a cairn, or a bridge between the worlds of god and men.

1/3 *týframra tíva þriggja*] 'of three divinely prominent deities.' For *týframr* (only here), Finnur suggests 'as able as a god, very able' ('dygtig som en gud, meget dygtig', LP, p. 576), which seems weak. Although OIce *framr* means 'famous' and is rare in the sense 'physically prominent' (LP, p. 150), it appears from Þjóðólfr's distinction between 'three' Æsir and one figure representing Þjazi, that *týframr* refers not only to the fame of these gods in their adventures but also to features which distinguish them as individual gods in the picture on his shield.

1/4 *naddkleif*] 'rivet-cliff.' From T; Finnur has *raddkleif* (i.e. 'voice-cliff', i.e. 'throat' or 'tongue', cf. LP, p. 454), based on a doubtful reading of W, though he refrains from rendering this compound in *Skj* B I, 14. Magnús refrains from even transcribing this line (p. 363, n. 92), although Faulkes translates *raddkleif* as 'voice-cliff' (*SSE*, p. 86). It seems best, however, to follow Holtsmark in reading *naddkleif* (p. 9).

1/6 *trygglaust far*] 'unsafe journey.' OIce *trygglauss* (only here) seems to mean 'without security' or 'untrustworthy'; *far* on this line may mean 'fate' or 'destiny' rather than 'track', but I have translated this word as 'journey' in order to convey something of the sense contained in its common use as 'passage' (cf. LP, p. 121 and Fritzner I, 133). See also note to 4/7–8. Holtsmark renders *trygglaust far* here as 'perfidious expedition' ('den troløse ferd', p. 9), yet without discussion of who betrays whom.

1/8 *Hildar vetts*] 'of Hildr's drum', i.e. of the shield. Konráð Gíslason, followed by Finnur, emends *vez* (1/8) to *fats* to make *hildar fats* ('war-clothes', i.e. 'shield').[3] So also Faulkes ('battle-sheet', *SSE*, p. 86). Parallels for this not entirely satisfying solution are the shield-kennings *fǫt Sǫrla* ('Sǫrli's clothes', in Hallfreðr vandræðaskáld's *Hákonardrápa* 9, *c.* 985) and *fǫt Hjarranda* ('Hjarrandi's clothes', in Snorri's *Háttatal* 53, *c.* 1220), but these kennings are firstly created with warriors', not valkyries' names and secondly refer probably to 'coats of mail', not 'shields'. Marold also emends to *fats*, but reads *Hildar fats* as 'Hildr's drinking-vessel' ('Gefäss der Hild', pp. 153–4). Her reading of *hildr* ('war') as a personified valkyrie makes a better context for *fat* (cf. *Vsp* 30, *Grím* 36 and *HHund* II 29), but Meissner records no parallels for this solution (p. 172, § 80.c). Kiil (p. 7) emends to *vats*, a presumed variant gen. sg. of *vǫttr*, 'glove' ('hanske'). Lindquist (p. 82), followed by Kock (*NN* § 1809) and Holtsmark (pp. 8–9), emends *hildar vez* to *hildar nets*, to make a compound 'war-net' on analogy with OE *wælnet* ('slaughter-net'), OIce *hrænet* ('corpse-net', or possibly *hjǫrnet*, 'sword-net', in a verse attributed to Gísli Súrsson, but

[3]Konráð Gíslason, 'Œgir og Ægir', *Aarbøger for Nordisk Oldkyndighed og Historie* (1876), 311–30, esp. 329, n. 13.

probably of the twelfth or thirteenth century, in *Skj* B I, 103, 33), *oddnet* ('spear-point-net', in a fragment, *ibid.* B I, 173, B 1) and *geirnet* ('spear-net', *ibid.* B II, 90, 1). See Meissner (p. 167, § 80.b). These parallels are all of the twelfth century or later; they are not exact, since swords, spears, spear-points and corpses are all elements of battle, not names for 'battle' itself; and Marold points out that *nets ok Þjaza* would be the only case of *skothending* (imperfect internal rhyme) on a line of *aðalhending* (perfect internal rhyme) in *Haustlǫng* as this poem is preserved. Hans Kuhn, however, regards a form **viaz*, which rhymes perfectly with *Þiaza*, as morphologically justifiable on the basis of the breaking of medial *e* in some tenth-century Norwegian runic inscriptions (p. 46, § 9). All things considered, it seems best to reject *fats* and *nets* and to retain MS *vez* as a spelling of *vetts*, the gen. sg. of n. *vett* (or *vétt*), a noun which elsewhere occurs only in *Lokasenna* and in *Ynglingatal*. The meaning of this noun is obscure ('lid'?) and must be inferred principally from the context of *Lok* 24 in which Loki accuses Óðinn of travelling through the nations dressed *vitca líki* ('in the likeness of a (male) witch'), and in particular of performing *seiðr*:

> Enn þic síða kóðo   Sámseyo í,
> oc draptu á vett [*or* vétt] sem vǫlor;
> *(Lok* 24/1–3)[4]

In this context, n. *vett* seems to refer to a lid or other resounding surface which *vǫlvur* ('sibyls') or witches could use as a drum. In more obscure contexts in *Ynglingatal*, Þjóðólfr twice uses *vitt*, apparently a variant of *vett*, when he describes as *vitta véttr* (for *vættr*) (? 'creature of the drums') two witches whose magic kills kings (Vanlandi in st. 3 and Aðils in st. 21).[5] Thus in *Haustlǫng*, Þjóðólfr's other surviving poem, it seems most appropriate to accept all MSS *hildar vez* as a kenning for 'shield' without emendation, assuming that if a valkyrie (*Hildar*) fulfils the role of a witch or *vǫlva* with a *vett* ('drum'), the drum in question must refer to a shield. There are no parallels for this solution, but the form *vez* for *vetts* in *Hildar vetts* ('of Hildr's drum') does the least violence to the text.

[4]'And they said that you performed witchcraft on the Lapp's isle and were beating on a drum like sibyls do.' Or 'on Samsø'; the vowel-length of *sámr* is hard to reconcile with the Olce element *sem-*, which usually means 'Lappish'.

[5]See also *Heimskringla I*, ed. Bjarni, pp. 29–30 (*Ynglinga saga*, ch. 13) and 59 (ch. 29).

2. *Not a short time ago did the wolf of the gentlewoman fly*
with a clatter towards the tellers of tales in a vulture's
worn-out shape; the eagle settled down where the Æsir
were bearing harvest-Gefn's horse (the Týr who would
imprison harvest-Gefn within rocks was not accused of
cowardice!) to the cooking fire.

2 Lines 1–4, the first half of this stanza (as R²T²), are also quoted separately by Snorri, in *Skáld*, ch. 60 (*SnE* I, 492), apparently in order to illustrate *gemlir* at 2/3 as a synonym for *ǫrn* ('eagle').

2/1 *Segjǫndum sagna*] 'the tellers of tales.' *Sagna* may at first seem to be the gen. pl. of *sǫgn* (f. 'tribe', 'band'). Jón Sigurðsson, followed by Meissner (p. 251, § 88.a), renders *sagna segjendr* (only here) as 'leaders of columns' ('agmina duces', *SnE* I, 307) and later *sagna hrœrir* (Loki's epithet in 9/1) as 'the mover of columns' ('agmina movens', *SnE* I, 313), because gods are seldom indicated with man-kennings either individially or generally. Accordingly, Finnur renders *segjǫndum sagna at móti* as 'towards the leaders of the band' ('skarens anførere', *Skj* B I, 14); Magnús, as 'towards the chieftains of the group' ('móti höfðingjum flokksins', p. 364, n. 93); and Faulkes, as 'to meet the commanders of the crew' (*SSE*, p. 86). Yet this popular rendering of *sagna* in two places in *Haustlǫng* puts strain on the meaning of *segja* in the first instance, and on the context of Loki's role in the second. It is more straightforward to take *sagna* as the gen. pl. of either *saga* or *sǫgn* (f. 'story'), and to greet the Æsir in this poem as the narrators of their own adventures to past men on whose tradition Þjóðólfr relies. Þjóðólfr's concern with sources is clear from *Ynglingatal* 6/1–4, in which he says that 'I had learned from wise men' (*fróða men of fregit hafðak*) on more than one occasion about the death of King Yngvi (*Skj* B I, 8). Holtsmark (p. 12) shows parallels for the 'stories' interpretation of *sagna* in the words OIce *segjandssaga* and *segjandssǫgn* ('hearsay-tale'). Einarr skálaglamm Helgason's kenning *sagna sviptir* in *Þórsdrápa* 3 (*c.* 985, *Skj* B I, 140), is probably a reference to Þórr as 'provoker of tales'. An interpretation of Þjóðólfr's kenning *sagna segjendr* as 'the tellers of tales', asks us to consider what type of religion was in use among the Norwegian heathens for whom this poem was composed, or what their concept of time was in relation to this religion. One answer is that Þjóðólfr's contemporaries (like the classical Greeks and Romans) imagined the tales of their gods to be set in the past, but were also capable, since their gods were still alive to them, of living or re-enacting these tales in the present. It is worth noting that the Germanic etymon of *Æsir* appears to have connoted deified mortals: PGmc **ansuz*, etymon of OIce *áss* or *ǫss* (and of OE *os*, cf. OE *ese* in *Metrical Charm* 4.23), is usually taken to have meant 'breath' or 'spirit', hence 'ghost' (cognate with OIce *ǫnd*).[6] The etymology of *ǫss* thus suggests that

[6]*AIEW* 25 (*an-*) and *ANEW* 16 (*áss*).

Þjóðólfr's community conceived of its gods in general as its 'ancestors', a *topos* which is represented in the ideology of Ingvi-freyr in *Ynglingatal*, Þjóðólfr's other surviving poem. A tradition of this kind, plus the temporal paradox that I have suggested above, may partly explain why Snorri Sturluson constructed *Gylfaginning* on the premise that 'historical Æsir' (men masquerading as mythical Æsir) handed down their own fictions about the old gods to King Gylfi and his descendants (cf. *Gylf*, pp. xii–iii, xxii–iv and 72).

2/2 *snótar ulfr*] 'the wolf of the gentlewoman,' i.e. Iðunn's thief Þjazi. There are no obvious parallels for this type of giant-kenning (Meissner, p. 256, § 88.b). However, as this kenning anticipates the robbery of Iðunn on behalf of Þjazi, it may be specific to this poem (cf. *ǫl-Gefnar hundr hrynsævar hrœva* in 11/1–2).

2/4 *glamma*] 'with a clatter.' This word, which cannot be part of a kenning in this half of the stanza, appears to be the genitive plural of *glamm* (n. 'clatter', 'roar', as in the nickname of the poet Einarr Helgason: *skálaglamm*, 'cup-clatter'),[7] used here in an adverbial sense with the plural as an intensifier. OIce *glammi* (m. 'wolf'), as in *Ragnarsdrápa* 10 (*stǫðva glamma mun*, 'to quell the wolf's desire', *Skj* B I, 2), does not fit the context of *Haustlǫng* 2/4, given that WUT have *ulfr* in 2/2.

2/4 *ó- fyr -skǫmmu*] 'not a short time ago.' Finnur bases the first two words on T *ofyr*, in preference to the variants *á* in R *á fyr* and U *á fyrir*, and reads this construction as tmesis for *fyr óskǫmmu*.[8] This reading is unacceptable, however, to Lindquist (p. 82) and Kock (*NN* § 1810), both of whom emend to *æ fyrir skǫmmu* (i.e. 'never a short time ago'), Kock doing so on the basis of the later variant AM 757 *æigi fíri*. Holtsmark, however, offers parallels for a tmesis here in Þjóðólfr's other work and in other instances both in Old Norse-Icelandic poetry and in Medieval Latin (pp. 10–11).

2/6 *ár-Gefnar mar*] 'harvest-Gefn's horse', i.e. 'ox'. Finnur (*Skj* B I, 14), Magnús (p. 364, n. 92) and Faulkes (*SSE*, p. 86) all keep R *mat* here (i.e. 'were bearing food to the cooking fire'), put *Gefnar* exclusively with *birgi-Týr* on the next line and treat *ár* separately as a word for 'ere' or 'long ago'. As a prefix to a name, *ár-* is rare (cf. LP, p. 30), only occurring with a female name elsewhere in *ár-Ilmr* (*Liðsmannaflokkr* 7, *c.* 1015). Holtsmark takes *ar-Gefn* to derive from **arð-Gefn*, 'plough-Gefn' ('plog-Gevn', pp. 13–14), yet the other part of her argument shows how the kenning *ár-Gefnar mar* works as a reference to the story of *Gefjun* and her eight sons whom she turned into oxen in order to plough land which she had received from King Gylfi of Sweden; Snorri tells this story in ch. 1 of *Gylfaginning* (*Gylf*, p. 7) and in ch. 5 of *Ynglinga saga* (ed. Bjarni, p.

---

[7]*Haralds saga Gráfeldar*, ed. Bjarni, *Heimskringla I*, pp. 208 and 219 (chs. 6 and 15).

[8]Finnur, 'Kenningers led-omstiling og tmesis', p. 10.

15), quoting a verse in each case which he attributes to Bragi Boddason and which is consequently taken to be part of Bragi's *Ragnarsdrápa* (*c.* 850):

Gefjun dró frá Gylfa   glǫð djúprǫðul óðla,
svát af rennirauknum   rauk, Danmarkar auka.
Bǫru ǫxn ok átta   ennitungl, þars gingu
fyr vineyjar viðri   vallrauf, fjǫgur haufuð.

(*Ragnarsdrápa* 13)[9]

The names *Gefn* and *Gefjun* appear to be cognate with *gefa* ('to give') and these goddesses probably descend from figures such as the *gabiae* ('givers') that were worshipped by Germanic auxiliaries in third- and fourth-century inscriptions in the lower Rhineland and in Roman Britain.[10] *Gefn* is listed by Snorri as a by-name of Freyja in *Skáld*, chs. 37 and 75 (*SnE* I, 350 and 557). Both Freyja and Iðunn are sought after by the giants: Iðunn, in *Haustlǫng* 9–12; and Freyja in *Þrymskviða*, in the story of the giant builder in *Gylfaginning*, ch. 42 (p. 34) and (with Sif, Þórr's wife) in the prologue to the story of Hrungnir's duel with Þórr in *Skáld*, ch. 17 (*SnE* I, 270). Thus it is likely that Þjóðólfr and other Norse-Icelandic mythological poets regarded Gefn, Gefjun and Iðunn as acceptable variant names for Freyja, the fertility goddess of the Vanir. Snorri elsewhere uses *ár* in association with the cult of Njǫrðr and Freyr, in combinations of the words *ár ok friðr* ('harvest-plenty and peace') in *Gylfaginning*, ch. 24 (*Gylf*, p. 24) and *Ynglinga saga*, chs. 9–10 (ed. Bjarni, pp. 23–5); this cliché was apparently transferred to the Christian Deity in the *Glælognskviða* of Þórarinn loftunga (*c.* 1032): *hann of getr af Goði sjǫlfum ár ok friðr ǫllum mǫnnum* ('he [St Óláfr] gets peace and harvest-plenty from God on behalf of all mankind', *Skj* B I, 301, 9). 'Harvest-Gefn', therefore, appears to be the meaning of *ár-Gefn* in the second half of *Haustlǫng* 2, in which this name probably qualifies both *mar* and *birgi-Týr* (see below) as the focal point of two kennings. This interpretation is argued in detail by Holtsmark (pp. 13–14). Reichardt (p. 164) and Kock (*NN* § 1810) also read *ár-Gefnar mar* in accordance with T; later, on metrical grounds, Kock decided for R *ar gnæfar* in order to make *Árgnæfa mar* ('the giant's horse'),

[9]My text is from *Heimskringla I*, ed. Bjarni, p. 15: 'Gefjun drew, gleaming, from Gylfi the deep-sea sun [jewel] of his estates, to the increase of Denmark, in such a way that steam came from her driven beasts. The oxen bore eight forehead moons [eyes] and four heads, when they trod ahead of her broad sea-wall-/choice-battle-spoil of a grassy island'. See also *Skj* B I, 3, 13. My reading *óðla* ('estates') for MS *aupla* is in keeping with A. Holtsmark, *Studier i norrøn diktning* (Oslo, 1956), pp. 164–8 and *Studier i Snorres Mytologi* (Oslo, 1964), pp. 69–71; and with Frank, *Old Norse Court Poetry*, pp. 103–8.

[10]Gutenbrunner, *Götternamen*, pp. 202 (*Alagabiae*) and 213–14 (*Gabiae* and *Garmangabi*); also in A. Riese, *Das Rheinische Germanien in den antiken Inschriften*, 2 vols. (Leipzig, 1892–1914) II, 325 and 329.

taking *Árgnæfi to be a giant's name (*NN* § 2004 and *Ska*, p. 9). Thereby, however, he kept T *mar* in preference to R *mat*, so as not to lose the ox-kenning 'Gef(ju)n's horse' which R *mat* would have precluded. A parallel for this type of ox-kenning is Þjóðólfr's *jǫtuns eykr* ('giant's draught-horse') in *Ynglingatal* 17 (*Skj* B I, 10). Kiil also reads *ár-Gefnar mar* (pp. 11–12). However, in keeping with his idea that this poem is influenced by the poet's knowledge of Lappish culture, Kiil takes this kenning to refer to a reindeer by which Iðunn draws herself through the wintry world of the giants, while she is in their keeping.

2/6–7 *ár-Gefnar byrgi-Týr bjarga*] 'the Týr who would imprison harvest-Gefn within rocks.' Given that I have read *ár-Gefnar mar* in 2/6, it might seem unnecessary to link *ár-Gefnar* on this line also with *byrgi-Týr bjarga* on 2/7. In the latter kenning, *birgi-Týr* occurs only here ('Týr of the rocks', hence 'giant') and its first element *byrgi-* appears to be redundant without an object for the implicit verb *byrgja* ('to shut in', cf. Sigrún and other brides who are *byrgðar í haugi*, 'shut within in the gravemound', with Helgi and his men in *HHund* II 46). *Ár-Gefn* would be the object of *byrgi-* if this word is used as a verbal prefix to *Týr* in *Haustlǫng* 2. Thus there is probably a semantic overlap involving *ár-Gefnar* between the kennings *ár-Gefnar mar* and *byrgi-Týr bjarga*. With this flexibility of meaning, the poet uses Gefn's name pointedly, not only to indicate the 'ox' which the Æsir are about to eat, but also to show that Þjazi plans to steal Iðunn from the Æsir even while he moves towards them.

2/8 *bleyði vændr*] 'accused of cowardice.' Here WT *vendr* (for *vændr*) is preferable to R *vǫndr*: *vændr* is the past participle of *væna* ('to hope for', 'to charge s-one with s-thing'); *vǫndr* (m. 'wand', 'switch') does not fit the context.

3. *Between its bones the dung-reindeer was divided with difficulty by the gods; something is the cause of this, said the wisdom-teacher of the divine powers encased in his helmet; the much-prophetic seagull of the surf of the slaughter-heap (Hœnir's friend was not gracious to him) began to speak from the ancient fir-tree.*

3 This stanza (as R²T²) is also quoted separately by Snorri, in *Skáld*, ch. 55 (*SnE* I, 468–70), in order to illustrate *hǫpt* at 3/3 as a synonym for *goð* ('gods').

3/1 *Tormiðlaðr*] 'divided with difficulty.' Finnur emends to -*miðluðr*, 'the one who hindered' ('den som hindrede', *Skj* B I, 14), because he needs to make sense of MSS *talhreinn* (see below). Kock defends *tormiðlaðr* as 'divided with difficulty' ('svårdelad', *NN* § 1015), from *miðla* ('to distribute'). The meat is probably hard to cut and share out because it is not yet cooked, due to a spell cast on the fire by Þjazi (Loki is still blowing on the fire in 4/3–4). A discussion of Norwegian cooking methods in the open in provided by Holtsmark (pp. 57–

8) and apparently followed by Faulkes, who translates *seyði* in 2/8 as 'earth-oven' (*SSE*, p. 86).[11]

3/2 *ta[ð]lhreinn*] 'dung-reindeer.' Holtsmark (pp. 15–16) emends the form *talhreinn* (in all MSS but R¹ *talhrein*) as *tall-hreinn*, 'dung-reindeer', where *tall* would derive by assimilation from *taðl, a suffixed form of OIce *tað* ('dung', 'manure'); ModNorw reflexes in *Landsmål* or *Nynorsk* dialect are *tad(d)*, *tadle* and (also in Swedish) *talle*, a word for 'muck' or 'hay'; Aasen, the *Nynorsk* lexicographer, said that *talle* is 'the bottom of a sheep-pen; the compressed layer which is gradually formed from the muck of the animal with the litter spread on top'.[12] The compound *ta[ð]lhreinn*, in this case, would allude to the ox-dung which was left to accumulate in the stall throughout the winter and then raked out to be spread on the fields in the spring (there were two ploughings in spring, one in autumn).[13] I choose *ta[ð]l-* also for the following reasons. Without emendation, *tal-* in MSS *talhreinn* is usually taken to represent *tál* ('deceit', 'allurement'), in which case *tálhreinn* would mean 'deceiving-deer' or the like (perhaps one such as the *stælhranas*, 'decoy reindeer', that the Nor-wegian skipper Ohthere mentioned to King Alfred in the 880s).[14] This idea is favoured by Kiil (pp. 14–15). Yet if we accept it, 3/1–2 *tálhreinn* would suggest that Þjazi is drawn towards the cooking fire like a deer into a trap. This unflat-tering image, however, sidelines the meaning of the rest of the sentence, which is that the cooked meat was difficult to cut or to distribute. In addition, *tálhreinn* by itself cannot be a kenning for an ox. Thus it is better to seek another solution. Finnur reads *hreinn* as an adjective (i.e. 'pure'), takes its compound to refer to Þjazi, and rearranges the words of 3/1–2 as *meðal-tálhreinn vas tormiðluðr beina tívum*: 'It was the deceitful one who hindered the gods in their meal' ('den svigfulde var den, som hindrede måltidet for guderne', *Skj* B I, 14). Magnús accepts Finnur's *meðaltálhreinn* and translates it as 'middling free with deceit, tricky' ('í meðallagi laus við tál, prettvís', p. 364, n. 94); Faulkes, as 'mid-dlingly free of deceit' (*SSE*, p. 86). Yet a meaning such as 'middling pure in deceit' throws no new light on Þjazi, nor do these scholars explain what point this meaning would have in its context (*meðal* works well enough as a preposi-tion with gen. pl. *beina*). Kock (*NN* § 1015), having defended *tormiðlaðr* above,

---

[11]Cf. also Simpson, *Everyday Life in the Viking Age*, pp. 70–1.

[12]Aasen, *Norsk Ordbog*, p. 798: 'Grunden i en Faaresti; det sammentrampede Lag som efterhaanden danner sig af Dyrens Møg med den derpaa udbredte Strøelse'. In the late-nineteenth-century (south-western) Norway from which Aasen drew words for his lexicon, *talle* appears to have been used only for sheep and goats.

[13]Cf. Simpson, *Everyday Life in the Viking Age*, p. 59; and Williams, *Social Scandinavia in the Viking Age*, pp. 164–8, esp. 165.

[14]*The Old English Orosius*, ed. Bately, p. 17.

emends MSS *talhreinn* to *tólhreinn* (i.e. 'tool-reindeer', on analogy with *okhreinn*, 'draught-deer', in *Ynglingatal* 16): 'between the bones the ox was hard for the gods to cut' ('mellan knotorna var oxen seg för gudarne att skära'). Although 'tool-reindeer' could be a kenning for an ox, 'dung-reindeer' in *ta[ð]lhreinn* is preferable, because in its later assimilated form with one *l* written for two, *tal-* in *tallhreinn* keeps all the letters of MSS *tal-*.

3/3 *kvað*] 'said.' All MSS have forms which represent *kvǫðu* ('they said'). As *kvǫðu* has two syllables, however, this form does not fit the metre; in addition, 'they said' makes no sense in the line; thus it is necessary to emend to *kvað* in agreement with *hapta snytrir*.

3/5–6 *margspakr mǫr valkastar bǫru*] 'the much-prophetic seagull of the surf of the slaughter-heap.' Given the general rhyming irregularities in *Haustlǫng*, Kock's emendation *margspakr* (all MSS) to *málspakr* (i.e. 'wise in speech') is unnecessary, even if it makes a *skothending*-rhyme for *mæla* on the same line (*NN* § 2504; followed by Kiil, p. 18). The word *margspakr* occurs but once elsewhere, as a term for King Haraldr hárfagri, in the *Glymdrápa* of Þorbjǫrn hornklofi (*Skj* B I, 21, 8; *c.* 890). Þjóðólfr's eagle-kenning in *Haustlǫng* is a vivid example of a *topos* for 'birds of battle' which is common to all early Germanic literature. This description of Þjazi seems to be related to the image of Óðinn in a helmet in the first half of this stanza, as well as to his epithet *hapta snytrir* ('wisdom-teacher of the divine powers') in 3/3 and to his role as *hrafnáss* ('raven-god') indicated in 4/4. Þjazi's role in this half of the stanza thus seems to be that of a prophesying bird such as Huginn or Muninn, who are Óðinn's oracular friends in *Grím* 20 and in Snorri's account of this stanza in *Gylf*, ch. 38 (pp. 32–3). Other such birds are the *fugl fróðhugaðr* ('learned-minded bird', *HHj* 2) who speaks to Atli Iðmundarson in *HHj* 1–4; and the two nuthatches who give Sigurðr advice in *Fáf* 32–9 and 40–4. OIce *mæla* in *Haustlǫng* 3/5, in addition, denotes the beginning of a formal speech. The 'ancient fir-tree' from which Þjazi speaks to Óðinn (*af fornum þolli*, 3/8) may also recall the world-tree Yggdrasill from whose top branches each day in *Grím* 32 an 'eagle's words' (*arnar orð*) are passed to the dragon Níðhǫggr down below (cf. 6/3, however, where this tree is an *eik*, 'oak'). In the light of these *topoi*, a mocking irony emerges in *Haustlǫng* 3: first Óðinn, the 'wisdom-teacher of the divine powers', fails to connect the spell on his cooking-fire with the eagle sitting in the tree; then the eagle, who has caused the spell, is presented in a traditional role as if ready to offer Óðinn some impartial advice. The effect of this augury-conceit is to emphasize the folly of the Æsir.

3/7 *Hœnis vinr*] 'Hœnir's friend.' This kenning for Loki occurs here and at 7/7 and is similar to *hugreynandi Hœnis* ('he who put Hœnir's courage to the test'), another kenning for Loki at 12/3. It is possible, as Holtsmark argues, that the name *Hœnir* is cognate with *hani* ('cockerel'), a reference to the world of the dead (cf. Holtsmark, pp. 47–53, esp. 49). But Þjóðólfr's effect in this stanza, particularly in the parenthesis *vasat Hœnis vinr hǫnum hollr*, may be based on another, more comic, implication of this word: 'the cockerel's friend was not gracious to the eagle'. OIce *hollr* is often used of gods, indicating the favours that others expect from them (*holl regin*, in *Lok* 4; *hollar vættir*, in *Oddr* 9; and of the Deity, *hollr seggjum* in the *Geisli* 34 of Einarr Skúlason, *c*. 1153). This aside in *Haustlǫng* not only looks forward to Loki's attempt to kill the eagle in 6/5–8, but also hints at Loki's own transformation into a bird to escape the eagle at the end of this story in st. 12. Above all, it seems to be with good intentions, namely through his friendship with Hœnir (whose name, incidentally, is missing from Ægir's guest-list in *Lokasenna*), that Loki starts out on his ill-judged road.

4. *The wolf of the fells (it fell to the portion of the raven-god's friend to blow) bade the stepping-Meili deal him his fill from the holy trencher (/ harpoon); the combat-fierce prince of wind-dolphins let himself sink down to where the trick-sparing defenders of the gods had come.*

4/1 *Fjallgylðir*] 'wolf of the fells.' OIce *gylðir* seems to be a common *heiti* or synonym for a wolf (Meissner, p. 258); Þjóðólfr uses *ǫlgylðir* ('alder-wolf', MS variant *hofgylðir*, 'court-wolf') to describe the fire that swallows King Óláfr *trételgja* ('tree-trimmer') in *Ynglingatal* 29 (*Skj* B I, 12). A 'wolf of the fells' in *Haustlǫng*, i.e. of open mountain-sides (with *fjall*), is likely to be a kenning for an eagle, despite Holtsmark's translation of *fjallgylðir* as 'fell-blower', a kenning for an eagle on the basis of Hræsvelgr in *Vaf* 37 ('fjellblåser', p. 18).

4/3 *af helgum skutli*] 'from the holy trencher.' Þjazi seems to use guile rather than outright effrontery to approach the gods, despite his predatory eagle's shape. OIce *heilagr* ('holy') is a portentous word and in *heilagt tafn*, 'holy sacrifice', it describes Baldr's death in Úlfr Uggason's *Húsdrápa* 14 (*c*. 995, *Skj* B I, 130). Its collocation with *skutill* ('table', 'trencher') in *Haustlǫng* 4 seems bathetic. Holtsmark treats the use of *heilagr* as a sign that the gods eat food which mortals have sent them through sacrifice (pp. 45–61, esp. 54–5). This is a plausible idea, but it is also possible that the collocation of *heilagr* with *skutill* in *af helgum skutli* is intended to reflect the words of Þjazi as he asks for a meal. Kock rejects this idea (*NN* § 1016), but his removal of the split parenthesis in *Haustlǫng* 3–4, between which the words *af helgum skutli* are found, strains the sense of this stanza by making Hœnir blow with rage from the table on which the food is served. So, if we keep the split parenthesis (as do Finnur, Holtsmark and Marold), *heilagr skutill* may be taken to represent Þjazi's words of flattery which Þjóðólfr reports to us in indirect speech.

4/2 *fet-Meila*] 'stepping-Meili.' The referent of this kenning is probably Hœnir (so Faulkes, *SSE*, p. 87). Snorri, in *Skáld* (ch. 15), calls Hœnir *hinn skjóta Ás, ok hinn langa fót, ok [WU] aurkonung* ('the fleet god and the long of foot and the dung-king', *SnE* I, 268). *Meili* is known as Þórr's brother (*Meila bróðir*) in *Hárb* 9 (and probably also in *Haustlǫng* 14). Since Olce *fet* implies a quick-step, Finnur (*Skj* B I, 15), Kock (*NN* § 1016) and Holtsmark (p. 18) take the subject to be Hœnir, whose name probably means 'cockerel' or 'cockerel-man' (cf. 3/7). Kiil, by a circuitous route in which he etymologizes *Meili* probably correctly as 'he who soils, makes stains', thus 'shitter' ('han som søler til, setter flekker', 'skjitaren'), attempts to show that *fet-Meili* refers to Óðinn, in his role as the rearer of the baby Meili or Váli (pp. 25–7). Magnús emends to *feðr Meila* ('Meili's father', p. 365, n. 95), also in order to make Óðinn the referent of this kenning. Marold (p. 157) interprets *fet-Meili* as a reference to Óðinn for another reason, because Óðinn, not Hœnir, answers Þjazi's request at the beginning of stanza 5. She cites as proof Óðinn's nicknames *Vegtamr* (*Bdr* 6 and 13), *Gangráðr* (*Vaf* 11 and 13) and *Gangleri* (*Grím* 46), together with Óðinn's repeated boast in *Vafþrúðnismál* that 'I have travelled in many places' (*fjǫlð ec fór*, st. 44, 46, 48, 50, 52 and 54). However, the meanings of these Odinic names, respectively 'way-tame', 'walking-counselled' and 'walking-weary', do not resemble that of *fet-Meili*, in that they focus on the exhaustion of walking, whereas *fet* ('step') suits the relatively quicker movement of a running fowl. The disparity noted by Marold, in Þjazi's addressing Hœnir and being answered by Óðinn, is not a problem if we take it to be another sign of Þjazi's politeness: one bird address-ing another. Hœnir is more amenable than either Óðinn or Loki, for his standard reply to questions when he was a hostage with the Vanir, Snorri says, was *ráði aðrir* ('let others decide').[15] Þjazi's request to eat 'his fill' from Hœnir's portion (when that arrives) must be comic, if we remember that Þjazi is imagined as an eagle and Hœnir apparently as a cockerel, a little barnyard fowl. Yet the comedy of this mismatch seems lost on Hœnir, Loki and Óðinn.

4/3 *hlaut hrafnásar vinr blása*] 'it fell to the portion of the raven-god's friend to blow.' While Þjazi makes his request, Loki continues to coax the flame into life, taking no other 'portion' from the ox but his job as its cook. I have taken 'por-tion' from *hlaut* (from *hljóta*, 'to obtain as a lot' or '... as a portion'). The 'raven-god' may be taken to be Óðinn, on the basis of Óðinn's friendship with Huginn and Muninn in *Grím* 20 and of Hofgarðarefr Steinsson's Óðinn-kenning *hrafnáss* (in *heilagt full hrafnásar*, 'the holy cup of raven-god', 'poetry', *Skj* B I, 295, 2). This god's friend may not be Loki, for Kock takes Hœnir to be the *hrafnásar vinr* (*NN* § 1016). However, as both Óðinn and Loki accuse each other of homo-sexuality (having *args aðal*, 'the nature of a queer', *Lok* 23–4), and as Frigg confirms that they were both male witches in days of old (*Lok* 25), it is even possible that Óðinn and Loki were imagined as former sexual partners.

[15]*Heimskringla I*, ed. Bjarni, p. 13 (*Ynglinga saga*, ch. 4).

4/5 *ving-rǫgnir -vagna*] 'prince of wind-dolphins.' This kenning appears to refer to Þjazi as an eagle. The first element, *ving*(-), is problematic, for this word seems unrelated either to OIce *vængr* or its ModE formal and semantic reflex *wing* (despite Kock's insistence in *NN* § 2505), or to any other known word. Magnús (p. 365), followed by Faulkes (*SSE*, p. 87), interprets this prefix as 'land' and puts it with *vagna*, to make 'land-whales', i.e. 'giants'. *Ving-*, however, is a prefix in several names, most notably *Vingþórr*, which is Þórr's name in his rage at losing his hammer Mjǫllnir (*Þrym* 1); *vin(d)gameiðr* ('the windy branch', presumably a backform from acc. **inn vinduga meið*), appears to be a name for the world-tree in *Háv* 138 and *Háleygjatal* 7 (*c.* 985); since Þórr's name identifies him with thunder and he appears to travel through the sky in a chariot in *Haustlǫng* 15–16, and since *Thor* was known as a god of the weather in Uppsala in (*c.* 1076),[16] it is possible that Þórr's *ving*-prefix was derived from the stem of **vindugr* (otherwise not recorded, but analogous with ModE *windy*). The word *vagna*, the other difficult part of this kenning, is unlikely to be the gen. pl. of *vagn* (m. 'waggon'), as Marold points out (p. 158), but rather that of *vagna* or *vǫgn* (f. 'whale', 'dolphin'). Kock (*NN* § 2505) takes *vagna* to be a giant-*heiti*, but as Marold says, this word needs a qualifier to mean 'giant' and Kock bases his argument on *vagna váttr* in 16/7–8, which is itself problematic. With *vagna* in 4/5 as the gen. pl. of 'dolphin', instead, I suggest that the phrase *ving-rǫgnir -vagna* may be read with *ving-* as a prefix transferred from *-vagna* (analogous to *hirði-* in *hirði-Týr herfangs* in 6/7–8): thus as *ving-vagna rǫgnir*, 'prince of wind-dolphins'.[17] The effect of this kenning for a large hunting bird is to change the mood of the stanza in its second half. As Þjazi moves nearer into view, his potential for ferocity (in *vígfrekr*, 'combat-fierce', only here) and above all, his size (implicit in *lét ofan sígask*, 'let himself sink down', 4/6) become clearer. Nonetheless, Óðinn and the others, now described as defenders of Ásgarðr (*varnendr goða*, 4/8), seem to be unaware of the danger. The word *vélsparir* (4/7) suggests that they have decided to make savings on acumen, the quality they need to detect the eagle's scheming (the fact that he is Þjazi, a giant, in disguise). Þjóðólfr heightens this sense of danger with the kenning *ving-rǫgnir -vagna* and possibly with an ambiguity in *skutill* in 4/3, which can also mean 'harpoon' (cf. *beita skutli*, 'to catch with a harpoon' in a probably twelfth-century loose-verse attributed to Þormóðr kolbrúnarskáld, *Skj* B I, 261, 4; and *brynju dyns háskutill*, 'high-harpoon of the din of the mail-coat', 'sword', in Anon (XIII) B 10). If Þjazi is imagined for a moment as a dolphin or whale, and the sky thus as the open sea, then the implication of this secondary meaning in *skutill* would be that it were better for the Æsir to harpoon Þjazi as soon as he comes within range.

---

[16]*Adam Bremensis Gesta*, ed. Schmeidler, p. 258 (IV.26).

[17]Finnur, 'Kenningers led-omstilling og tmesis', p. 2.

4/7–8 *þars vǫru farnir*] 'to where they had come.' The danger of this moment becomes clearer if we relate this use of *farnir* to *far* in the gods' *trygglaust far* ('unsafe journey') which Þjóðólfr claims to see on the shield in 1/6.

5. *Swiftly the handsome lord of the land bade Fárbauti's boy deal out the whale of the cracking rope of spring-times among the thanes, and after that the Æsir's prank-wise disobliger served up four bull-portions from the broad table.*

5/1–2 *foldar dróttinn*] 'lord of the land.' In this stanza the scene appears to be presented from Óðinn's perspective: Óðinn, as if lord of the estate surrounded by thanes in his hall, cheerfully orders the guest to be served; Loki, as if a serving-boy fostered there away from his father, obeys with bad grace. Óðinn's marriage with Jǫrð ('earth') is expressed in twenty kennings for the earth (Meissner, p. 87, § 1.a) and is elsewhere implicit in kennings for Þórr (their son) in six instances (*ibid.*, p. 258, § 88.a). It is worth noting, however, that Meissner records no other kenning such as *foldar dróttinn* in which this marriage is indicated through Óðinn (rather than through Þórr or the earth). In this light, it is possible that Þjóðólfr alludes to Óðinn as *foldar dróttinn* in order to present him as if he were a mortal chieftain with both 'land' (*fold*) and 'retinue' (*drótt*).

5/2 *Fárbauta mǫg*] 'Fárbauti's boy.' *Fárbauta mǫgr* denotes Loki elsewhere only in Úlfr Uggason's *Húsdrápa* 2, in which Loki wrestles with Heimdallr both underwater in seal's shape for possession of a mythical jewel. *Fárbauti* is probably Loki's father, for this noun's ending is masculine and Loki's mother seems to be known as *Laufey* (*Lok* 52, *Þrym* 18 and 20). Snorri calls Loki *sonr Fárbauta jǫtuns* ('son of Fárbauti the giant') in *Gylf*, ch. 33 (p. 26). OIce *mǫgr* means both 'son' in particular and 'boy' in general: this ambiguity of meaning, similar to that of the unique kenning *foldar dróttinn* above, appears to allow Þjóðólfr to present Loki both as a mythological figure and as a serving-boy in Óðinn's hall (cf. note to 5/6–7).

5/3 *þekkiligr*] 'handsome.' Kock (*NN* § 3037) emends to *þægiligr*, with a similar meaning ('agreeable'), to achieve *skothending* on this line. Although this emendation is more persuasive than others made by Kock in *Haustlǫng*, it seems best to keep all MSS *þekkiligr*. The phrase with which *þekkiligr* is linked is likely to alliterate with it on the same line, i.e. *með þegnum*. This domestic portrait of Óðinn as a young landed chieftain in the midst of his his thanes is likely to be painted from the point of view of Óðinn himself, for it is not consistent with other images of this god in *Haustlǫng*.

5/2, 5/4 *vára þrymseilar hval*] 'the whale of the cracking rope of spring-times', i.e. an ox. As *hvalr* shows, the kenning in this part of the stanza must represent an ox, the food that Óðinn generously orders Loki to serve up to his avian guest. Yet there are two problems: one, the form, meaning and semantic context of R *vǫro* W *vara* T..*ra*; two, the meaning of the noun *þrymseil* of which *hvalr* appears to be the compound base. First, it is possible to emend the WT forms to *Várar*, the gen. sg. of f. *Vǫr*, goddess of pledges and oaths (*Gylf*, ch. 35, p. 29) and then to place *Várar* with the elements of the ox-kenning on the next full line, to make *þrymseilar Várar hvalr*, 'whale of the Vǫr of the bowstring', hence 'Skaði's whale', hence 'ox'. So Finnur (LP, p. 649), Meissner (p. 111, § 30), Magnús (p. 365, n. 96) and Faulkes (*SSE*, p. 86). Skaði is a goddess with bow and arrow, and this formulation deals with the contextual difficulty of *Vára[r]*, but it is still not clear why Skaði should hunt oxen rather than wild game. It is also possible to read R *vǫro* as *Vǫru*, dat. of *Vǫr*. This course is followed by Kock (*NN* § 137), by Kiil (p. 34) and by Marold (p. 158), who links *Vǫru* with *foldar dróttinn þekkiligr* to make 'Herr der Erde angenehm der Vár'. Kiil suggests that Óðinn in this stanza is pleasing to the goddess of oaths because he allows Þjazi into the banquet, but *Vǫru þekkiligr* is too brief as an adjectival phrase to justify its position split by an enjambement between lines 2 and 3 (even if *Vǫru þekkiligr* should go with *foldar*, i.e. 'pleasing to the Vǫr of the land'). The third and strongest reading is to accept W *vara* without emendation as *vára*, gen. pl. of n. *vár* ('spring'), and then to place *vára* with *þrymseilar hval* on the next full line. Olce f. *seil* in *þrymseil* means 'line' or 'rope'; *þrym-* could derive from *þrymja* (either 'to lie, extend' or 'to thunder, crash, crack') or from a noun **þrymr* (?'roar'; cf. f. *þruma*, 'peal of thunder') such as can be reconstructed on the basis of Þrymr, the name of the giant who steals Þórr's hammer in *Þrymskviða*: thus either 'extending rope' or 'thundering rope' or even Olsen's 'rope of Þrymr' (**Þryms seilar*, pp. 325–6). Holtsmark takes *þrymseil* to refer to a bell-harness with which an ox might be decorated prior to sacrifice in the rituals which Þjóðólfr may have known (pp. 22–3). Marold follows Olsen, rendering 'whale of Þrymr's rope' ('Wal des Seiles des Þrymr', p. 159) on the basis of *jǫtuns eykr* ('giant's draught-horse'), which is Þjóðólfr's kenning for an ox in *Ynglingatal* 17. At any rate, the 'whale' of the 'rope' in *Haustlǫng* 5 appears to be the ox: the seventeenth-century *Edda*-text of Magnús Ólafsson, otherwise known as the *Laufás-Edda*, says that *vxi kiennist j fornv(ysum) þrymseilar hvalur* ('in old poems an ox is known as *þrymseilar hvalur*').[18] According to this later interpretation of *Haustlǫng* 5/4, *þrymseilar hvalr* indicates 'ox' without the help of *vára* or whatever this word is at the end of the previous full line. Kock and Marold thus put the latter word with other elements in this stanza, with Marold making up the necessary qualifier by personifying *þrym-*. Yet it is awkward to read Þrymr's name in this kenning when a qualifier may be had in the otherwise free-floating *vára*. Hence Finnur's suggested 'bow-string' ('buestræng', LP, *s.v.* *þrymseil*) in order to get Skaði out of an emended *Várar* ('whale of the Vǫr of

---

[18] *Two Versions of Snorra Edda from the 17th Century, Edda Magnúsar Óláfssonar (Laufás Edda)*, ed. Anthony Faulkes (Reykjavík, 1979), p. 310.

the bowstring'). In my turn, however, I suggest that W *vara* (and T *..ra*) may be kept unemended as *vára* ('of spring-times', gen. pl. of n. *vár*), in order to qualify *þrymseilar hval* without the introduction of a goddess or giant: i.e. 'whale of the cracking rope of spring-times'. Although *vára* could be left out if 'cracking rope's whale' were enough to suggest an 'ox' on its own, the addition of 'spring' to this image gives it a seasonal context which may be compared with Þjóðólfr's description of the ox as (apparently) *tallhreinn* ('dung-reindeer', 3/2) and as *okbjǫrn* ('yoke-bear', 6/4) and *okhreinn* ('yoke-reindeer', *Ynglingatal* 16). Given that these three other kennings appear to refer to the ox in ploughing time, i.e. in the spring, it is reasonable to suppose that the image of this time of year mattered to Þjóðólfr in its own right. Ploughing, then seeding, took place in April (or May, depending on the severity of the weather).[19]

5/6-7 bragðvíss ósvífrandi ása] 'the Æsir's prank-wise disobliger.' The precise meaning of R *ósvífrandi* in this kenning is unknown, as is that of W *ósviptandi*. A use of OIce *svipta* in W *ósviptandi* ('to sweep', 'to clear', cf. Fritzner III, 626) might imply that Loki was reluctant to serve all four portions. On the other hand, the words *ósvífinn* and *ósvífr* ('coarse, disobliging', the second also a name), all of which appear to be related to *ósvífrandi*, make this R reading slightly preferable to that of the W-text. Towards the end of *Skáldskaparmál* (ch. 67), furthermore, Snorri lists the word *ósvífruðr* among various *heiti* for *óvinr* or 'enemy' (R; U has *ósvipuðr* and two leaves in W in a different hand have *ósvifrungr*: cf. *SnE* I, 536, n. 6). Magnús thus translates *ósvífrandi ása* as the Æsir's 'unyielding opponent', but treats this phrase as a kenning for Þjazi ('ósvífinn andstæðingur', p. 365, n. 96; so Faulkes, *SSE*, p. 87). Þjazi in this case would anger Loki by snatching all four ox-portions off the broad table at once (Snorri seems to have understood the stanza this way). Yet even if this image is a tribute to Þjazi's size, it is worth noting that the words *át okbjǫrn* in the following stanza (at 6/3-4) do not refer to four ox-steaks, but to one. Does Þjazi put the other three portions by for a while while he devours the first one? Only then does Loki thwack him with the stick – a slow reaction to such an obvious impertinence. It seems more probable, in this way, that Loki himself is the referent of *ósvífrandi ása*. The words *svífa* ('to swing', 'to turn'), *svífask* ('to set oneself in motion', cf. Fritzner III, 621), Nynorsk *svivar* ('rambler', 'vagrant': Aasen's 'Omflakker', p. 784), ModE *swivel*, might imply that Loki as an *ósvíf(r)andi*, the opposite to these terms, is the Æsir's stubbornly unstirring servant. Kiil comes to much the same meaning by reading *óss víprandi ása* and by using Norwegian dialect forms to translate these words as 'the gods' randy pantomime artiste', a reference to Loki's later game with the goat in front of Skaði ('gudenes geile pantomimiker', pp. 36-8). Sveinbjörn and Finnur (LP, p. 449) and Meissner (p. 256, § 88.b), countered by Holtsmark (p. 23) and Marold (pp. 159-60), take the referent of this kenning to be Þjazi, not Loki. Yet an

[19]Williams, *Social Scandinavia in the Viking Age*, p. 165.

apparent ambiguity in *ósvífrandi* between 'enemy' and 'disobliger' suggests that Loki is imagined as both the fatal enemy of the Æsir (consistent with the allusion to *Fárbauti*, his giant-father, in 5/2) and as their ill-tempered servant called upon to serve his master's guest. This ambiguity is in keeping with the presentation of Óðinn in 5/1–4 as both the divine partner of the earth and an ebullient lord in his hall. But there is no doubt that Þjóðólfr is now beginning to warn us about Loki's impending treachery with Iðunn (in 10–11).

5/8 *þjórhluti fjóra*] 'four bull-portions.' The R scribe has written *hlifi ora* for *hluti fiora* (the form contained in W and T). Otherwise it is worth noting Þjóðólfr's interest here, as also in 1/5–8, in the precise number of participants in the story. This interest suggests that he indeed had a shield to work with on which four shapes were painted representing Óðinn, Hœnir, Loki and Þjazi.

6. *And hungry then (that was long ago) Mǫrn's father*
ferociously ate the yoke-bear off the oak-tree's roots,
before the deep-counselled Týr who was watching over the
war-booty struck the very bold foe of the field down
between the shoulders with a pole.

6/1 *sliðrliga*] 'ferociously.' OIce *slíðr* ('fierce, cruel') is the name of a river of knives and swords in the underworld in *Vsp* 36, while a compound *sliðrbeitr* ('cruel-cutting') describes the *sax* ('knife') with which Gunnarr asks the Huns to cut out the heart of his brother Hǫgni in *Akv* 21. Thus there is probably a sense in *sliðrliga* (only in *Haustlǫng* 6/1) of Þjazi's eagle's beak piercing the ox-flesh which he eats.

6/2 *vas þat fyr lǫngu*] 'that was long ago.' See note 2/4. This parenthesis, juxtaposed with *svangr* ('hungry'), suggests either that Þjóðólfr's community regarded itself as no longer in any danger of famine, or that it has been a long time since Þjazi last ate. Kiil (p. 39) may be right to point out that Þjóðólfr would not have known the word *lǫngu* in its back-mutated form, but would have said *svangr vas þat fyr langu*, with the correct *aðalhending* (and likewise **stangu* in 6/8); however, in matters of morphology it is better to stick to forms characteristic of the later Icelandic language without which this poem would not have survived.

6/4 *okbjǫrn*] 'yoke-bear.' Close to *okhreinn* ('yoke-reindeer', *Ynglingatal* 16): see note 5/2, 5/4. Þjóðólfr's ox may indeed have resembled a 'bear' if the breed of cattle to which *okbjǫrn* refers was anything like the Highland Longhorn, known for its shaggy hair.

6/4 *faðir Mǫrna[r]*] 'Mǫrn's father', i.e. Þjazi. RW *morna* may be emended to read *Mǫrnar* on the basis of all MSS. *mornar* in 12/8, although a gen. pl. *Mǫrna* (?'giantesses') would be acceptable here without emendation. Although OIce *mǫrn* seems to mean 'giantess', Holtsmark (pp. 24–5) identifies this word also with the wild river Månn in Mandal in Vest-Agðir at the southern end of Norway, to the east of Kvinesdal from which Þjóðólfr of *Hvinir* is likely to have come.[20] That a river might be called a giant's daughter is apparent from *Lok* 34, in which Loki accuses Njǫrðr (i.e. the ocean) of having acted as a piss-trough for *Hymis meyiar* ('Hymir's girls', i.e. rivers). Hymir is the giant with whom Þórr goes on a fishing-trip to catch the world-serpent in *Hymiskviða*. There is also a now notorious image in Eilífr Goðrúnarson's *Þórsdrápa* (*c.* 985) in which a giantess' menstrual flood pours over Þórr like a river:

Harðvaxnar leit herðar   hall-lands of sik falla
(gatat) *mar* (njótr in neytri   njarð- rǫð fyr sér -gjarðar);
þverrir lét, nema þyrri   (Þórns barna) sér Marnar
snerriblóð, til svíra   salþaks megin vaxa.

(Þórsdrápa 7)[21]

The giantess, hence also the river, in this difficult passage appears to be called Mǫrn, and there may be some humour in Eilífr's use of the *njarð*-prefix, which seems to alternate between qualifying Þórr's belt and describing what happens to him when the giantess' flood swamps his head and shoulders ('(strength-) belt's user [Þórr] could not get for himself more profitable Njǫrðr-recourses than this').[22] Mǫrn in these contexts seems to be a Norwegian name for both a river and a giantess. Finally, the plural *Mǫrnir* (of which the unemended RW

---

[20]See Berg and Berg, *NAF Veibok*, p. 4, A3, A4. Other rivers by this name in the southern half of Norway are the Måna in Fidjadalen in southern Rogaland (*ibid.*, p. 7, D3), the Måna near Rjukan in eastern Telemark (*ibid.*, p. 17, D1) and the Måna above Romsdalsfjorden in Møre and Romsdal (*ibid.*, p. 47, D2).

[21]*Skj* B I, 141: 'He saw the ocean [*emend.* R *maðr*] of the rock-terrain fall over his hard-grown shoulders; (strength-)belt's user [Þórr] could not get for himself more profitable Njǫrðr-recourses than this: the diminisher of the ogre's (/ Þorn's) children [giants] declared that unless Mǫrn's swift-flowing blood [river] dried up, his power would grow to the peak of hall-hatch [to heaven] itself'. This text is only partly based on Finnur's; I am grateful to J. P. Grove for allowing me to use his text and translation of this poem, which he presented in a seminar in University College London; and Daphne Davidson also provides an excellent discussion of this stanza in 'Earl Hákon and his Poets', pp. 522 and 533.

[22]The placing of this *njarð*-prefix is discussed by Davidson (*ibid.*, p. 544) and by Konstantin Reichardt (who also links it with *gjarðar*) in 'A Contribution to the Interpretation of Scaldic Poetry: Tmesis', in *Old Norse Literature and Mythology: A Symposium*, ed. E. C. Polomé (Austin, TX, 1969), pp. 200–26, esp. 212–13. Kock links it with *ráð* in *gatat meir njótr in neytri njarðráð fyr sér gjarðar*: 'now the girdle-clad one knew furthermore of no better plan for himself' ('numera visste sig den jördelklädde icke någon bättre råd', NN § 449). It is likely, in my view, that *njarð*- covers both possibilities.

morna T *niorna* may be a gen. pl. example) appears to mean 'trolls' in *Vǫlsa þáttr*, a tale in *Flateyjarbók* in which some heathen householders offer these beings and their other gods a horse's prick.[23] It is not clear whether or not Mǫrn, a giantess (and river), should be regarded as synonymous with Skaði.

6/5–8 *djúphugaðr hirði-Týr herfangs*] 'the deep-counselled Týr who was watching over the war-booty', i.e. Loki. The adjective *djúphugaðr* prepares us for the trap that Loki, already *bragðvíss* in 5/6, springs on Þjazi at the end of the stanza. The syntax of *hirði-Týr herfangs*, whereby *hirða* ('to watch over, guard') in *hirði-* needs *herfangs* as its object, provides a means by which *ár-Gefnar byrgi-Týr bjarga* may be read in 2/6–7.

6/6 *dolg ballastan vallar*] 'the very bold foe of the field', i.e. Þjazi. Marold renders this kenning as 'the strongest enemy in the world' ('der stärkste Feind der Welt', p. 160), apparently taking these words to be Þjóðólfr's indication of the risk which Loki takes in attacking Þjazi. Yet these words appear to be Loki's, given the superlative *ballastan*, which better suits the exclamation of a bystander (cf. the words of Beowulf's mourners: *cwædon þæt he wære ... manna mildust ond monðwærust, leodum liðost ond lofgeornost*, in *Beowulf* 3180–2) than Þjóðólfr's comment about Þjazi's boldness relative to that of other giants (cf. note to *af helgum skutli, Haustlǫng* 4/3). Olce *dolgr* may mean 'warrior', or perhaps 'zombie', as in the *dauðir dolgar* ('dead ?warriors') to which Helgi Sigmundarson alludes in *HHund* II 51. Yet in *Haustlǫng* 6, *dolgr* appears to mean 'foe' or 'enemy', as in *Jóta dolgr* ('the foe of Jutes'), Þjóðólfr's epithet for King Dómaldi of Uppsala in *Ynglingatal* 5 (cf. *Ála dolgr* and *Eistra dolgr*, 'Áli's foe' and 'foe of the ?Prussians', *Ynglingatal* 22 and 26 respectively). The noun *vǫllr*, in conjunction with these warlike terms and with reference to its use to describe Vígríðr, the site of Ragnarǫk, in *Vaf* 18, may be read as 'battle-field'.[24] Note the shift in scenery in this half of *Haustlǫng* 6: the epic words *herfang, dolg* and *vallar* suggest a battlefield on which the ox becomes a prize and Þjazi the 'very bold' warrior who wishes to steal it. Þjóðólfr here appears to give us an insight into Loki's mind, building up from external views of him first as the protective friend of Hœnir (3/7–8); then as Óðinn's friend, given the job of blowing on the fire (4/3–4); then as a disgruntled serving-boy, ordered by his master to serve a guest (5/5–8). The poet's image of Loki in 6/7–8 as the keeper of booty taken on a raid, thus as a victorious defensive warrior, now seems to represent Loki's view of himself (cf. Óðinn's apparent *amour propre* in 5/3).

[23]*Stories from the Sagas of the Kings*, ed. Anthony Faulkes, w. introduction, notes and glossary (London, 1980), pp. 56–9 and 97 (n. 56/3).

[24]Holtsmark discusses this word in 'Kattar sonr', *Saga-Book* 16 (1963), 144–155, esp. 146–7.

7. *Then set fast was the cargo of Sigyn's arms, whom all the divine powers glare at in his bonds, to the foster-father of the ski-goddess; the sailyard stuck to the mighty spectre of the giants' world, and the hands of Hœnir's loyal friend to the end of the pole.*

7/2 *farmr Sigynjar arma*] 'the cargo of Sigyn's arms', i.e. Loki. WT *sigyniar* is preferable to *signyiar* of the R-scribe, who seems to have treated 7/1–2 as part of the Vǫlsung-legend in which 'the cargo of Signý's arms', i.e. her brother Sigmundr, 'became a fast friend of his foster-son', i.e. of Sinfjǫtli, Signý's son by him (m. *fóstri* may mean either 'foster-father' or '-son').[25] Snorri begins his first account of the Vǫlsung-legends in *Skáld* ch. 39 (*SnE* I, 356), not far from where he quotes *Haustlǫng* 1–13 in ch. 22 (*SnE* I, 306–14). Here, as elsewhere in *Haustlǫng*, the R-text of *Skáldskaparmál* is less reliable than W and T. The collocation *farmr arma* is elsewhere attested in *farmr Gunnlaðar arma* ('the cargo of Gunnlǫð's arms', Steinþórr) and in *farmr arma galdrs hapts* ('cargo of the arms of the spell-god', Eilífr's *Þórsdrápa* 3, *Skj* B I, 140), both kennings for Óðinn as the thief of the mead of poetry (cf. Loki as *sagna hrœrir* in the note to 9/1). The irony of *farmr Sigynjar arma* as a kenning for Loki is that he is the properly the cargo of Þjazi's arms; yet, as Þjóðólfr shows with the words *er ǫll regin eygja í bǫndum* (7/3–4), Loki will indeed be cradled by Sigyn when, at the end of his career as a friend of the gods, the Æsir chain him beneath the earth under the drops of a serpent's poison. In the words of the poet of *Vǫluspá*, *þar sitr Sigyn þeygi um sínom ver velglýjuð*, 'there Sigyn sits, though not perfectly gleeful, at the side of her husband' (*Vsp* 35); in Snorri's prose, *Sigyn kona hans stendr hjá honum ok heldr mundlaugu undir eitrdropa*, 'Sigyn his wife stands by him and holds a handbowl beneath the drops of poison' (*Gylf*, ch. 50, p. 49).

7/1–4 *við fóstra ǫndurgoðs*] 'to the foster-father of the ski-goddess', i.e. to Þjazi, who is also known as 'father of the ski-lady' (*faðir Ǫndurdísar*) in Bragi's *Ragnarsdrápa* 20 (*Skj* B I, 4). Skaði is known as *ǫndurgoð* only in *Haustlǫng* 7 and in Snorri's prose in *Gylf*, ch. 23 (p. 24). She is known as *ǫndurdís* in the same prose, and also in Eyvindr skáldaspillir's *Háleygjatal* (c. 985), in which Eyvindr says that *sunu marga Ǫndurdís við Óðni gat* ('many sons did Ski-lady

[25]On Signý and the Vǫlsungar, see *Die prosaische Edda im Auszuge nebst Vǫlsunga-saga und Nornagests-þáttr*, ed. and gloss. Ernst Wilken, 2nd ed., 2 vols. (Paderborn, 1912) I, 147–234 (pp. 152–63); and *The Saga of the Volsungs: the Norse Epic of Sigurd the Dragon Slayer*, trans. Jesse L. Byock (Berkeley, CA, 1990), pp. 38–47; and Richard North, 'Metre and Meaning in *Wulf and Eadwacer*: Signý Reconsidered', in *Loyal Letters: Studies on Mediaeval Alliterative Poetry & Prose*, ed. L. A. J. R. Houwen and A. A. MacDonald, Mediaevalia Groningana 15 (Groningen, 1994), 29–54, esp. 40–1.

get with Óðinn', st. 4), after referring to her by name:

> Þann skjaldblœtr   skattfœri gat
> Ása niðr   við Jarnviðju,
> þás þau mær   í Manheimum
> skatna vinr   ok Skaði byggðu.
>
> (*Háleygjatal* 3)[26]

Snorri calls Skaði *ǫndurgoð eða ǫndurdís* ('ski-goddess or -deity') and says that she married Njǫrðr after the death of Þjazi – unsuccessfully, for she left him to live in Þrymheimr *ok ferr hon mjǫk á skíðum ok með boga ok skýtr dýr* ('and goes about a great deal on skis with a bow and hunts wild animals', *Gylf*, p. 24).

7/4 *í bǫndum* 'in his bonds.' With an economy of language whereby the phrase *í bǫndum* elegantly complements both *varð fastr* (7/1) and *sá er ǫll regin eygja* (7/3), Þjóðólfr conveys two images with the same expression: Óðinn and Hœnir staring at Loki as he disappears into the sky, with his staff gripped by the magical 'bonds' of Þjazi; and all the Æsir beholding Loki as this time they bind him themselves. There is probably some anticipation of the latter scene in the binding of Loki that takes place in st. 11/3–4.

7/5 *loddi rǫ́* 'the sailyard stuck.' The preterite *loddi*, following close on *í bǫndum*, also does duty for two parts of its own sentence: for the *rǫ́* which sticks to Þjazi (7/5); and for the *hendr* of Loki which, presumably without magical constraint, desperately stick to the *rǫ́* (7/8). The rapid sequence of these key terms *í bǫndum* and *loddi* at the join of the stanza's two *helmingar* produces a chiasmic effect which accelerates the pace of the narrative. In addition, it is possible that *rǫ́* ('sailyard', 'yardarm', but also 'corner', 'ship's berth'), here used metonymously to describe the *stǫng* ('pole', 6/8 and 7/8), conveys an image of Loki 'sailing' out of sight as if on board ship. This image might be consistent not only with Loki's status as *farmr* (lit. 'cargo') in 7/2, but also with the conceit in Þjazi's kenning *ving-rǫgnir vagna* ('prince of wind-dolphins') in 4/5.

7/6 *reimuð Jǫtunheima* 'spectre of the giants' world', i.e. Þjazi. The meaning of *reimuðr* (only here) is not entirely clear. Turville-Petre associates *reimuðr* with *reim* ('cord') and translates as 'mighty ruler' through a rather tenuous comparison between *reim* and *bǫnd* and *hǫpt*, both words describing gods as 'bonds' (p. 9). Kock attempts to connect this word with OE *arœman* and OHG *irreimen* (i.e. *uzraimian*, 'to rise up'), thus rendering *reimuðr* as 'one who raises himself up high' ('en som reser sig högt upp', *NN* § 158). Holtsmark, against Kock and followed by Marold (p. 160) and Faulkes (*SSE*, p. 87), connects this

---

[26]*Heimskringla I*, ed. Bjarni, p. 21 (*Ynglinga saga*, ch. 8): 'The kinsman of the Æsir [?Óðinn], worshipped with a shield, begot that tribute-bringer with Iron-wood giantess, when the glorious pair, the friend of warriors and Skaði, lived in the homes of *Man* [?man/?love]'. See also *Skj* B I, 60, 3.

word with *reimleikr* ('haunting') and the expression *þar er reimt* ('the place is haunted') and translates *reimuðr* as 'ghost' ('skrømt', pp. 26–7). Yet Kock's meaning is not irreconcilable with theirs, if a ghost is seen to 'rise up': for example, a sibyl whom Óðinn raises from the dead in *Bdr* 4 *nauðig reis* ('was forced to rise') and the same motion may be attributed to the sybil of *Vǫluspá* in that *nú mun hon søcqvaz* ('she must now sink') at the end of her interview in *Vsp* 66. In this respect, Þjóðólfr's choice of *reimuðr Jǫtunheima* to describe Þjazi reveals the alarming speed with which this supernatural figure hoists Loki into the sky and disappears over the mountains.

7/7 *holls vinar Hœnis*] 'Hœnir's loyal friend', i.e. Loki. The effect of this kenning is to recall 3/7 (see note), in which it is implied that Loki takes a violent dislike to Þjazi out of protectiveness towards Hœnir (i.e. 'cockerel'), a smaller bird to whom, as we see in 4/1–4, the eagle speaks first. Now Loki's epithet tells us that he suffers for his loyalty. Loki suffers because he was *hollr* to Hœnir but not to Þjazi. Þjóðólfr also appears to play for comic effect on the relative size of the creatures in his tale: from Hœnir, apparently the cause of Loki's misfortune; to Loki; then to Þjazi, whose enormous size was implicit in 4/5–6 and is now clear both in the adjective *rammr* ('mighty, powerful') and in *Jǫtunheima*, a word which represents Þjóðólfr's first explicit use of *jǫtnar* ('giants') in this poem.

8. *With a wise deity now the blood-?woodpecker flew happy in his booty over such a long way that the wolf's father was ready to tear asunder; then Þórr's confidant ('Ariel' was heavy and near dead with exhaustion) was obliged to beg the giant's meal-companion for whatever deal he could get.*

8/3 *fangsæll sveita nagr*] 'blood-?woodpecker happy in his booty.' The meaning of *nagr* is unknown, though it appears in other eagle-kennings (*blóðs nagr*, in a verse attributed to Eiríkr viðsjá (*c.* 1014), *Skj* B I, 199, 1; and *sára nagr*, in Þorkell Gíslason's twelfth-century *Búadrápa*, in *Skj* B I, 538, 11). Kiil connects *nagr* with Nynorsk *snag(e)*, ModIce *snagi* ('snag'), and suggests that it means 'falcon' because this bird has a 'tooth' behind the point of its upper beak (p. 52). However, as Marold points out (p. 160, n. 341), this suggested sense is too close to the meaning of the kenning as a whole. As the base of a kenning for an eagle, *nagr* probably denotes a bird which is not a bird of prey. Holtsmark avoids discussion (pp. 27–8). If the meaning of this noun is similar to that of the verb *gnaga* ('to gnaw'), with which it seems to be cognate, I suggest that 'woodpecker', a bird which might be thought to 'gnaw' through tree-bark, is a possible meaning of *nagr*. Two implications of Þjóðólfr's use of *fangsæll* are firstly, that Loki, previously the keeper of *herfang* (6/7–8), may now be regarded as *fang* or captured plunder himself; and secondly, that Þjazi appears to have planned Loki's abduction as a necessary step towards his aim (stated in st. 9) of having Iðunn in the world of the giants.

8/3–4 *slitna sundr ulfs faðir mundi*] 'the wolf's father was ready to tear asunder.' The placing of *slitna* just before and of *sundr* just after the caesura (the break) in 8/3–4 gives us a metrical illustration of Loki's predicament. Loki's epithet *ulfs faðir* alludes to the wolf Fenrir (or *Fenrisúlfr*) which Loki begets on a giantess (cf. *ól úlf Loki við Angrboðo*, 'Loki begot a wolf with Grief-boder', *Hynd* 40) and which the gods must eventually bind in magical fetters (*Gylf*, ch. 34, p. 27), until the day of Ragnarǫk when the wolf breaks free (*Vsp* 49) and swallows the sun (*Vaf* 46–7) and Óðinn whole (*Vaf* 53 and *Vsp* 53). Þjóðólfr may give Loki this epithet in conjunction with *slitna* in order to show the irony of Loki's predicament in comparison to that of his monstrous son: the wolf wants to break his bonds and later does so (cf. *festr mun slitna, enn freki renna*, 'the bond will tear and the wolf will run', *Vsp* 49), whereas Loki hopes that his bond will stay unbroken.

8/5 *varð Þórs of rúni*] 'Þórr's confidant was obliged.' Kock emends MSS *vard* to *nam* to secure at least partial *skothending* in this line (*NN* § 3038), but since he is ready to accept the imperfection of *nam* in this case, it is not clear why he cannot accept *varð*. Nor is it at first clear why Þjóðólfr calls Loki 'Þórr's confidant' in this stanza. Loki is a road-companion of Þórr in Þórr's bridal journey to Þrymr in *Þrymskviða* and in their adventures with Útgarða-Loki in *Gylf*, chs. 45–7 (pp. 37–43), but otherwise there is little evidence of a friendship between them. Eilífr, a century later than Þjóðólfr, may allude to a friendship between Loki and Þórr in *vilgi tryggr geðreynir Gauts herþrumu* ('not at all trustworthy temper-tester of the war-Gautr [Óðinn] of thunder ': i.e. 'of Þórr'), a kenning for Loki in *Þórsdrápa* 1 (*Skj* B I, 139); yet although the context in this stanza requires Þórr, the meaning is not clear and Meissner takes the referent of *Gauts herþrumu* to be Óðinn (p. 254, § 88.a). Holtsmark (p. 28) sees an irony in the combination of *Þórs of rúni* with *ulfs faðir* in that Þórr (rather than Viðarr) will one day kill the wolf Fenrir in Ragnarǫk. Her idea seems to be based on the word *úlfr* in *gengr Óðins sonr við úlf vega* ('Óðinn's son goes to fight the wolf', *Vsp* 56), which occurs in all MSS of *Vǫluspá*, but which may have been miscopied for *orm* ('serpent'; cf. *Lok* 58, in which Loki says that Þórr will not dare to fight the wolf). With this idea, however, Holtsmark draws our attention away from *Haustlǫng* by begging the question of how well Þórr gets along with Loki. Holtsmark is probably right, on the other hand, to see another irony in *Þórs of rúni* whereby Loki's friendship with Þórr does not help him when he must beg this giant for mercy.

8/6 *þungr vas Loptr*] '"Lofty" was heavy'. The fact that Loki is now airborne makes the name *Loptr* ('air, sky') appropriate. Loptr is Loki's name also in *Lok* 6 and 19, *Hynd* 41 and in Eilífr's parenthesis *drjúgr vas Loptr at ljúga* ('Loki was able at lying', *Þórsdrápa* 1), which may give a sense of Loki's truthfulness in *Haustlǫng* 8, particularly as Þjóðólfr calls Loki *sagna hrærir* ('rouser of tales') shortly after in 9/1. I have translated *Loptr* as 'Lofty' to show the bathos of Þjóðólfr's association of *Loptr* with *þungr* ('heavy').[27]

8/6 *sprunginn*] 'near dead with exhaustion.' This word is difficult to translate, for literally it means 'burst open'. Oddly, Magnús omits this word in his note (p. 366, n. 99). Faulkes' translation ('had collapsed') describes the imminent prospect, not the current state of Loki as he hangs off the end of the pole (*SSE*, p. 87). The name *Sprengisandur*, that of a desert in north-eastern Iceland, appears to refer to the state of the first men who crossed it, and thus Turville-Petre's translation ('about dead of exhaustion', p. 10) seems about right.

8/7–8 *mǫlunaut miðjungs*] 'the giant's meal-companion.' R *mildings* ('the prince's', cf. *mildingr* in a verse of Markús Skeggjason, *SnE* I, 514) may have been copied for *miðjungs*, a form which is found in WT *miðivngs*, which is in any case required by the *aðalhending* with *biðja* on 8/8, but which is not entirely understood. Olce *miðjungr* is found as a *heiti* for a giant in the *Þulur* (IV.b.6), yet it is also the basis of four surviving warrior-kennings (see Meissner, p. 348, § 88.v). Of kennings for men in *Skáldskaparmál*, Snorri says that *kennt er ok við jǫtna heiti, ok er þat flest háð eða lastmæli* ('there are also kennings using giant-synonyms, and mostly that is mockery and slander', *SnE* I, 334). But Snorri does not rule such kennings out entirely, and so with *miðjungr* it is likely that we have a word for 'giant'. The form *mǫlunaut* (R *malo navtr)*, as Marold points out (p. 161), appears to be a compound (such as *mǫnudagr*) older than the composition of *Haustlǫng*, for one would expect *mála*- rather than *mǫlu*- (all MSS have *malo*). As a kenning for Þjazi, *mǫlunautr miðjungs* is appropriate for two reasons: first, the image of a bird as a 'meal-companion' recalls the augury-motif in 3/5–8 whereby Þjazi is conceived as a bird of battle, ready to give the gods some advice if they give him a meal; and second, Þjóðólfr's portrayal of Þjazi as a 'giant's meal-companion' makes a mocking contrast with Þjazi's role in 4/14 as an eagle importuning Hœnir for some of his meal, for Hœnir means apparently 'cockerel' (see note to 3/7). This contrast reveals again the immense size of Þjazi compared to that of Loki hanging on beneath him.

8/8 *friðar biðja*] 'beg for a deal.' The meaning of Olce *friðr* ('peace') is as problematic as that of its cognate OE *friþu*. Once again, however, some light may be thrown on *Haustlǫng* by the Alfredian text on the voyages of Ohthere (i.e. Óttarr), a Norwegian skipper, also *c.* 890, which was interpolated into Orosius' *Historia adversus paganos*: Ohthere told Alfred that he dared not enter the territory of the Beormas *for unfriðe*, which, as Christine Fell has indicated,

---

[27]On the complex question of Loki's names, see Anatoly Liberman, 'Saxo and Snorri on Útgarðaloki, with Notes on Loki Laufeyjarson's Character, Career and Name', in *Saxo Grammaticus: Tra storiografia e letteratura*, ed. Carlo Santini, I Convegno di Classiconorroena 1 (Rome, 1992), 91–158, esp. 150–8.

probably means 'because he had no treaty' with them.[28] As this usage appears to represent common ground between Old English and Norse, it is reasonable to suppose that OIce *friðr* in Þjóðólfr's time meant (i.a.) 'contract of peace' or '(peace-) deal'.

9. *The kin-branch of Hymir bade the rouser of tales, who was mad with pain, to bring him a girl, the one who knew the old-age medicine of the Æsir; the thief of the gods' Brísing-girdle later got the gods' lady of the brook of the well-spring's cornfield into the courtyards of the rock-Níðuðr.*

9/1 *sagna hrœri*] 'the rouser of tales.' The same problem is faced here as with *sagna segjendr* in 2/1: does f. *sǫgn* mean 'tale' or 'band of men'? Although Finnur reads ' men' ('mænderne', *Skj* B I, 16) and Turville-Petre 'tribes' (p. 9), Holtsmark (p. 28) and Marold (p. 161) are probably right to read 'tales': Loki is not known as a leader of men, unlike Óðinn, who has names such as *Heriann* ('war-leader', *Grím* 46 and *Vsp* 30), or Freyr, whom his servant calls *fólcvaldi goða* ('commander of the gods' hosts', *Skí* 3). Nor is OIce *hrœrir* ('rouser', 'mover') common as the basis of warrior-kennings: Meissner (p. 296, § 88.m) records only one example, probably from the late thirteenth century, in a kenning for 'swordsman' attributed to Skarpheðinn Njálsson in *Njáls saga* (*lǫgðis branda hrœrir*, *Skj* B II, 214, 12). 'Rouser of tales', instead, better conveys Loki's role as a liar (cf. *drjúgr vas Loptr at ljúga*, *Þórsdrápa* 1 and note 8/6). *Hrœrir* appears elsewhere, however, in Einarr skálaglamm's kenning *Óð[h]røris hafs alda* ('wave of the sea of soul-rouser') in *Vellekla* 5 (*c.* 985, *Skj* B I, 117), as a name for the divine mead of poetry. Einarr's is one of many surviving kennings which refer to the myth in which Óðinn steals the mead of poetry from the giant Suttungr: first by seducing Suttungr's daughter Gunnlǫð, who keeps the mead in a cave; then by drinking it, changing his shape into that of a bird (an eagle or a heron)[29] and flying back to Ásgarðr with Suttungr, disguised as an eagle, in hot pursuit; and finally by spewing this mead into vats which the Æsir have prepared (cf. *SnE* I, 218–24 and Meissner, pp. 427–30, § 100). The mead in Einarr's kenning is thus described as a sea, a poem as one wave from this sea,

---

[28]*The Old English Orosius*, ed. Bately, p. 18. Christine Fell, '*Unfrið*: an Approach to a Definition', *Saga-Book* 21 (1982–5), 85–100, esp. 94–5.

[29]The implication of Óðinn's reference in *Háv* 13–14 to his being 'fettered with the feathers' of 'the heron of oblivion' in Gunnlǫð's place. See Ursula Dronke, 'Óminnis hegri', in *Festskrift til Ludvig Holm-Olsen*, ed. Bjarne Fidjestøl (Øvre-Ervik, 1984), pp. 53–60.

while the function of the mead, to 'rouse the soul to poetry', is implicit in the elements *hrœrir* and *óðr* ('soul', 'poem'). With *sagna hrœrir*, therefore, it is possible that Þjóðólfr mocks Loki not only as a liar, but also as the mead of poetry which the eagle Þjazi has stolen from the gods as if he were Óðinn in flight from the giants.

9/2 *sorgœra[n] mey*] 'mad with pain'...'a girl.' RW has *sorg eyra*, T *sorg eura*. The context supports an emendation to *sorgœran*. -*eyr*- for -*œr*- is attested elsewhere, viz. *Óðreyrir*, Snorri's spelling of *Óðrœrir* or *Óðrerir* in the *Bragarœður* (*Gylfaginning*, ch. 58; normalised to *Óðrerir* in SnE I, 222). As it stands, *sorgœra* would appear to be a f. sg. acc. indef. adjective qualifying *mey*, in which case it would be Iðunn, not Loki, who was 'mad with pain'.

9/3 *ellilyf ása*] 'the old-age medicine of the Æsir.' Snorri does not cite Iðunn's *ellilyf* in his prose version of this story in the *Bragarœður* (*Gylfaginning*, ch. 56, SnE I, 208–212), but he makes an attempt to gloss this word in the preamble to his quotation of st. 1–13 in *Skáld* (ch. 22), when he defines Iðunn as *gætandi eplanna* ('keeper of the apples') and her *eplin* ('apples') as *ellilyf Ásanna* ('old-age medicine of the Æsir', SnE I, 304). It is not certain what kind of apples Snorri's *epli* would have been or when apples as we know them would have arrived in Scandinavia. Skírnir, Freyr's servant in *Skírnismál*, offers *epli ellifo* ('eleven apples') to Gerðr as part of his master's marriage gifts in * Skí* 19 (she refuses them in st. 20). Snorri seems to have known *Skírnismál*, for he quotes the last stanza after paraphrasing it in *Gylf*, ch. 37 (pp. 30–1). Since Snorri equates *epli* with *ellilyf* in *Skáldskaparmál*, it is likely that he read 'epli elli*lyfs*' in his version of *Skí* 19–20. Literally *ellilyf* does not tell us what fruits, herbs or plants Iðunn uses to keep the Æsir perpetually young, but the elements of her name, *ið*- ('again', cognate with Latin *iterum*) and -*unnr* (from *unna*, 'to yield'), show that she was probably a goddess of fertility and renewal (see note to 10/3–4).[30]

9/4 *áttrunnr Hymis*] 'the kin-branch of Hymir.' Hynir is the name of the giant with whom Þórr goes fishing for the world serpent and from whom he steals a kettle or cauldronon behalf of Ægir, a god of the sea (*Hymiskviða*), and whose *meyiar* ('girls', probably 'daughters') urinate into Njǫrðr's mouth, according to Loki (*Lok* 34). By connecting Þjazi to Hymir, Þjóðólfr reveals Þjazi's true identity as a giant and therefore as an enemy of the gods. This revelation mimics that of Loki.

---

[30]*AR* II, 334 (§ 559); and *Altnordisches etymologisches Wörterbuch* (Leiden, 1961), s.v. *Iðunn* (p. 283): 'die Erneuende, Verjüngende'. The *ið*-prefix may have an etymon in an antique inscription dedicated to the *gabiae* ('givers') '*Id*bangabis' or '*Idi*angabis' in Hagen, Bonsdorf Pier In the lower Rhineland: see Gutenbrunner, *Die germanischen Götternamen*, p. 218.

9/5–6 *brunnakrs bekkjar dísi goða*] 'the gods' lady of the brook of the well-spring's cornfield', perhaps a riddle for *goða dís unnar iðu* ('gods' lady, i.e. goddess, of the wave of the eddy, i.e. (of) *Iðu-unnr*'). The lines in which this *ofljós* kenning appears are perhaps the most tantalizing in *Haustlǫng*. *Hvernig skal kenna Iðunni?* is Snorri's question before he quotes st. 1–13 (*SnE* I, 304), and one which we might put less rhetorically. Yet some problems in 9/5–8 are relatively straightforward. First, the larger context requires that the referent of the kenning which describes Loki's theft in 9/5–8, whatever it is, must be Iðunn, for she is named in st. 10 when she arrives in the world of the giants. Second, the kenning for Loki in this half of st. 9, since it is probably longer than *girðiþjófr* ('girdle-thief') in 9/7, is likely also to involve the word *Brísings* if not *goða* in 9/6: thus we may read 'thief of the gods' Brísing-girdle' as Loki and leave *Brísings goða girðiþjófr* for the time being out of play (on the *Brísingamen*, see note to 9/6–7 below). Third, the place to which Loki brings Iðunn seems to be indicated relatively straightforwardly in *í garða grjót-Níðaðar* (see note to 9/8 below). This leaves us with the kenning for Iðunn, which, by this rough process of elimination, appears to be *brunnakrs bekkjar dísi (goða)*. By a roundabout process, Kiil takes this kenning to refer to Iðunn as a goddess of angelicas (pp. 56–60). Holtsmark (pp. 29–30) argues that Iðunn's *Brunnakrs bekk* is a phrase dependent on a proper noun meaning 'well-acre's bench' ('Brønnakersbenk'), a reference to 'the sacrificial spring' ('blotkjelda') through which Iðunn enters Þjazi's domain (the world of the dead). This argument also appears far-fetched, although Finnur (*Skj* B I, 16), Magnús (p. 367, n. 100), Turville-Petre (p. 11) and Faulkes (*SSE*, p. 87) all favour this translation. Marold's is the clearest discussion of this problem so far, with these and six more interpretations listed in addition to her own (pp. 162–5). Rather than listing the others again here, I shall focus on the ambiguities in vocabulary and syntax in 9/5–8, with reference to Marold. First, as we have seen, the word *goða* ('of the gods') may go with *Brísings girðiþjófr*. Nonetheless, it is possible to include *goða* in the kenning for Iðunn without altering the various meanings of *brunnakrs bekkjar dísi*. The potential variety of meanings in this kenning depends on two things: on *bekkr* (gen. sg. *bekkjar*), which means either 'brook' (i.e. 'beck') or 'bench'; and on whether we read either R *brvN* (i.e. *brunnr*, 'well', 'well-spring') or W *brvn* (i.e. *brún*, 'brow') or T *bran* (probably for *brvn*). With one less likely permutation removed ('brow-acre's brook'), we are left with Iðunn as the 'lady' either (1) 'of well-acre's brook' (*brunnakrs bekkjar dís*), or (2) 'of brow-acre's bench' (*brúnakrs bekkjar dís*). The second of these interpretations is easier to explain than the first, although I have not followed it: as proposed by Bugge (p. 2) and Lindquist (p. 85), the 'brow's acre' is a head of hair whose 'bench' (i.e. where the hair sits) is a necklace; and the 'lady of the necklace' is Freyja or her hypostasis Iðunn. For Iðunn to be seen clearly in this kenning, however, we must also add *Brísings (goða)*, sharing these words with Loki's epithet *girðiþjófr* on 9/7. That is to say, Iðunn is the 'lady of the (gods') Brísing-necklace' and her kenning is properly *dís bekkjar brúnakrs Brísings (goða).* The anatomical part of this kenning is suspected by Marold (p. 162) on the grounds that it runs contrary to Þjóðólfr's usual style, which favours mythological rather than general details. Yet the syntax of these lines seems to resemble that of 2/6–7, in which Þjóðólfr appears to qualify both *mar* and *byrgi-Týr bjarga* with *ár-Gefnar*, a phrase which does duty for two kennings. So it is possible that he uses *Brísings (goða)* in the same way in 9/6–7, qualifying both Iðunn and Loki with these words. Thereby Þjóðólfr would suggest, with an economy of diction similar to that in st. 2, that Loki finds it no less easy to steal Freyja or Iðunn than he did Freyja's *Brísingamen* on an earlier occasion (on Óðinn's behalf, in *Sǫrla þáttr*, chs. 1–3). This second interpretation ('of brow-acre's bench', *brúnakrs bekkjar dís*) appears to work; were it not for Þjóðólfr's tmesis of Iðunn's name as *Ið-* and *-unnr* in 10/3–4, I might follow it here. Yet Þjóðólfr, with this tmesis, puts *-unnr* on the headstave of 10/3–4 apparently in order to show that 'wave', the meaning of this word, is a part of Iðunn's identity (cf. Marold, pp. 163–4). Given this emphasis of *unnr* in Iðunn's name in st. 10, it seems better, therefore, to take *bekkjar* in 9/5 as the gen. sg. of *bekkr*, 'brook'. Since the formulation 'brow-acre's brook' makes little sense, we may read (1) *brunnakrs bekkjar dís* and translate these words as 'lady of well-acre's brook'. Kock (*NN* § 1017) and Holtsmark (p. 29) interpret *brunnakrs bekkjar* as a genitive of motion (i.e. 'to well-acre's brook'), on the assumption that this place, whatever it is, can be found in the world of the giants. Yet this interpretation, as Marold points out (pp. 162–3), creates an awkward parallelism between *brunnakrs bekkjar* and *í garða grjót-Níðaðar* in 9/8. Marold takes *brunnakrs bekkjar* with *dís* and accepts the mystery of an otherwise unrecorded 'Brunnakr' as Iðunn's place of origin; she is probably right to add *goða* to this kenning to establish the 'lady' as a 'goddess'. Iðunn, in this way, in (1) *brunnakrs bekkjar dís,* may be pictured with water about her: a vague image, but one which seems to be required by the tmesis of her name in st. 10.

Can 'well-acre's brook' mean something more specific, however? First, Olce *akr* (ModE *acre*) appears to denote a cornfield rather than wasteland (which is better expressed in *vǫllr*). Olce *brunnr* means a 'well' or 'well-spring' (cf. *Vsp* 19–20 and *Háv* 111). In this light, *brunnakr*, as 'well-spring's cornfield', suggests jets of water which resemble stalks of corn; and with 'brook' this compound kenning might thus work as a riddle for 'wave of the eddy' or 'eddy's wave', as *ið(u) unnr*, two words with which Þjóðólfr surrounds *með jǫtnum* in 10/3–4. Thus Þjóðólfr may have intended the formulation *brunnakrs bekkjar dís goða* to suggest a pun on a folk-etymology of Iðunn's name: *iðu unnar dís goða* ('goddess (of the) wave of the eddy', with a descriptive gen. after *dís*). What is a kenning if not a riddle? There are at least three similar cases in other Scaldic poems. Elsewhere a name-riddle is attempted, with a play on *svan-* ('swan'), in Bragi's kenning for Svanhildr, the former wife of Jǫrmunrekkr in *Ragnarsdrápa* 6 (*c.* 850, *Skj* B I, 2): *flaums foglhildr* ('river-current's bird-*hildr*'). A second riddle may be seen in a kenning for Þorgrímr Freysgoði in a verse attributed to his killer, Gísli Súrsson, who may have wished to confess his guilt to his sister, Þorgrímr's widow, who overheard his verse as she sat nearby: Gísli (*Skj* B I, 97, 8) calls the dead man *tál-gríms vinar fǫlu*, 'deception-*grímr* of the friend of the giantess', i.e. 'Þór-*grímr*', because Þórr (or divine aid working for him) deceives Hrungnir into standing on his shield, thereby killing him (cf. *Haustlǫng* 16). A third name-riddle appears in *gammleið*, either the 'sky' ('vulture-road') which Þórr allows to persuade him to set off for Geirrøðr's dwelling in Eilífr's *Þórsdrápa* 2 (*Skj* B I, 139), or a kenning specifically for m. acc. *lopt* ('air'), which may also be taken as *Lopt* ('Loki'). Þjóðólfr's apparent riddle for 'Iðunn' in *Haustlǫng* 9 is more *ofljóst* than these kennings, in that his clue, the element of the name that he wishes to reveal, is postponed to the following stanza: his emphasis of *-unnr* in 10/4 is not only the starting-point of our deductions, but was perhaps also a clue for his audience to follow, an incentive to return to the puzzle of *brunnakrs bekkjar dísi* in 9/6–7. It is possible, furthermore, that the delayed position of this clue in 10/4 is intended to illustrate how slowly the Æsir wake up to Iðunn's disappearance.

9/6–7 *Brísings goða girðiþjófr*] 'the thief of the gods' Brising-girdle', i.e. Loki. The words *Brísings girði-* allude to the *Brísingamen* ('necklace of the *Brísingar*') which elsewhere the goddess Freyja is said to own in *Þrym* 13, 15 and 19, in *Gylf*, ch. 35 (p. 29), in *Skáld*, ch. 8 (*SnE* I, 264–6) and in *Sǫrla þáttr*, chs. 1–3 (*Flat* I, 275–6). The last source, in particular, contains the story of how the dwarves made the *Brísingamen* for Freyja on condition she sleep with them, and how Loki then stole it from her on Óðinn's behalf. The word *goða* thus appears to be necessary to qualify *Brísings girðiþjófr* to the extent that the dwarves, not the gods, are the first owners of this necklace. Two stories survive in which Loki steals the *Brísingamen* from Freyja: one is the tale in *Sǫrla þáttr*; the other is preserved in Úlfr Uggason's *Húsdrápa* (*c.* 995), an older source which Snorri quotes in *Skáld*, ch. 16 (*SnE* I, 268):

> Ráðgegninn bregðr ragna   rein- at Singasteini
> frægr við firna slœgjan   Fárbauta mǫg -vári;
> móðǫflugr ræðr mœðra   mǫgr hafnýra fǫgru,
> kynnik, áðr ok einnar   átta, mærðar þóttum.
>
> (*Húsdrápa* 2)[31]

Snorri also alludes to this verse in *Skáld*, ch. 8 (*þá deildi hann við Loka um Brísingamen*, 'then he strove against Loki for the *Brísingamen*', *SnE* I, 264). In

---

[31]*Skj* B I, 128: 'Straightforward in counsel, the land-guardian of the powers [Heimdallr] wrests the Singa-stone away from the crime-cunning son of Fárbauti [Loki], famous for doing so; strong in heart, the son of eight and one mothers [Heimdallr] is first to take possession of the dazzling sea-kidney. I proclaim this in tales of glory'.

this story, which Úlfr apparently saw carved on the new kitchen panels of Hjarðarholt, Óláfr Hǫskuldsson's new farm in Iceland, it is implied that Heimdallr wrests a jewel such as the Brísingamen from Loki, whose epithet *firna slœgr* ('cunning in crimes') shows that he probably stole it from its owner (Freyja). In addition, a *Brosinga mene* (*bros-* perhaps a miscopying of *breos-*?) was known to the poet of the Anglo-Saxon *Beowulf*, who treats a version of the Loki-Heimdallr story in an entirely euhemerised context:

> Nænigne ic under swegle   selran hyrde
> hordmaðum hæleþa,   syþðan Hama ætwæg
> to þære byrhtan byrig   Brosinga mene,
> sigle ond sincfæt;   searoniðas fleah
> Eormanrices,   geceas ecne ræd.
>
> (*Beo* 1197–1201)[32]

Holtsmark (p. 29) associates *Brísings goða girðiþjófr* with the Loki-Heimdallr story, but it is more likely that *Sǫrla þáttr*, the clearest example of Loki's theft of Freyja's necklace, contains the variant to which Þjóðólfr may allude in this kenning for Loki in *Haustlǫng* 9. By revealing one of Loki's previous offences, this kenning hints at the ease with which he steals Iðunn (who is probably a hypostasis of Freyja, the owner of the *Brísingamen*) out of the world of the gods.

9/8 *í garða grjót-Níðaðar*] 'the courtyards of the rock-Níðuðr.' Finnur (LP, *s.v*) lists the nominative of the name in this kenning as *Níðaðr*, thus keeping it distinct from the *Níðuðr* who is known to us as the mutilator and captor of Vǫlundr the craftsman in *Vǫlundarkviða*. Yet, as Marold indicates (p. 165 n. 369), there is no real reason to regard *Níðaðr* and *Níðuðr* as separate forms. Given the likely identity of one with the other, it seems that Þjóðólfr not only knows a poem such as *Vǫlundarkviða*, but also makes an allusion to Níðuðr as the king who hamstrings his supernatural captive Vǫlundr in order to ensure that he works for him as an endless source of wealth. This allusion is consistent with Freyja's ownership of the *Brísingamen*, and it implies that Þjazi will use Iðunn similarly as a generator of youth and prosperity in the world of the giants (cf. OIce *iðn*, 'industry'). In the next stanza it appears that Iðunn is characterized as the coming of spring. This is the prize which the giant Þjazi appears to have been hoping for as early as in *Haustlǫng* 2/6–7 (see note).

[32]*Beowulf and The Fight at Finnsburg*, ed. F. Klaeber, 3rd ed. (New York and London, 1950), p. 45: 'Nor have I heard of any better hoard-treasure of men beneath the sun since Hama carried off the necklace of the Brosings to the bright city [Rome? Ravenna?] – he fled the crafty enmities of Eormanric, chose eternal counsel'.

10. *Those who dwell in the bright mountain-tops did not become downcast after that; this was when Eddy-Wave had newly arrived from the south among the giants; all the kin of Ingvi-freyr (the divine rulers were looking rather ugly) deliberated in the assembly, grey-haired and old,*

10/1–2 *bjartra borða byggvendr*] 'those who dwell in the bright mountain-tops.' RT have *biartra* (gen. pl. 'bright'), W *brattra* ('steep'), and all MSS have *borþa*. Finnur (*Skj* B I, 16) and Kock (*NN* § 3039 and *Ska*, p. 10) read *brattra barða* (i.e. 'steep mountains'), emending *borþa* to *barþa* on the grounds that OIce n. *barð* ('ship's prow') is used in the Icelandic place-name *Barðaströnd*, a mountainous coast with a sheer drop to the sea. The word *borð*, however, is sufficiently wide in meaning to describe not only 'shield' (so Turville-Petre, 'dwellers of the bright shields', p. 11), but also the *beranda borð* ('carrying-margin') of a drinking-vessel in *Gylf*, ch. 46 (p. 41), i.e. the sides between its rim and the liquid inside. There are other instances of *borð* in which this word means 'margin' or 'side'. Thus it is possible that Þjóðólfr uses *borð* as a metonym for 'mountain-tops' (so Holtsmark, pp. 30–1 and Marold, p. 165). It is hard to choose between RT *biartra* or W *brattra*, given that both 'bright' and 'steep' are appropriate adjectives for mountains (Holtsmark stays undecided; Marold reads *brattra borða*). However, since *bjartr* also means 'illustrious', its gen. pl. *bjartra*, which makes both a good image and contrast with the mood of *hryggvir* ('downcast') in 10/2, is preferable.

10/3 *þá vas*] 'that was when.' I have expanded sense for context. Kock first emends all MSS *þa* to *þátt* (from *þekkja*, i.e. 'loved', *NN* § 2504), then to *þat* ('that', *ibid.*, § 3039 and *Ska*, p. 10). Neither emendation is called for.

10/3–4 *Ið- með jǫtnum -unnr*] 'Eddy-wave among the giants.' Finnur is right to say that a tmesis in these lines is the only interpretation that works.[33] Furthermore, there is little doubt that Þjóðólfr splits Iðunn's compound name, then puts -*unnr* on the headstave of 10/4, in order to emphasise his interpretation of *Iðunn* as a goddess connected with water. The scribes of RWT all spell this name *iðvǫr*, in which -*vǫr* is a fourteenth-century spelling of *unnr* ('wave'). In this way, *ið(a)*- ('eddy') and -*unnr* ('wave') would act as a key to the riddle which Þjóðólfr has posed in his kenning for Iðunn in 9/5–6, *brunnakrs bekkjar dís* ('lady of the brook of the well-spring's cornfield', cf. note 9/5–6). Elsewhere I have argued that Þjóðólfr intended to stress the meanings of *ið*- ('again') and *unna* ('to yield'), which correspond to the true etymology of Iðunn's name.[34] Perpetual renewal may be one of the themes in Iðunn's role, as I have attempted to show with the

[33] Finnur, 'Kenningers led-omstilling og tmesis', p. 10.
[34] See my *Heathen Gods in Old English Literature*, Cambridge Studies in Anglo-Saxon England 22 (C.U.P., forthcoming).

implication of *grjót-Níðuðr* in 9/8, but it is clear that 'eddy' and 'wave' are the primary meanings that come out of the tmesis in 10/3–4. If these meanings are intended to give us an image of a flood after winter in the spring-time thaw, so much the better, for Holtsmark may not be far from the truth when she interprets (this part of) *Haustlǫng* as a seasonal drama (pp. 64–73, esp. 66–9). There is an implication of increased sunlight in *nýkomin sunnan* and *bjartra borða*, while the fact that *ið(a)-* ('eddy') and *-unnr* ('wave') are placed about *með jǫtnum* on 10/3–4 may give us a further image of meltwater cascading over rocks in the Norwegian mountains. If Iðunn is synonymous with the spring in this stanza, however, it should be remembered that spring-time for the giants is the same as winter for the gods. Their physical wellbeing may be seen declining rapidly in the next *helmingr*.

10/5 *gættusk at þingi* 'deliberated in the assembly.' Finnur (*Skj* B I, 16) emends all MSS *gorðoz* to *gættusk* ('they deliberated') for two reasons: we (but perhaps not Þjóðólfr) need *skothending* for *áttir* on the same line, which *gǫrðusk* does not provide; and each time the gods gather for a crisis meeting in *Vǫluspá*, they *um þat gættuz* ('deliberated about that', *Vsp* 6, 9, 23 and 25). The last instance of *gættuz*, in particular, concerns a meeting in which the Æsir try to discover

> hverir hefði lopt alt   lævi blandit
> eða ætt jǫtuns   Óðs mey gefna.
>
> (*Vsp* 25/5–8)[35]

As this scene refers to a variant version of Iðunn's, i.e. Freyja's, abduction to the world of the giants, it seems justifiable to reject MSS *gorðoz* in favour of *gættusk* also in *Haustlǫng* 10/5. Snorri's version of this scene depends on *Haustlǫng*: *gerðusk þeir brátt hárir ok gamlir. Þá áttu þeir Æsir þing* ('they quickly became grey-haired and old. Then the Æsir held a meeting', *SnE* I, 210–11). The parallel in *Vǫluspá* shows that it is probably worthwhile emending *gorðoz* to *gættusk* in this poem. Holtsmark keeps *gǫrðusk* (p. 30); Kock first keeps *gættusk* (*NN* § 1018), then pointlessly emends to *mættusk* ('they met each other', *ibid.*, § 3039).

10/6 *allar áttir Ing[v]i-freys* 'all the kin of Ingvi-freyr.' In its context, this kenning must refer not only to the Æsir, but also to all creatures subject to ageing, as members of the Vanir. Is this conceit mere poetic licence, or does it rely on a tradition? Nearly all the poetic and prose evidence in Old Norse-Icelandic literature is at odds with this conceit (except for an unexpected aside in *Þrym* 15 that Heimdallr knew the future *sem vanir aðrir*, 'as other Vanir [do]'). The poet of *Vǫluspá* appears to describe the Vanir as upstarts, relative newcomers to the religious privileges of the Æsir (*Vsp* 23); and after a futile cult-war between these two tribes of gods (*Vsp* 24), Njǫrðr and his children (Ingvi)-Freyr

---

[35]'which ones of them might have mingled all the sky with poison and given Óðr's girl [Freyja] to the giants'.

and Freyja are elsewhere said to live as hostages among the Æsir (*Vaf* 38–9 and *Lok* 34–5); a *ljóðháttr*-formula in *Skírnismál* places the Æsir, *álfar* ('elves') and Vanir in separate categories (*Skí* 17 and 18). Snorri enlarges on these references in *Gylf*, chs. 23–4, in *Skáldkaparmál* (i.e. *Gylfaginning*, ch. 57, *SnE* I, 216) and in *Ynglinga saga*, chs. 1–4. Through Snorri and Eddic poems, this tradition of Æsir-Vanir rivalry seems to be well-established. On the other hand, *Haustlǫng*, probably a poem from the late ninth century, is one of the oldest extant Scaldic poems and may be based on a tradition even older than those represented in the poems on which Snorri relied in the thirteenth century. Freyr's *ing*-prefix in *Ing[v]i-freys* in 10/6 is an ancient stem: not only is it preserved in other, mostly later, Icelandic sources (in the stem and dynastic ideology of *Ynglingatal*, Þjóðólfr's other surviving poem, *Ingvi-freyr* in *Háleygjatal* 13, *Ingunar-freyr* in *Lok* 43 and *Yngvi-Freyr* in *Ynglinga saga*, Prol. and ch. 11); but also in *Beowulf* (*eodor Ingwina*, l. 1044, and *frea Ingwina*, l. 1319, both 'prince of the friends of Ing'), in *The Old English Rune Poem* (*Ing wæs ærest mid East-Denum gesewen secgun*, 'Ing was first seen among men, among the East-Danes', ll. 67–8) and in the name of a Bernician ancestor (*Inguec* in the ninth-century *Historia Brittonum* and *Ingui* in the *Anglo-Saxon Chronicle, s.a.* 547); in the inscription *Inguz* found in a ninth-century site in Wijnaldum (W. Friesland) and in *Ingo*-prefixes in Frisian and Merovingian Frankish royal names; in the fourth-century Gothic form *Inggws* and its eighth-century derivative *Enguz*; and lastly, the oldest instance, in the *Ingvaeones* cited by Pliny and Tacitus in the first century, a tribe which Tacitus, in particular, locates in the coastal (i.e. Scandinavian) area of Germania.[36] There are problems in linking this *ingvi-*

---

[36] *The Old English Rune Poem: a Critical Edition*, ed. Maureen Halsall (Toronto, 1981), p. pp. 21–32 (text and MS) and 86–93 (notes); *MS A: A Semi-Diplomatic Edition with Introduction and Indices*, ed. Janet Bately, in *The Anglo-Saxon Chronicle: A Collaborative Edition*, gen. ed. D. N. Dumville and S. Keynes, vol. 3 (Cambridge, 1986), p. 22; *Die Stammtafeln der angelsächsischen Königreiche*, ed. Erna Hackenberg (Berlin, 1918), pp. 109–10; *Vita Vulframni episcopi Senonici auctore Pseudo-Iona*, ed. Wilhelm Levison, Monumenta Germaniae Historica, Scriptores Rerum Merovingicarum 5 (Hanover and Leipzig, 1905), 666 and 670; *Gregorii Episcopi Turonensis Libri Historiarum X*, ed. Bruno Krusch and Wilhelm Levison, *ibid.* 1.1 (Hanover, 1951), 75 (II.29); Jan Zijlstra, 'Onderzoek Wijnaldum: Supplement "Finns Fibula"', *Friese Bodemvondsten* 2 (1991), 17–22; *Alkuin-Briefe und andere Traktate im Auftrage des Salzburger Erzbischofs Arn um 799 zu einem Sammelband vereinigt: Codex Vindobonensis 795 der österreichischen Nationalbibliothek Faksimileausgabe*, ed. Franz Unterkircher, Codices Selecti 22 (Graz, 1969), 10–13 (date) and fol. 20v; C. J. S. Marstrander, 'De Gotiske Runeminnesmerker', *Norsk tidsskrift for sprogvidenskap* 3 (1929), 25–175, esp. 40 (date), 39–65 (discussion) and 63 (conclusion); *C. Plini Secundi Naturalis Historia*, ed. C. Mayhoff, 4 vols. (Leipzig, 1892–1909) I, 347 (IV.28); *The Germania of Tacitus*, ed. R. P. Robinson (Middletown, CT, 1935), p. 273 (ch. 2).

prefix exclusively to Freyr which I have discussed elsewhere.[37] Here, for the time being, it is enough to suggest that Þjóðólfr alluded to an older tradition, whereby all gods had once been considered Vanir, in order to show the dependence of the Æsir and all living things on the gifts of Iðunn, the goddess now held by the giants.

10/7–8 *(vǫru heldr) ok hárar gamlar*] '(they were rather..) and greyhaired and old.' The *ok* in this formulation presents a problem, for it appears to lack a verb complementary to *hárar gamlar*. Kock first treats *ok* as a conjunction misplaced from a position between *hárar* and *gamlar* (*NN* § 1018 and 3039), then emends to *auk* ('besides', 'in addition', *Ska*, p. 10). It is easier, however, to treat *vǫru* as one verb governing two predicates at the same time, i.e. *heldr hamljót* and *gamlar* (with *hárar* qualifying *ættir*, the subject of the second use of *vǫru*), in a manner similar to that of *loddi* in 7/5 and of other 'double-duty' words and phrases in 2/6 (*ár-Gefnar*), 7/4 (*í bǫndum*), 11/5 (*vélum*), 13/2 (*skǫpt*), 13/6 (*minni*), 14/3 (*hyrjar*) and 17/3 (*ímun-*). The conjunction *ok* in this case links the first predicate of *vǫru* to the second, i.e. *regin vǫru heldr hamljót ok hárar ættir Ing[v]ifreys (vǫru) gamlar*. No doubt Þjóðólfr is constrained to this elliptical construction of 10/5–8 by the tough demands of *dróttkvætt*. Yet by making two statements at once, in this way, he succeeds in giving an impression of confusion in these lines.

11. *until they met the hound of of the falling sea of corpses of the nursing-Gefn and bound the servant who had led her *with a spear of* the tree of venoms; 'you shall be tricked out of your mind', angry, he spoke, 'with trickery, unless also with trickery, Loki, you lead the glorious joy-increasing girl of the gods back here.'*

11/1–4 Scribal errors] An unusual repetition of *aðalhending* rhymes in this *helmingr* (see note below) may have caused at least one scribal distortion, in copyings up to and perhaps including the common archetype of the texts in RWT. This miscopying concerns an apparent duplication of 11/2 WT *ǫlgefnar* into *avlgefnar* on 11/4 (another sequence of errors may have produced R *þiR* and WT *þir* on 11/3). Otherwise lines 1–4 are reasonably intelligible, although both Finnur (*Skj* B I, 16) and Magnús (p. 368, n. 102) decline to translate them.

11/1–4 *-sævar hræva læva; hund fundu lund- bundu*] Some scholars will find it difficult to accept all these rhyming words as part of Þjóðólfr's composition. At first glance, and for a long time after, it appears that he takes his *aðalhending* rhymes to excess in st. 11, and particularly in R *sævar hræva* which is repeated

---

[37]In *Heathen Gods in Old English Literature* (C.U.P., forthcoming).

in *læva* 11/3 yet which is not metrically required in 11/1. But it is worth noting that *aðalhending* in odd lines is found elsewhere in *Haustlǫng*, in 11.25% of these lines (with *fljótt-dróttinn* in 5/1, *slíðrliga síðan* in 6/1, *þás-ása* in 9/3, probably *véltr-vélum* in 11/5, *hófu-skófu* 13/1, *biðils-sviðnar* in 13/3, *móðr-blóða* in 14/7, *grund-hrundin* in 15/3 and *gekk-ekkja* in 15/7). This figure rises to 16.25%, furthermore, if *Haustlǫng* was composed before the back-mutation of *a* to *ǫ* in syllables with a following *u* (*skalk-gjǫldum* in 1/1, *rǫgnir-vagna* in 4/5, *vǫru-hárar* in 10/7 and *varðat-hǫrðum* in 17/5). Thus, although the text of this poem is always subject to doubt, it seems that Þjóðólfr was more relaxed with the rules of *dróttkvætt* than later Scaldic poets. This being so, it is possible that he wished to emphasise the meaning of st. 11 through an unusually intense repetition of both *aðalhending* rhymes. The meaning of this stanza is the Æsir's threat to use magic in order to drive Loki mad. Given that this type of magic is induced through *galdr* ('incantations'), Holtsmark suggests (p. 33) that the rhymes in *Haustlǫng* 1–4, if proper to the original version of this poem, may have been created in order to reproduce the repetitions of *galdralag*. Seven examples of the incantatory effect of this metre may be found in Skírnir's threat to drive Gerðr mad in *Skírnismál*: *kranga kosta laus, kranga kosta vǫn* (st. 30); *eða verlaus vera* and *þic [MS þitt] geð grípi, þic morn morni* (st. 31); *gambantein at geta, gambantein ec gat* (st. 32); *manna glaum mani, manna nyt mani* (st. 34); and *mær af þinom munom, mær af minom munom* (st. 35). This is the effect that Þjóðólfr appears to contrive as a metrical illustration of the spell which binds Loki, for there is a suggestion of incantation not only in the mumbo-jumbo of *-sævar hræva læva* and *hund fundu lundar bundu*, but also in *véltr nema vélum* in 11/5.

11/1–2 *hrynsævar hræva hund ǫl-Gefnar*] 'the hound of the falling sea of corpses of nursing-Gefn', i.e. Þjazi. The wolf-kenning *hræva hrynsævar hund* has one late parallel in *benja tík* ('bitch of wounds', *Skj* B I, 460, 11). The only parallel for a kenning in which 'wolf' is linked with 'lady' is found in the first kenning for Þjazi, *snótar ulfr* ('wolf of the gentlewoman', 2/2). Since the latter type of kenning is so rare, it is reasonable to suppose that it denotes Þjazi in both instances, and that Þjazi himself tells the Æsir where their goddess Iðunn is when they find or meet him by chance or by appointment. Thus Holtsmark (p. 33), although Kock (*NN* § 233) argues that this whole kenning may be read as a designation for Loki parallel to his epithet (Kock's) *leiðiþí* in 11/3. Marold is reluctant to say whether Loki or Þjazi is intended (p. 165). Kock finds a case of parallelism elsewhere in *Haustlǫng* to support his argument (*fjaðrar leikblaðs reginn* and *Mǫrnar faðir* in 12), but he cannot discount the implication of *snótar ulfr*, the one parallel that matters, that Þjazi, not Loki, is 'the hound of the falling sea of corpses of nourishing-Gefn'. It is unlikely that the *ǫl*-prefix in *ǫl-Gefn* means 'ale' as Marold supposes, despite the *topos* in *Sigrdrífumál* and other eleventh- or twelfth-century poems that valkyries or goddesses serve beer to gods and heroes. As Holtsmark shows, this *ǫl*-prefix is probably derived from the mystical word *alu* (cognate with *ala*, 'to nurse', 'nourish (a child)'), which is found in runic inscriptions in Norway and elsewhere before the Viking Age. *Ǫl-Gefn*, Þjóðólfr's name for Iðunn (cf. *ár-Gefn*, 2/6) may thus reveal her regenerative property of which the Æsir now stand in desperate need.[38] The disclosure of theft from the thief himself is a motif to be found also in *Þrymskviða*, in which Þórr knows the whereabouts of his hammer only when Loki finds this out for him from Þrymr, the giant who has stolen it (*Þrym* 7–8).

11/3 *leiðiþir*] 'leading-servant', 'the servant who had led', i.e. Loki. R *þiR* and WT *þir* justify the reading of an acc. *þir* ('servant') in this kenning for Loki. Elsewhere *þirr* is found twice in *Skáldskaparmál*: as a synonym for *þræll* in ch. 65 ('thrall', 'slave', *SnE* I, 532); and with the same meaning in the *Þulur* in ch. 75 (*ibid.*, p. 562). OIce *þirr* appears to be a variant of OIce *-þér*, a form which is found in *Eggþér* (*Vsp* 42), the cognate of OE *Ecgþeow* (Beowulf's father, in *Beo* 263 and in fifteen further instances). However, *þirr* does not resemble OIce *-þér*, in that both instances in *Skáldskaparmál* show *r* in the stem of this word. Kock (*NN* § 223) cites OE *þeow* ('servant') and makes an intriguing comparison between *leiðiþir* and OE *latteow* ('teacher', < *lad-þeow*, 'leading-servant'). His translation of acc. *leiðiþi* as 'the one who had taken and led' ('den som tagit och fört') is not as exact as his morphology, however. Later he reads R *lvnd avlgefnar* as *lund-allgegnir* and takes *læva* with *leiðiþi*, to read 'and wholly honest in mind they bound the leader full of treachery' ('och helt ärliga i sinnet bundo förarn full av svek', *NN* § 2721). Yet in order to get *leiðiþi*, Kock must also remove the final letter of R *þiR* or WT *þir*. Marold accepts Kock's awkward *leiðiþi* (pp. 165–6). However, since the later servant-*heiti* in *Skáldskaparmál* give *þirr* with *r* in the stem, Kock's form cannot be trusted. With a sounder instinct for philology, Holtsmark (p. 32) suggests *þjóf* instead of *þir* on this line. Her reading is preferable on metrical and contextual grounds, for a word for 'thief' in this context not only better suits Loki's crime in st. 9/5–8, but also provides the desirable *skothending* with *læva* on 11/3. Faulkes appears to accept this emendation (*SSE*, p. 88). It is possible to explain R *þiR* and WT *þir* as derived from a mistranscription of *þiof*, first with a misreading of *f* as a lower-case *r* (producing *þior*, acc. 'bull', cf. 5/8), then with gradual omission of the *o* (cf. *q⁷þu* for *qvoþu* in R², the quotation of *Haustlǫng* 3/1–4 in *Skáld*, ch. 55, *SnE* I, 470). Since the R scribe of nom. *þiR* shows a tendency elsewhere to insert a supernumerary -*r* (viz. R *þungrs* WT *þungs* 8/6; R *navtr* T *nautz* 8/7; R *þatri* WT *þatti* 16/8; and R *tyrs* WT *tyss* 20/2), it is possible that his *þiR* is miscopied ultimately from *þiof* rather than *þiofr*. Further, if we follow Holtsmark's reading *leiði-þjóf*, we get a compound which recalls *girðiþjófr*, Loki's epithet in 9/8 (also on the first three syllables of its line; cf. *naddkleif* 1/4 and *bifkleif* 13/8, 20/8; *birgi-Týr* 2/7 and *hirði-Týr* 6/7). In short, Holtsmark's emendation has

---

[38]On *alu*, see Richard North, '"Wyrd" and "weard ealuscerwen" in *Beowulf*', *LSE* n.s. 25 (1994), 69–82, esp. 77–82.

much to recommend it, apart from the fact that we have an elsewhere unknown form *þírr* in *Skáldskaparmál*. So there is nothing for it but to read acc. *leiðiþír* in 11/3. There is no *skothending* on this line, as a result, but Loki's role as a 'servant' in this case tells a story of it own, provides Loki with a pretext to lead Iðunn into the wrong place and is paralleled, furthermore, in Loki's role as Þórr's *ambót* ('maid') when he accompanies this reluctantly transvestite god to Jǫtunheimar in *Þrym* 20. On analogy with the 'double-duty' use of *birgi-Týr* in 2/7, furthermore, I suggest (with Kock, *NN* § 223) that *ǫl-Gefnar* in 11/2 quali- fies *leiðiþír* as well as *hrynsævar hræva hund* (11/1–2).

11/3–4 *læva lundar geiri bundu*] 'they bound [Loki] *with a spear of* the tree [branch] of venoms', i.e. with a *lævateinn* ('poison-branch'). Here I read *lundar geiri* for RWT *lvnd avlgefnar* 11/4. Holtsmark (p. 32) and Marold (p. 166) both keep *avlgefnar*, linking it with *leiði*-compound. Yet, as *avlgefnar* is the only repetition with no metrical justification in 11/1–4, this form is probably wrong and represents the first scribal distortion in these lines. The manner in which *avlgefnar* may have been copied is revealed elsewhere in the R-text, where the scribe writes *herfangs ofangs ofan* in 6/8 (*Skj* A I, 16), repeating *-fangs* in *ofangs* because the first three letters of *-fangs* resemble the *fan* of *ofan*. Similarly, I suggest that the scribe who wrote *avlgefnar* in an earlier exemplar did so be- cause the preceding words *læva* 11/3 and *lvnd* 11/4, rhyming with and thus perversely resembling *hræva* 11/1 and *hund* 11/2, encouraged his eye to skip back to *ǫlgefnar* in 11/2, the word following *hund*. It is anyone's guess what the word was that this scribe would have replaced with *avlgefnar*. On the weak assumption that some letters were the same, and in analogy with *geirr*'s figura- tive use in *svigðis geirar* ('ox's spears', Þjóðólfr's kenning for 'horn' in *Ynglingatal* 1, *Skj* B I, 8), I conjecture *ar* for the first syllable and *geiri* for the second and third. The letters *-ar* may be taken as the gen. sg. ending of f. *lund* ('grove', also 'tree'), while *geiri* is suitable as the dat. sg. of m. *geirr* ('spear'). So, after R *leiþe þiR* WT *leiþe þir*, which I discuss in the note above, 11/3–4 may be emended as 'læva lundar geiri bundu' ('they bound *with a spear of* the tree [branch] of venoms'). This kind of branch is probably a *lævateinn*, such as a magical sword in *Fjǫl* 26 and similar to the *gambanteinn* with which Skírnir threatens to make Gerðr mad in *Skí* 32, and with which Hárbarðr (i.e. Óðinn) says that he defeated a giant in *Hárbarðsljóð*:

> harðan iǫtun   ec hugða Hlébarð vera,
> gaf hann mér gambantein,
> enn ec vélta hann ór viti.
>
> (*Hárb* 20)[39]

---

[39] 'a hard giant I thought Hlébarðr was, he gave me a *gamban*-branch, yet I tricked him out of his wits.'

It is thought that *gamban-* is a assimilated form of *gand-band*, with a meaning such as 'witch-staff-binding'. The likely presence of *band-* in this word, plus the use of *véla* ('to trick'), shows that Óðinn probably paralyses the giant with a form of magic that attacks his mind. Snorri says that when Óðinn broke into gravemounds to steal the gold of their dead occupiers, *batt hann með orðum einum þá, er fyrir bjoggu* ('he bound with some words those who dwelt there', *Ynglinga saga*, ch. 7).[40] Óðinn is also the *galdrs faðir* ('father of incantation') in *Bdr* 3 and there are many other instances of his skill in witchcraft (principally in *Háv* 146–63). Holtsmark cites later instances of magical 'binding' in Norwegian folklore (p. 33). It has long been thought that Loki is immobilised with this kind of influence in *Haustlǫng* 11, for the use of *véla*, n. pl. *vél* ('trickery') and *binda* ('to bind') in st. 11/4–5 resembles that of *véla* and *-ban[d]* in *Hárbarðsljóð*. Given that the Æsir probably hear of Iðunn's whereabouts from Þjazi, not from Loki, in 11/1–2, it is appropriate that they must bind Loki with magic and threaten him with madness before he is ready to risk another encounter with the giant.

11/6 *[v]reiðr*] 'he [Ingvi-freyr], angry.' The fact that no name is given in association with *[v]reiðr* in this line is an indication that the masculine subject must be sought in the previous sentence. This is a long sentence, extending from st. 10/5 to 11/4. Although it refers to Loki and probably also to Þjazi too, its only unambiguous m. proper noun is contained in *Ingvi-freys* in st. 10/6. There have been other suggestions concerning the concealed referent of *[v]reiðr*. Given that Óðinn is associated with the type of magic with which the Æsir appear to bind Loki, it might be thought at first that he is the 'angry' spokesman. Óðinn seems to know magic in *Háv* 146–63 and he also appears to be a leader of Æsir in st. 5. Holtsmark, however, suggests that Þórr speaks these lines (p. 35), given that *hann siáldan sitr er hann slíct um fregn* ('he seldoms stays sitting when he hears of such a thing', *Vsp* 26). This suggestion may be supported with other instances of Þórr's wrath: also in *Vsp* 26, Þórr is *þrunginn móði* ('swollen up with rage'); and in particular, *[v]reiðr var þá Vingþórr* in *Þrym* 1 ('?Wind-Þórr was enraged'). Snorri, perhaps rendering in his prose some formulae that he knew in a poetic version of Þórr's adventure with Útgarða-Loki, frequently uses *reiðr* of Þórr: *þá varð hann reiðr* ('then he became angry', *Gylf*, ch. 45, p. 38); *þá varð Þórr reiðr* (*ibid.*, ch. 46, p. 41); *Nú em ek reiðr!* ('Now I am angry!', *ibid.*, ch. 46, p. 42); and also in Þórr's fishing-trip with Hymir, with *þá varð Þórr reiðr* (*ibid.*, ch. 48, p. 44). 'Wrath' thus seems to be the abiding characteristic of Þórr more than of other gods. That Þórr boasts elsewhere of having killed Þjazi himself (*ec drap Þiaza, inn þrúðmóðga iotun*, 'I killed Þjazi, the mighty-hearted giant', *Hárb* 19), may also mean that Þórr, speaking on behalf of the Æsir, is the *[v]reiðr* who threatens Loki with madness in *Haustlǫng* 11. Yet other gods can become angry (*reið varð þá Freyia* in *Þrym* 13; and of Óðinn,

---

[40]*Heimskringla I*, ed. Bjarni, p. 19.

notoriously, Adam of Bremen *c.* 1076 says *Wodan id est furor*);[41] Freyr, in particular, is said to be *ofreiði*, 'exceedingly angry', in *Skí* 1–2. Given that Freyr is Skírnir's master, that Skírnir in *Skírnismál* later threatens Gerðr with the same kind of magic to which Loki subjected in *Haustlǫng* 11, and that Iðunn seems to have the role of Freyja (Freyr's sexual partner, *Lok* 32) in her abduction to the world of the giants, it appears likely that Ingvi-freyr himself is intended to supervise the questioning of Loki in st. 11.

11/5 *nema vélum*] 'with trickery, unless also with trickery.' Kock takes the word *vélum* in this line to refer to the trickery that Loki is asked to perform (*NN* § 224), Finnur, to the trickery that Loki may otherwise expect to suffer (*Skj* B I, 16). Kock's syntax (adopted by Holtsmark, p. 34) is more straightforward than that proposed by Finnur, but as Finnur's reading cannot be ruled out, I suggest that we take *vélum* both ways as a word which complements two sentences at once. The word *véltr* seems to be the past part. of *véla* ('to trick'), despite Holtsmark's preference for *veltr* as the past part. of *velta* ('to set rolling', 'to roll s-one over') on the grounds that thieves and other undesirables in Norway were sometimes pushed over cliff-tops: in her view, the Æsir threaten Loki with this fate (p. 34). Although *véla* appears to mean 'to trick', the evidence of the words *véltu goð Þjaza* (Kormákr's line in *Sigurðardrápa* 6) and of *véla* in *Hárb* 37, in which Þórr boasts that he fought berserks' brides in Hlésey and *vélta þióð alla* ('tricked the whole nation [to its death]'), suggests that *véltr* in *Haustlǫng* 11 can mean 'driven (fatally) mad'.

11/6 At this point the W-text runs out. From here to the end of st. 13, the text of *Haustlǫng* is based on RT alone.

11/7–8 *munstœrandi mœra mey [hapta]*] 'the glorious joy-increasing girl of the gods', i.e. Iðunn. The word *hapta* (gen. pl. 'of the gods', a rhyme with *aptr*) is supplied by Finnur to fill the textual lacuna in both R and T (*Skj* B I, 16). So Magnús (p. 368, n. 102) and Faulkes (*SSE*, p. 88). Sveinbjörn Egilsson, followed by Holtsmark (p. 32), supplies *deyja* ('to die', a rhyme with *mey*). The other problem in this line is R *mora* T *môra*. Finnur, followed by Holtsmark (p. 32), by Magnús and by Faulkes, emends this word to *mœra*, which he puts with *mey* (i.e. 'glorious girl', f. acc. sg. indef. of *mœrr*). Kock, however, considers the syntax and metre awkward with *mœra* and emends again to *mœrra* (gen. pl), which he puts together with Finnur's *hapta* (*NN* § 2005). It seems better to follow Finnur's judgement in both *hapta* and *mœra*. Although *deyja* is explicitly faithful to Snorri's prose version of the story at this point, *var honum heitið bana eða píslum* ('he was promised death and torture', *SnE* I, 212), there are two arguments against the use of this word: the participle *véltr*, as we have seen (note to 11/5), may connote the death of its victim without *deyja*; and the role of

[41]*Adam Bremensis Gesta*, ed. Schmeidler, p. 257 (IV. 26).

hapta in *mæra munstærandi mey hapta* is paralleled by that of *goða* in *brunnakrs bekkjar dís goða* (Þjóðólfr's kenning for Iðunn in 9/5–6; cf. note to these lines). The respect for Iðunn which is apparent in these *ofljós* kennings is belied, however, by Þjóðólfr's use of *ása leika* to describe her in the next stanza.

12. *I heard this, that afterwards, he who was putting Hœnir's courage to the test, increased by a hawk's flying-fur, betrayed the playmate of the Æsir back and that the ruler-deity of the feather's swinging leafblade, the loon-minded father of Moørn, laid an eagle's vigorous wing-draft right onto the child of the bird of prey.*

12/1 *Heyrðak*] 'I heard.' An epic formula which is an example of the untypically narrative rather ornamental character of this *dróttkvætt* poem. In addition, the use of this formula might imply that Þjazi's pursuit of Loki (and Iðunn) is not depicted on Þjóðólfr's shield. With *þats of fátt* in 13/5–8, however, Þjóðólfr makes it clear that his shield does have on it an image of the burning of Þjazi over Ásgarðr. Thus the two elaborate wing-kennings in 12/4 and /6, which imply a painted image of birds flying, may show that Þjóðólfr is here inferring Þjazi's pursuit of Loki from a picture of two birds above a fire.

12/1 *svá, þat*] 'this, that.' The older form of the subordinating conjunction *þat* for *at* seems to be preserved on this line in order to avoid an elision with *svá*.

12/2 *ept*] 'back.' Finnur reads as *opt* ('often') in order to support his parenthesis (see note below). Holtsmark emends *ept* to *aptr* because the construction with *aptr* in 11/8 appears to be similar and because she is reluctant to give *ása* and *leiku* equal stress (p. 36). But *ept*, as she points out, is acceptable as a reduced form of *eptir* (apparently used like *aptr* in *Vsp* 61).

12/2 *ása leiku*] 'the playmate of the Æsir', i.e. Iðunn. OIce f. *leika* means a 'playmate' or 'play-sister'; the vb. *leika við* ('to play with') may have a sexual connotation when linked with *mær*, as in one of Hárbarðr's boasts to Þórr:

> *léc ec við ina línhvíto   oc launþing háðac,*
> *gladdac ina gullbiǫrto,   gamni mær unði.*
>
> (*Hárb* 30)[42]

Given that Iðunn is described as a *mær* in *Haustlǫng* 9/2 and 11/8, it is likely that '(sexual) playmate of the Æsir' is one of the meanings of *ása leika* in 12/2. Thus Iðunn seems to represent (i.a) the active sexuality on which the Æsir (and

---

[42]'I played with the linen-white woman and arranged a secret meeting, gladdened the gold-bright woman, the girl enjoyed pleasure.'

Þjóðólfr's community) rely for their youth and regeneration. If n. *leika* ('play-thing', 'doll') is also to be understood in this kenning for Iðunn, it is possible that Þjóðólfr makes an allusion to her transformation into a shape such as the *hnotar líki* ('form of a nut') into which, in Snorri's version of this story, Loki changes Iðunn when he steals her back from Þjazi, carrying her thus in his claws (*SnE* I, 212). Finnur emends RT *asa* to *ǫsu* (acc. of *æsir*) and reads *ǫsu leikum*, with *síðan sveik opt ǫsu leikum* as a parenthesis and with an emended *fló* (for RT *flvg* in 12/4) as the main verb in the clause introduced by *svá þat*. He also emends all MSS *ept* to *opt* and renders this parenthesis 'later he often deceived the Æsir with his play-acting' ('senere sveg han ofte aserne ved sit spil', *Skj* B I, 16; followed by Magnús, p. 368, n. 103: 'síðan lék hann æsi oft sviksmalega'). However, T *leiko* (i.e. acc. of *leika*, 'playmate', play-sister') is probably to be preferred to R *leikom* in this line. The R-scribe may have written a suspension mark for *m* in R *leikom* ('with games') because of *vælom* (i.e. *vélum*, 'with trickery'), which he had written four lines earlier in 11/5. The effect of Finnur's parenthesis, which depends on emendations and on a less reliable text, is to slow the narrative pace of this stanza by interrupting it with an ornamental aside. Holtsmark (pp. 35–6), Kiil (p. 74) and Faulkes (*SSE*, p. 88) avoid the parenthesis and treat only *sveik* as the main verb. Unusually for him, Kock follows Finnur's parenthesis, although he leaves *síðan* outside in the main clause (*NN* § 159 and *Ska*, p. 11).

12/3 *hugreynandi Hœnis*] 'he who was putting Hœnir's courage to the test', i.e. Loki. *Hugreynandi* resembles Loki's role as *geðreynir* in *vilgi tryggr geðreynir Gauts herþrumu* ('not at all trustworthy temper-tester of the war-Gautr [Óðinn] of thunder ': i.e. 'of Þórr'), in *Þórsdrápa* 1 (cf. note to *Þórs of rúni*, 8/6). Yet *hugreynandi Hœnis* in *Haustlǫng* 12/3, in combination with *vinr Hœnis* in st. 3/7–8 and 7/7, implies a sentimentality between Loki and Hœnir which is lack-ing in Loki's relationship with Þórr: Loki attacked Þjazi out of loyalty to Hœnir and now Hœnir fears for Loki's safety. Holtsmark (p. 36), followed by Marold (p. 166), suggests that Hœnir's courage is tested by the results of Loki's trickery, the theft of Iðunn. But why 'Hœnir's courage', as opposed to that of the other Æsir? Hœnir can hardly be presented as a faint-hearted god when it is so likely that he be the mythic personification of a cockerel, a fighting bird. The effect of Hœnir's implied love for Loki, oddly enough, is to make Loki into the hero of *Haustlǫng* 1–13.

12/4 *hauks flugbjalfa*] 'with a hawk's flying-fur.' In R *havðs flvg bialba*, the word *havðs* (for *hauðrs*?) makes no sense as the gen. sg. of n. *hauðr* ('earth'), although *bialba* seems to be written for *bialfa*. T *haucs flug bialfa* is preferable (so Marold, p. 167, Holtsmark, p. 35). Finnur, followed by Kock, emends RT *flvg* to *fló* ('flew', cf. note to 12/2). However, *flug-* qualifies *bjalfi* ('fur', 'skin') as the first element of a compound which denotes a bird's wing.

12/5–8 The problem with these lines is the apparent clutter of words with which Þjazi, again in eagle's shape, is described as he swoops down on Loki. In the centre of this *helmingr* is the kenning which denotes Þjazi in relation to his eagle-disguise, *leikblaðs reginn fjaðrar* (cf. note to 12/6); at the outskirts, the once-attested adjective *lómhugaðr* at the start of the sentence appears to qualify *faðir Mǫrnar* at the end.

12/5–8 *lómhugaðr faðir Mǫrnar*] 'the loon-minded father of Mǫrn', i.e. Þjazi. See the note to 6/4, where RT *faðir morna* is emended to *faðir Mǫrna[r]* on the strength of a comparison with this epithet on 12/8. OIce m. *lómr* means either 'deception' or the sea-bird 'loon' or 'loom' (the *Colymbus arcticus or septentrionalis*, cf. Fritzner II, 558). Þjóðólfr uses *lómr* in the first meaning in *lómi beittr* ('hunted by deception'), a phrase which describes King Guðrøðr in *Ynglingatal* 34 when, drunk and incapable one night, he is assassinated by a servant of his wife Ása, whose father he had killed a couple of years earlier; in the same stanza the murderer is called *enn lómgeði* ('the deception-spirited', only here), who *launsigr at jǫfri bar* ('through secrecy achieved a victory over the warrior', *Skj* B I, 13). Þjóðólfr's adjective *lómhugaðr* in *Haustlǫng* 12 is treated as if it is a variant of *lómgeðr*, by Finnur ('svigsindet', *Skj* B I, 16), Kock ('slug', *NN* § 74), Holtsmark ('med listig hug', p. 36), Magnús ('svikull', p. 368, n. 103), Kiil ('svikefull', p. 77), Faulkes ('with deceitful mind', *SSE*, p. 88) and Marold ('der verräterisch gesinnte', p. 167). This idea of Þjazi suits his trickery in st. 2–8, but it does not fit the context of st. 12, in which it is Loki, not Þjazi, who has successfully (so far) carried out a deception. Is this use ironic, therefore, or is it Loki's *lómr* on which Þjazi's *hugr* is focussed when he tries to catch him? This second option strains the sense of *-hugaðr*, which means 'courageous' or '(well) disposed', or lit. 'minded', but not 'mindful' as would be needed here if this compound were to show Þjazi 'mindful of (Loki's) deception'. In this respect *lómhugaðr* may be compared with OIce *úlfhugaðr* ('wolf-minded', i.e. 'savage', 'rapacious'), which is a more common adjective (and also comparable to Eormanric's *wylfen geþoht*, 'wolfish intention', in the Old English poem *Deor*). Given that *úlf-* in this Norse adjective represents a wild animal, and given the fact that *lómhugaðr* Þjazi is disguised as a bird in *Haustlǫng* 12, it seems more likely that *lómr* in the latter compound denotes the 'loon' or 'loom', a member of three distinct families of northern sea-bird which are 're-markable for their clumsy gait on land' and are also known as 'divers' or 'sprat-loons' from their diet of fish near the coastal cliffs where they live.[43] The eagle is called a *sárlómr* ('wound-loon') in *Óláfsdrápa* 8, in a poem which is attributed to Hallfreðr vandræðaskáld, but which was probably composed in the twelfth century (*Skj* B I, 569). In *Skáldskaparmál*, Snorri says of Þjazi that when Loki

[43]Alfred Newton, *Encyclopaedia Britannica*, vol. 11 (London, 1911), s.v. 'Loon'.

arrived to snatch Iðunn, *var hann róinn á sæ* ('he had gone rowing out to sea', *SnE* I, 212). With 'loon' in *lómhugaðr*, it is possible that Þjóðólfr gives Þjazi the 'mind' or 'intention' of a diving fish-eating predator which nests in a noisy cliff-dwelling community of sea-birds. The overarching syntax of *lómhugaðr faðir Mǫrnar*, furthermore, with the adjective on one side and the noun phrase on the other of *ǫglis barn*, 'child of the bird of prey', gives an illustration of Þjazi closing the gap on Loki as they come within sight of Ásgarðr.

12/6 *leikblaðs reginn fjaðrar*] 'the ruler-deity of the feather's swinging leafblade', i.e. Þjazi. Olce *reginn* refers to Þórr in 15/5 (*hofreginn hógreiðar*, 'temple-deity of the easy-riding-chariot') and also appears to be the singular of n. pl. *regin* or *rǫgn*, which describes the gods probably as 'rulers'. On the basis of *ving-vagna rǫgnir* for *ving-rǫgnir vagna* in 4/5, Finnur reorders *fjaðrar leikblaðs reginn* the kenning as *fjaðrar blaðs leikreginn* and renders 'wing-swinger' ('vinge-svinger', *Skj* B I, 16) and 'he who sets the wing's play into motion' ('han som sætter vingens leg i bevægelse').[44] Other commentators (Kock, § 138; Holtsmark, p. 36; Marold, p. 167) avoid the tmesis; Marold, in particular, because she regards *leik-* as a verbal prefix to *blað*. Since Þjazi and Loki are in the air in this stanza, it seems best to read this implicitly verbal use of *leik-* as a reference to the 'swinging' movements of a pair of wings (cf. the *túnriðor*, 'ghosts', whom Óðinn sees *leika lopti á*, 'swinging through the air', in *Háv* 155).

12/7–8 *ern arnsúg*] 'an eagle's vigorous wing-draft.' The adjective *ern* ('vigorous', 'brisk') agrees with either a nom. or acc. indefinite masculine noun, depending on whether it qualifies Þjazi or *arnsúg*, the direct object of his verb *lagði*. Finnur, Magnús and Faulkes all put *ern* with the kenning based on *reginn* in 12/6, whereas Kock makes it a predicate yet still in agreement with Þjazi (*NN* § 138); however, both Holtsmark (p. 36) and Marold (p. 167) are probably right to read it as agreeing with *arnsúg* in 12/8. What the latter word means is hard to define. The first element *arn-* denotes an 'eagle', a plain word reminding us of the type of bird into which Þjazi is again transformed (cf. *ǫrn* in 2/5). The second element *súgr*, cognate with ModE *sough(ing)*, appears to allude to an audible rush of air. Elsewhere *arnsúg* is found only in Snorri's prose adaptation of this stanza: *ok dró arnsúg í flugnum*, 'and he moved with an eagle's soughing in his flight' (*SnE* I, 212). Holtsmark (p. 37) links Þjóðólfr's image of Þjazi with Hræsvelgr, the *iǫtun í arnar ham* ('giant in eagle's shape') at the end of heaven whose wings start the wind across the world (*Vaf* 37). Faulkes accepts this idea and translates *lagði arnsúg* as 'directed a storm-wind' (*SSE*, p. 88). Holtsmark's suggestion is ingenious, but draws us out of the immediate context, which seems to be Þjazi's rapid flight-dive onto the tail of Loki in disguise as a (young) hawk or falcon. In order to make this image clearer, I have treated *arn-* as a separate gen. noun and have added 'wing-' to 'draft', my translation of *súgr*. The rela-

[44]Finnur, 'Kenningers led-omstilling og tmesis', pp. 1–3.

tively fast pace of this stanza, plus an overwhelming distribution of nouns and other words in favour of Þjazi in its second half, gives us an impression of Loki reaching Ásgarðr with only seconds to spare.

13. *Quickly the shafts while the enticer-gods shaved them started to burn, and the son of the suitor (there was a flurry in his journey) of Greip singes. A memorial of that is painted on my bridge of the foot-soles of the Lapp of the fells. I have received the coloured cliff of the shield-rim, painted with tales, from Þorleifr.*

13/1–2 In this full line, n. pl. *skǫpt* ('shafts') is both the nom. subject of *hófu brinna* ('started to burn') and the acc. object of *ginnregin skófu* ('the enticer-gods shaved (them)'); the conjunction *en* ('while', 'when') serves to link these two statements, which, in prose word-order, would run as follows: *fljótt hófu skǫpt brinna, en ginnregin skófu (skǫpt)*. Þjóðólfr may blend these statements together in this full line in order to give a syntactical illustration of the frantic speed of *fljótt* ('quickly'). This technique appears to repeat the flurried effect of 10/7–8 (see note), yet with the Æsir this time poised to regain their advantage by killing Þjazi.

13/2 *ginnregin*] 'the enticer-gods.' The *ginn*-prefix may be cognate with ModE 'be*gin*' and thus denote 'aboriginal' in its primary meaning. The *regin* of Æsir (and Vanir) are said to be *ginnheilǫg goð* ('?aboriginal-sacred gods') in *Vsp* 6, 9, 23 and 25. On the other hand, it is hard to exclude the meaning of the verb *ginna e-n til e-s* ('to entice s-one into s-thing') in Þjóðólfr's *ginnregin* in *Haustlǫng* 13, given the fact that Loki is not only escaping from Þjazi, but also leading him on into the fire which Æsir are about to kindle. That the death of Þjazi is planned by the Æsir rather than secured by them as a lucky bonus to Iðunn's rescue, may be seen in one of Kormákr Ǫgmundarson's mythological asides in *Sigurðardrápa* (*c.* 960): *véltu goð Þjaza* ('the gods tricked Þjazi [to his death]', *Skj* B I, 69, 6).

13/3–4 *sonr biðils Greipar*] 'the son of Greip's suitor', i.e. Þjazi. This is an example of the rare type of kenning in which a giant's family provenance is indicated by a giantess' name (cf. Meissner, p. 256, § 88.b). This kenning may also presume some knowledge of the tale of Þórr's journey to Geirrøðr, for Greip is known elsewhere as the sister of Gjálp, both daughters of Geirrøðr, in a stanza which Snorri quotes in *Skáld*, ch. 18 (*SnE* I, 288) from a now lost Eddic poem on Þórr and Geirrøðr in order to support his prose rendition of Eilífr's *Þórsdrápa*. These legends are various: Þórr kills both Greip and Gjálp in an Eddic **Geirrøðarkviða*, presumably before they have children (they are not named in *Þórsdrápa* 13–14); and yet these girls are also said to be two of the nine mothers of (probably) Heimdallr in *Hym* 37. It is possible, nonetheless, that Þjóðólfr knew Þjazi as Geirrøðr's grandson (and Skaði as the old giant's great-granddaughter). Þjazi's father, the *biðill Greipar* in *Haustlǫng* 13, is known as Allvaldi in *Hárb* 19; and as Ǫlvaldi in a tale told by Snorri in *Bragarœður* (*SnE* I, 214), in which Ǫlvaldi's three sons Þjazi, Iði and Gangr divided up their father's gold, when he died, by each son holding as much gold as he could in his mouth. What lies behind the image in Þjóðólfr's kenning of Allvaldi calling on one of the daughters of Geirrøðr? It should be noted that the parenthesis *sveipr varð í fǫr* ('there was a flurry in his journey') occurs just after *sonr biðils* (prompting thoughts over the role of Þjazi's father as a suitor) and just before *Greipar* (the lady's name). The effect of this word-order, with the parenthesis doing duty for two stories, may be to compare Þjazi's position with that of his father in the house of Geirrøðr, his putative father-in-law, whose treatment of guests, at least in Þórr's case (molten ingots as food projectiles), could be regarded as insane. Through his kenning with *Greip*, Þjóðólfr appears to be suggest that Þjazi has an even smaller chance of survival.

13/4 *sveipr varð í fǫr*] 'there was a flurry in his journey.' It is possible that Snorri renders *sveipr* in the words *en ǫrninn mátti eigi stǫðva er hann misti valsins; laust þá eldinum í fiðri arnarins ok tók þá af fluginn* ('and yet the eagle could not stop when he missed the falcon; the flames then struck the eagle's feathers and then his flight came to a standstill', *SnE* I, 212). At any rate, Magnús renders *sveipr varðr í fǫr* as 'his flight stopped' ('flug hans stöðvaðist', p. 369, n. 104). Faulkes also seems to have Snorri's prose-text in mind when he translates this phrase as 'there is a sudden swerve in his travel' (*SSE*, p. 88). Yet OIce *sveipa* means 'to enfold' or 'wrap', as when Sigurðr 'enfolds' Guðrún in his arms 'in the bedlinen' (*sveipr í ripti*, *Sigsk* 8). Figuratively, therefore, the noun *sveipr* may mean 'disturbance' or 'commotion'.

13/5–6 *Þat...á brú minni*] 'a memorial of that...on my bridge.' The word *minni* at the end of line 6 appears to be either the f. dat. sg. posessive adjective qualifying *brú* ('my') or the n. noun *minni* ('memorial', 'toast') in agreement with *þat* at the beginning of the sentence, or possibly both at once. In the dative, n. pl. *minni* describes the pictures which Úlfr Uggason's sees on Óláfr's new kitchen panels in *Húsdrápa*: *hlaut innan svá minnum* ('this is how commemorative pictures have been allocated within', *Skj* B I, 129, 6, 8 and 9, 4). If there is a pun on Þjóðólfr's line, its effect is to look forward to the next sentence, in which Þjóðólfr, having called the images on his shield a 'memorial', indicates that the shield is also his, by stating the name of the Þorleifr who gave it to him.

13/5–6 *á fjalla Finns ilja brú minni*] 'on my bridge of the foot-soles of the Lapp of the fells', i.e. on my shield. Meissner lists ten examples in which words for 'bridge' or 'road' form the basis for shield-kennings (pp. 169–70, § 80.b). Þjóðólfr's kenning is one of seven listed by Meissner which allude to the story of Hrungnir, how this giant is tricked into standing on his shield in order to defend himself from Þórr (p. 166, § 80.a). The other kennings are *Þrúðar þjófs* *ilja blað* ('leaf of the foot-soles of the thief of Þrúðr', *Ragnarsdrápa* 1, *Skj* B I, 1); and from the twelfth or thirteenth centuries: *Hrungnis fóta stallr* ('pedestal of the feet of Hrungnir', *Skj* B I, 73, 14); *mellu kindar brú* ('bridge of the race of the giantess', *ibid*. B I, 604, 3); *Hrungnis ilja þilja* ('plank of the foot-soles of Hrungnir', *ibid*., B II, 69, 30); *Aurnis spjalla ilflet* ('foot-sole floor of the friend of Aurnir', *ibid*., B II, 122, 19); and *Leifa vegr* ('Leifi's [giant's] road', *ibid*., B II, 208, 6). Evidently the myth of Hrungnir was a popular source of shield-kennings. In this case, however, it seems that Þjóðólfr uses this kenning to anticipate his treatment of Þórr's duel with Hrungnir in the next section of *Haustlǫng*: this is why we are probably justified in regarding st. 14–20 as his continuation of 1–13.

13/7–8 This refrain is repeated at 20/7–8 and may have helped to unify *Haustlǫng* in a form even longer than that which survives in *Snorra Edda*. Another refrain from the earlier pre-Christian period is that in Bragi's *Ragnarsdrápa* 7/3–4 and 12/3–4: *Ræs gǫfumk reiðar mána Ragnarr ok fjǫlð sagna*, 'Ragnarr has given me the moon of the chariot of Rær [the sea-king's ship's moon: shield] along with a multitude of stories' (*Skj* B I, 2–3). Úlfr, as we have seen, also relies on his half-line *hlaut innan svá minnum* to bind together the episodes of *Húsdrápa* (*Skj* B I, 129, 6, 8 and 9, 4).

13/7–8 *baugs bifum fáða bifkleif* 'the coloured cliff of the shield-rim, painted with tales.' With *hringr*, Olce *baugr* appears to mean 'shield' in *bauga hrings þrymdraugr* ('spirit of the thundering of the ring of armlets'), a kenning for 'warrior' in Hallfreðr's *Óláfsdrápa* 14 (*c*. 1020, *Skj* B I, 571; cf. Kock, *NN* § 2722). *Baugr* is a vague term and sufficiently wide in meaning ('ring', 'brace-let', 'jewel'), perhaps, to permit 'shield-rim' in the context of *Haustlǫng* 13, albeit Meissner (pp. 166–71, esp. 171) records no shield-kennings with *baugr* as the baseword apart from the dubious *naddbaugr* ('rivet-jewel', *Skj* B I, 153, 13). The stem *bif-* appears to mean 'tremble' (< Olce *bifask*), but may also mean either 'image', or 'colour', or both. Marold (pp. 167–8) lists the inconclusive attempts so far to elucidate this word and refrains from translating it herself. 'Colours' for *bifum* is to be assumed from the context (Finnur, *LP*, p. 46), although Kock (*NN* § 157) and Kiil (p. 82) prefer 'images'. Holtsmark (p. 40) finds the words *bifi* and *bifa* listed in *Skáldskaparmál* (*SnE* II, 550 and 613) under *máls heiti* ('synonyms for speech'), and translates 'painted with tales' ('malt med fortellinger'); yet she also shows reflexes of this stem in ModIce *bifur* ('fright', 'antipathy') and Nynorsk *biv* ('trembling', 'respect'). Her reading of *Haustlǫng* as the serious reflection of ritual drama, with Þjóðólfr 'pervaded by religious fear at the annual festivals for *ár ok friðr*', is helped by these modern reflexes of *bifum*: 'the images fill him with religious awe, they are frightening'.[45] Nonetheless, Holtsmark's translation of *bifum* as 'tales' is

---

[45]'Idun og Tjatse', p. 40: 'gjennomrystet av religiøs frykt ved de årlige fester til *árs ok friðar*...Billedene fyller ham med religiøs age, de er fryktelige'.

preferable to the other solutions, as Marold recognises (p. 168), since it is supported by two words outside the poem. The next tale, and possibly the next image on the shield as Þjóðólfr's eye moves round it, concerns Þórr's duel with Hrungnir.

14. *And yet one may see on the ring of fire where giants'*
dread paid a call on the cavern-tree of the fire of the
grave-mound of stone-enclosures; Earth's son drove
towards the play of iron, while Moon's path (the passion of
Meili's blood-kinsman swelled) clattered beneath him.

14/1 *sér*] 'one may see.' Kock (*NN* § 2985 and *Ska*, p. 11) emends RWUT *ser* to *lítk* (for *lít ek*, 'I look'), in order to secure some kind of *skothending* rhyme (with *jǫtna*). Given Þjóðólfr's apparent metrical freedom elsewhere, however (2/5, 3/5, 5/3, 7/5, 8/5, 9/5, 10/3, 11/3, 12/1, 13/5, 13/7, 14/1, 15/3, 15/7, 18/5, 20/6, 20/7), this emendation seems relatively undesirable.

14/1–2 *jǫtna ótti*] 'giants' dread', i.e. Þórr. This Þórr-kenning belongs to the 'giants' killer' type of which Meissner lists thirty-four examples (pp. 254–5, § 88.a). However, this is the only kenning among this total in which Þórr is imagined as the 'fear' of the giants rather than as their 'killer' or 'foe' (i.e. *jǫtna dolgr*, 'giants' foe', in a verse attributed to Eyvindr (allegedly *c.* 965), *Skj* B I, 64, 9). Similar to *jǫtna ótti* is Bragi's Þórr-kenning *ǫflugbǫrðu ægir* ('powerful-?bearded woman's [giantess'] frightener') in *Ragnarsdrápa* 15 (*Skj* B I, 3), as well as *gýgiar grœtir* ('causer of the giantess' weeping') in *Hym* 14. Yet these kennings are like all the others in that they look at the giants from Þórr's point of view. No poet succeeds more than Þjóðólfr with *jǫtna ótti* in imagining Þórr entirely from the perspective of the giants.

14/3–4 *á hyrjar baugi*] 'on the ring of fire', i.e. on the shield. It is not certain to what extent OIce *baugr* can work as a synonym for 'shield' independent of a qualifier (cf. Meissner, p. 171, § 80.b.; *pace* Marold, p. 169, n. 407). If this use of *baugr* is compared with *baugs bifkleif* in the foregoing stanza ('coloured cliff of the shield-rim'; see note to 13/7–8), it seems at first that *baugr* may work as a shield-synonym on its own (so Kiil, pp. 83–4). Yet the word *á* in 14/3, the preposition necessary for *baugi*, lies separated from *baugi* by *hyrjar*, a word which also involves *hellis* at the beginning of this full line. Thus Þjóðólfr's term for 'on the shield' is necessarily more complicated than *á baugi*. Probably because of the position of *á*, which is separate from *baugi*, Åkerblom (p. 270), Kock (*NN* §§ 139 and 2722) and Marold (p. 169) get 'shield' by linking *baugi* with the intervening word *hyrjar* ('of the fire', i.e. 'of (gold-)red colour'). This type of kenning is not paralleled exactly, but as Kock points out, *hyrjar baugr* could mean 'the fire-red shield' ('den eldröda skölden', *NN* § 139), on analogy with *rauðr skiǫldr* ('red shield') in *HHund* I, 33 and elsewhere.

14/3–4 *hellis bǫr hyrjar haugs grjót[t]úna*] 'the cavern-tree of the fire of the grave-mound of stone-enclosures', perhaps a riddle for '*hringa*-giant' which alludes to the stem of *Hrungnir* (cf. 9/5–6). W *baur* and *haugs* in this kenning are preferable to R *biaur* (T *maur*) and *havg: baur*, because this word seems to mean 'tree'; and gen. *haugs*, because acc. *haug* creates two awkward syntactical alternatives. First, although both Finnur (*Skj* B I, 17), Magnús (p. 349, n. 65) and Marold refrain from translating '*baur(r)*' (p. 168 and n. 403), it seems clear that W *baur* is written for acc. *bǫr* ('tree'): Meissner lists thirty examples of warrior-kennings of the type 'tree of battle' in which *bǫrr* is the baseword (p. 267, § 88.h.; e.g. *vígs bǫrr*, in the *Háttalykill* of Rǫgnvaldr Jarl of Orkney and Hallr Þórarinsson (*c.* 1145), in *Skj* B I, 501, 29b). Kock accepts this meaning (*NN* § 139 and *Ska*, p. 11), although he temporarily emends *bǫr* to *bǫr[g]* ('boar') to achieve 'cliff-cave's boar' ('klipphålans galt'), on analogy with basewords such as 'bear', 'calf', 'whale', 'reindeer' and 'wolf' (*ibid.* § 1018, anm. 2). The *i*-infix in the R-form *biaur* may be explained as a result of a scribe's eyeskip forward to the *ia*-combination in *hyriar* on the same line (he or she also writes *ginnivnga* presumably for *ginnvnga* in 15/4). The *m* in the T-form *maur* is probably the result of an obscurity or miscopying of the *b*-form in the (now lost) fourteenth-century exemplar of the T-scribe, who failed to correct the error when he copied this text in *c.* 1600. The kenning *hellis bǫrr* is paralleled as a giant-kenning by *hella mildingr* ('chieftain of caverns', *Skj* B I, 239, 2), *hellis gramr* ('cavern-prince', *ibid.* B II, 438, 14) and *hellis Gautar* ('cavern-Gautar', *ibid.* B I, 480, 7; II, 422, 14). Although there is no parallel giant-kenning for *hellis bǫrr* of the type 'cavern-tree', it is still possible to take *hellis bǫrr* as a reference to a 'giant' on analogy with the common use of 'tree' basewords in man-keninngs. Second, if we accept acc. *haug* in RUW, we must revise the syntax of this *helmingr*: either (with Finnur and Kock, *NN* § 139) by making *haug grjót[t]una* and *hellis bǫr* both the objects of *lét of sóttan* ('paid a visit (to)'; R *sottvm*); or by making *haug grjót[t]una* the object of *sér* in the main clause, and reordering the sentence as *eðr of sér haug grjót[t]úna á hellis hyrjar baugi, es jǫtna ótti lét of sóttan hellis bǫr* ('and yet one may see the mound of stone-enclosures on the ring of fire, where giants' dread paid the cavern-tree a visit'). The first alternative is awkward because it puts Hrungnir and Hrungnir's presumed abode into the same category of meaning; the second alternative overloads the main clause at the expense of the sub-clause (and also appears to take the figures of Þórr and Hrungnir out of the painting on the shield). Thus Marold (pp. 168–9) is probably right to prefer the W-reading *haugs* and to take this word as part of a longer kenning for Hrungnir. Kiil splits up *grjóttúna* into *grjóttún* and *á* (a second prep. governing *baugi*) and translates *á hyrjar haugs grjóttún* as 'on the fire-mound's stone-enclosure (i.e. crater of a volcano?)', in order to suggest that Hrungnir is a fire-giant ('på eldhaugens steintun (d.e. vulkan-krateret?)', pp. 83–4). As with most of Kiil's arguments to do with *Haustlǫng*, this idea takes liberties with the text and forces the sense. As Marold shows, the apparent overload of rock-elements in this kenning, in *hellis bǫr haugs grjót[t]úna* ('cavern-tree of the grave-mound of stone-enclosures'), may be compared with that of water-elements in *brunnakrs bekkjar goða dís* in 9/5–6. My question is now whether or not there is likewise a clue to Hrungnir's name in the extended kenning *hellis bǫr haugs grjót[t]úna*, as there appears to be a clue to Iðunn's name in *brunnakrs bekkjar goða dís*. Firstly, the form *griotvna* or *griotuna* (all MSS) may be emended to *grjóttúna*, given that neither *grjó* nor *úna* appears to be a self-standing word and given that 'stone-enclosures' appears to be an appropriate abode for Hrungnir, the stone-headed giant. Magnús thus reads *Grjóttúna* (p. 349). Snorri appears to treat *griotvna* as a place-name (*á Grjótúnagǫrðum*, *SnE* I, 272), as do all the editors of this poem since. Yet there is no instance of this compound word as a place-name outside *Haustlǫng* or Snorri's *précis* of this poem, nor does Þórr cite any *Grjótún*, *Grjótúnir* or *Grjótúnagarðar* when he alludes to his duel with Hrungnir in *Hárb* 15 and *Lok* 61 and 63. In this light, it seems that Snorri gave up the task of unravelling the elements of *griotvna*, rather as Sveinbjörn Egilsson, Theodor Wisén, Finnur, Kock, Holtsmark and Marold all take an otherwise unknown *Brunnakr* to be the name of Iðunn's place in 9/6 (see Marold, pp. 162–3). What is then to be done with the gen. of *grjót[t]únir*, if this compound is not a place-name? Given that *Nóatúnir* ('ships' enclosures: sea') is the name of Njǫrðr's abode, which appears to be the 'ocean' (*mar*, in his dialogue with Skaði, *Gylf*, p. 24), it is likely that *grjót[t]únir* also denotes the element which 'encloses', in this case, 'the rocks'. Although *Nóatúnir* provides the only parallel for a sea-kenning with *túnir*, Meissner lists about seventy kennings of this type (such as *foldar fjǫturr*, 'earth's fetter', *Skj* B I, 200, 4; *grundar garðr*, 'ground's court-wall', *ibid.* B I, 207, 3; or *margra jarða meingarðr*, 'harm-court-wall of many estates', *ibid.* B I, 533, 30). It is possible, in this case, to take *grót[t]úna* as a kenning for the sea, whose 'grave-mound' (in *haugr*) is the sea-bed, where seamen settle when they drown. Meissner gives just over three hundred examples (in 317 instances) of the 'sea-fire' type of gold-kenning (pp. 229–37, §§ 87.o.–q). Thus the words *hyrr haugs grjót[t]úna* may refer to 'gold' as 'fire of the sea-bed'. The nature of this 'gold' becomes clear if we use the word *baugi* ('ring') adjacent to this kenning on 14/4 as a qualifier or clue to the kenning's referent, the giant (the name *Hrungnir* is not cited until 15/8). Gunnarr of the Burgundians shows that underwater gold is imagined as rings, when he denies Atli his treasure in *Atlakviða*:

> í veltanda vatni   lýsaz valbaugar,
> heldr enn á hǫndom gull   scíni Húna bǫrnom!
>
>   (*Akv* 27)[46]

---

[46]'In the churning water the choice-rings shall gleam rather than gold may shine on the hands of the children of the Huns!'.

In these lines, in which Gunnarr reveals that he has dropped his hoard of treasure into the Rhine, his treasure is imagined as *valbaugar* and *gull á hǫndom*. Thus the word *hringar* may be understood in Þjóðólfr's apparent gold-kenning *hyrr haugs grjót[t]úna* in *Haustlǫng* 14/3–4, not only because of *baugi* at the end of the same line, but also because, as Gunnarr's words show, gold on the river-bed, at least, is imagined specifically as 'rings'. In conjunction with *hellis bǫr*, this long *ofljós* kenning in *Haustlǫng* may thus refer to its subject as *hellis bǫr hringa*: 'cavern-tree, i.e. giant, of *hringar*'; thus '*Hrung*nir', the name of the giant himself. This solution to the problems of 14/3–4 is not the only meaning to be taken from these lines, for, as *Grjót[t]únir*, this compound could be read as a place-name appropriate to where this stone-headed giant lives, without any attempt to probe Hrungnir's kenning for a deeper meaning. Thus Marold's image of Hrungnir waiting for Þórr on his *haugr*, like Þrymr in *Þrym* 6 or Eggþér the giantess' herdsman in *Vsp* 42, is good as far as it goes. But if we go further with this kenning in *Haustlǫng* 14, as the Iðunn-kenning in 9/5–6 and 10/3–4 suggests we might, then it is possible to see a more intricate, and more playful, attempt to conceal Hrungnir's name, as if it were Hrungnir's stone shape, within the rocks of his dwelling.

14/5–8 This half-stanza (as R²T²W²) is also quoted separately by Snorri, in *Skáld*, ch. 23 (*SnE* I, 316), apparently in order to illustrate *Mána vegr* at 14/8 as a kenning for *himinn* ('sky').

14/5 *at isarnleiki*] 'to the play of iron', i.e. to battle. Meissner (p. 199, § 81.q) lists fifty-three examples of battle-kennings of which the baseword is *leikr* ('play', 'game'); Þjóðólfr's phrase *at isarnleiki* is found once elsewhere (in the *Erfidrápa Óláfs helga* of Sigvatr Þórðarson (*c.* 1040), *Skj* B I, 242, 14); *járnleikr*, a contracted form, also occurs (in *Hǫfuðlausn*, attributed to Egill Skalla-Grímsson but probably of an eleventh- or twelfth-century date, in *Skj* B I, 32, 8; cf. *stála leikr*, 'play of steel (blades)', in *ibid.* B II, 433, 16). As standard as Þjóðólfr's kenning seems, it is worth noting that his use of *isarnleikr* has special force as an early intimation of Þórr's iron-age hammer, when compared with stone, the ancient material of rock-dwellers such as the 'cavern-tree' Hrungnir.

14/6 *Jarðar sunr*] 'Earth's son', i.e. Þórr. Þórr is called *Grundar sveinn* ('Ground's lad') in st. 17, and is elsewhere known as *Iarðar burr* ('Earth's boy') in *Þrym* 1 and probably in *Lok* 58 (sc. *burr*); and as *Hlǫðyniar mǫgr* and *Fiǫrgyniar burr* ('earth's son, boy') in *Vsp* 56 (cf. Meissner, p. 253, § 88.a). Thus Þjóðólfr accounts for a third of the surviving kennings in which Þórr is designated by his mother's name (it is odd that no such kenning appears in the extant *Þórsdrápa*).

14/6 *dunði*] 'clattered.' Elsewhere Olce *dynja* describes the supernatural journeys of Óðinn to Hel on Sleipnir (*fram reið Óðinn, foldvegr dunði*, 'forwards rode Óðinn, the earth-road clattered', *Bdr* 3) and of Loki in a bird's shape to and from Þrymr's mountain stronghold (*fló þá Loki, fjaðrhamr dunði*, 'Loki then flew, his feather-shape clattered', *Þrym* 5 and 9). Since in these instances *dynja* seems to refer to the sound of a horse's hooves on earth and a bird's wings flapping in the air, 'Moon's path clattered' (rather than 'boomed' or 'resounded') is perhaps the most suitable translation for *dunði Mána vegr* in *Haustlǫng* 14.

14/7 *móðr svall*] 'passion swelled.' This aside appears to be an allusion to previous incidents in this story such as those which Snorri recounts in *Skáld*, ch. 17: Hrungnir's sanctioned but insolent sojourn with the Æsir, his drunkenness and threats to steal Freyja and Sif and to lay waste to Ásgarðr, and his agreement with Þórr to meet him with weapons for a duel. This image of Þórr's 'swelling' anger may be compared with Bragi's description of Hǫgni's rage, *þá svall heipt í Hǫgna* ('then hatred swelled in Hǫgni'), in *Ragnarsdrápa* 10. Þjóðólfr's use of *móðr* with Þórr resembles that of the poet of *Vǫluspá*, in whose poem Þórr *þrunginn móði* ('swollen up with rage', *Vsp* 26) strikes the giant-builder dead because the giant has managed to secure the goddess Freyja as part of his bargain with the Æsir. Eyvindr, apparently the last named Norwegian Scald, in one of the verses attributed to him allegedly in *c.* 961–2, says that *malmhríðar svall meiðum móðr* ('passion swelled in the trees of the metal-storm [warriors]', *Skj* B I, 63, 6); while in a verse from *Heiðreks saga ok Hervarar*, a later poet, probably from the thirteenth century, says that *enn harðsnúinn hugr í brjósti svellr Hervǫru* ('a staunch courage swells up in Hervǫr's breast', *ibid.* B II, 264–5). These Norse expressions may be compared with phrases for the 'welling mind' in the Old Saxon *Heliand*, in which Simon Peter *gibolgan uuarð* ('was blown out with rage') when he saw Christ arrested in Gethsemane, and *uuell im innan hugi, that hie ni mohta ênig uuord sprecan* ('purpose welled up within him in such a way that he could not say a word', *Heliand* 4865–8); and in Old English poetic vocabulary, in which Beowulf becomes *torne gebolgen* ('swollen with anger') when he goes to fight the dragon (*Beo* 2401).[47] In the light of these similarities, it appears that the diction concerning Þórr in *Haustlǫng* is older than that which, for example, we see in Eilífr's late-tenth-century *Þórsdrápa* (where Þórr is described as being no more than *stríðlundr*, 'stern in disposition', in st. 9; and where the poet confines himself to saying that the heart of Þórr and Þjálfi *skalfa við ótta* and *skelfra við ótta*, 'did / does not shake with dread', in st. 10 and 21; *Skj* B I, 141 and 144).

14/7 *Meila blóða*] 'of the blood-kinsman of Meili', i.e. of Þórr. Þórr says that he is *Meila bróðir* ('Meili's brother') in *Hárb* 9 (cf. note to *Haustlǫng* 4/2). Perhaps consequently, but probably also through the influence of *moþur* at the beginning of 14/7, the scribes of RWT at this point write *meila broþvr* or *broþur* (the U-scribe writes *blodi*, followed by *blode* in AM 757). However, when this *helmingr* is quoted separately in *Skáld*, ch. 23 (*SnE* I, 316: R²W²T²), the scribes write *bloþa*, a *lectio difficilior* which is more likely to represent the genuine form.

[47]See North, *Pagan Words*, pp. 63–98, esp. 88–91.

14/8 *Mána vegr und hǫnum*] 'Moon's path beneath him'. Meissner (p. 107, § 18.g.-h) records thirteen expressions in which the sky is the 'land', 'beach', 'path' or otherwise place of *máni* ('the moon', in twenty mostly Christian examples, the commonest being *mána fold*, 'the moon's land'); and four more in which the sky is the place of the *tungl* ('star', probably 'moon', in four examples). Given the likely early date of *Haustlǫng*, there appears to be every reason to regard the 'moon' in this stanza as a personification equal in solidity to Þórr, whose name means 'thunder'. It appears to be Þjóðólfr's purpose here to introduce us to Máni, Þórr and Hrungnir as both persons and natural phenomena at one and the same time, with an image in this stanza of Þórr clattering like thunder through the upper atmosphere to strike an opponent who waits below with the passivity of rock.

15. *All the sanctuaries of falcons (/ of the abyss) did burn, while down below, thanks to Ullr's father-in-law, the ground was kicked with hail, when the bucks drew the temple-deity of the easy-riding-chariot forward (at the same time Svǫlnir's widow split asunder) to meet Hrungnir.*

15/1–4 Finnur orders this *helmingr* as two statements, *ǫll ginnunga vé knǫttu brinna fyr Ullar mági* linked to *en endilǫg grund vas hrundin grápi*. In order to secure this arrangement, he must extract *Ullar..fyr mági* from its context by punctuating the first full line as *knǫttu ǫll, en, Ullar, endilǫg, fyr mági* (*Skj* B I, 17). This staccato is an awkward arrangement, for it fractures the first two lines and slows down the momentum achieved in the previous stanza. I have followed Kock's syntax, which is more straightforward: by keeping the phrase *Ullar..fyr mági* where it is, he turns *en Ullar* plus 15/2–3 into a long parenthesis and thereby reveals the contrast in these lines between Þórr's hurtling progress up above and the hailstorm this journey causes down below (*NN* § 140).

15/1–2 *Ullar fyr mági*] 'thanks to Ullr's father-in-law', i.e. because of Þórr. Many place-names show that a god named *Ullr* or *Ullinn* was worshipped in southern and western Norway (and in Sweden) before the Viking Age, including Ullgjell (apparently 'Ullr's ravine') on the Lista peninsular down the Fedafjorden south of Kvinesdal, from which Þjóðólfr of *Hvinir* probably came.[48] Snorri says that Ullr was the son of Sif, Þórr's wife, by a previous husband, that he was good with a bow and on skis, and *ok fagr álitum ok hefir hermanns atgervi. Á hann er*

---

[48]Berg and Berg, *NAF Veibok*, p. 3, D3 (cf. also 22, C3 *et al.*). There is cluster of *Ull*-names in Þjóðólfr's part of Norway : cf. *AR* II, 153–63, esp. 154–8, §§ 444–5, diagram IV.

gott at heita í einvígi ('also fair in feature with the accomplishments of a war-rior. He is good to call on for single combat', *Gylf*, p. 26, ch. 31). Þórr is known as *Ulls mágr* in a poem about Þórr composed by Eysteinn Valdason (*c.* 1000, *Skj* B I, 131, 3) and Eilífr refers to Þórr as *ítr Ullar gulli* ('splendid nurturer of Ullr') in *Þórsdrápa* 18 (*ibid.* B I, 143). Given that the cognate OE *wuldor* glosses Latin *gloria* in about nine hundred instances, and given that the common allit-eration of *wuldor* with OE *wlite* ('beauty', 'countenance') is clearly a counter-part of the relationship between *Ullr* and Olce *litir* (< *Wullr* and *wlitir*) in Snorri's description of Ullr as *fagr álitum* ('fair in feature'), it is likely that Ullr's name still meant 'brilliance' in the late ninth century and that he contin-ued to be worshipped through his association with light in northern lands.[49] His family connection with Þórr in *Haustlǫng* 15 may be cited not (only) because he was apparently a patron of duels, but because 'brilliance' and 'thunder' are kindred phenomena in the summer sky. Ullr's name thus helps to portray Þórr's duel with Hrungnir as a thunderstorm with lightning in the mountains.

15/2 *endilǫg grund*] 'the ground down below.' Cecil Wood, followed by Marold (p. 170), puts *endilǫg* with n. pl. *ǫll* in the first line, both qualifying *ginnunga vé* in the last line of the *helmingr*; but 'the distantly extending sanctuaries of the falcons', Marold's translation of these lines ('die sich weithin erstreckenden Heiligtümer der Falken'), hardly does justice to the meaning of *endilǫg*, which refers not to an expanse extending upwards or to one side, but to an abysmal drop from the stand-point of the observer.[50] Contrary to the view of Wood and Marold, *endilǫg* is more likely to agree with f. sg. *grund*, especially if Kock's relatively straightforward arrangement of these lines is preferred to Finnur's. Þjóðólfr uses this adjective to emphasise a contrast between perspectives of heaven and earth.

15/3 *grápi hrundin*] 'kicked with hail.' Olce *hrinda* means 'to push': as when the giantess Hyrrokkin takes the stern of Baldr's funeral ship and *hratt fram* ('pushed it forwards'); or when Þórr, shortly afterwards, kicks a dwarf and *hratt honum í eldinn* ('cast him into the fire', *Gylf*, p. 46). By association, a gerund of *hrinda*, f. *hrundning*, means either 'pushing' or 'kicking'. Thus it seems best to translate *hrundin* in 15/3 as 'kicked', given that *gráp* is a more forceful type of hail, and given that Þjóðólfr may imagine this hail to be kicked downwards by the hooves of Þórr's billy-goats.

15/4 *ginnunga vé*] 'the sanctuaries of falcons (/ of the abyss)', i.e. the sky. At first it might seem that Þjóðólfr describes *Ginnungagap*, the cosmic abyss of Norse mythology to which the poet of *Vǫluspá* (*gap var ginnunga*, 'there was a

[49]See North, *Heathen Gods in Old English Literature* (C.U.P., forthcoming).
[50]Cecil Wood, 'Skaldic Notes', *Scandinavian Studies* 32 (1960), 153–8, esp. 153–4.

chasm of abysses', st. 3) and Snorri (*Gylf*, chs. 5 and 8) allude; or better still, *Ginnungahiminn* ('Yawning-heavens'), which is apparently Snorri's name for the sky created out of Ymir's skull in *Gylf*, ch. 8 (p. 12). Although *ginnunga* (R *ginnivnga*) *vé* in *Haustlǫng* 15 recalls *Ginnungagap* (as Marold believes, p. 170), it is not likely that Þjóðólfr derived *ginnunga* from this name. Instead, *ginnunga* appears to be the gen. pl. of OIce *ginnungr* ('falcon'), and provides an image of the sky in keeping with the third part of Snorri's statement in *Skáld*, ch. 59 (*SnE* I, 486) that *lopt heitir ginnungagap ok meðalheimr, foglheimr, veðrheimr* ('the sky is called Ginnunga-gap and middle-home, bird-home and weather-home'). Meissner (p. 108, § 20.b) lists four similar sky-kennings with a flying creature as the baseword: *býskeið* ('bee's course', a compound of uncertain meaning in Egill's *Sonatorrek* (*c*. 960), *Skj* B I, 36, 18); *gagls leið* ('gosling's road', in the twelfth-century *Plácítúsdrápa*, *Skj* B I, 614, 28); *gammleið* ('vulture-road', *Skj* B I, 139, 2; cf. note to 9/5–6); and perhaps *svana flugrein* ('swans' flight-land', in the twelfth-century *Harmsól* of Gamli kanóki, *Skj* B I, 559, 44). *Ginnunga vé* differs from the other examples in that, with *vé* ('sanctuaries'), this kenning appears to reveal the heavens as a collection of temples or idols worshipped by the birds who fly there. That Þórr sets these sanctuaries on fire as he races by (with *brinna*, 'burn') describes not only the lightning that he causes in the sky, but also his lack of subtlety.

15/5 *hafrar fram drógu*] 'the bucks drew forward.' R *hafrir* must be emended to *hafrar*, but is preferable to W *hofðv* T *hafdi* which seem to have been written for *hafrar* by an earlier scribe's attention to *þá er* and to what appears to be a subject of this subordinate clause (pl. in W, sg. in T) in *hofregin*. Snorri tells us in *Gylf*, ch. 21 (p. 23) that Þórr's goats are named *Tanngnjóstr* and *Tanngrisnir* ('tooth-gnasher' and 'tooth-grinder', presumably because they gnash the bit); Snorri may use *Haustlǫng* as a source when he also says that Þórr has *reið þá er hann ekr, en hafrarnir draga reiðna. Því heitir hann Ǫkuþórr* ('the chariot that he drives, while the billy-goats draw the chariot. For this reason he is called Driver-Þórr'). The poet of *Þrymskviða*, who may also know *Haustlǫng*, alludes to these goats in the pasture before they are harnessed for Þórr's journey to Þrymheimr:

> Senn vóro hafrar   heim um reknir,
> scyndir at scǫclom,   scyldo vel renna.
> (*Þrym* 21/1–4)[51]

15/5–6 *hofregin hógreiðar*] 'the temple-deity of the easy-riding-chariot', i.e. Þórr. The *regin*-suffix in all MSS *hofregin* is probably the acc. of *reginn*, a noun which is paralleled within this poem by *leikblaðs reginn fjaðrar*, Þjóðólfr's kenning for Þjazi in 12/6. OIce *reginn* would appear to be the m. sg. of the

[51]'Together the bucks were driven home, hurried into their harnesses, they had to run fast.'

common n. pl. *regin* or *rǫgn* ('(ruling) deities', 'powers'), but it is worth noting that *hofregin* in 15/5 could otherwise be the n. pl. form and denote Þórr with at least one unnamed attendant (such as Loki or Þjálfi). Þórr and Þjálfi go together to visit Geirrøðr in *Þórsdrápa*, Þórr and Týr to see Hymir in *Hymiskviða* and Loki with Þórr to see Þrymr in *Þrymskviða*. Snorri furthermore includes Þjálfi in Þórr's duel with Hrungnir and Mǫkkurkálfi in his prose rendition of this story in *Skáldskaparmál*. As Þjóðólfr, however, names no-one else in the duel in *Haustlǫng*, it is reasonable to suppose that his *hofregin* refers to Þórr alone (see also note 17/2). As regards the form of this compound, Finnur, in his Copenhagen dissertation of 1884 on critical problems in Old Norse-Icelandic Scaldic verse, emended *hof* to *haf* in *hógreiðar hafreginn* ('the deity lifted by the easy carriage', i.e. 'the transported deity').[52] He saw no reason to revise this emendation later either in *Skjaldedigtning* (B I, 17) or in his revision of *Lexicon Poeticum* (p. 219), in each of which he retains acc. *hafregin* for Þórr. Magnús follows Finnur in reading *hafregin*, 'a god who is raised, lifted' ('ás, sem er hafinn, sem er lyft', p. 349, n. 66). Kock defends *hofregin* (*NN* § 1019), but then goes too far in taking this compound as sufficient to refer to Þórr on its own and *hógreiðar* to go with *hafrar* on 15/5 (*ibid.* § 2985 D). With Marold and Faulkes (*SSE*, p. 80) it seems best to keep *hofregin hógreiðar* together, and to take this kenning as a reference to Þórr in one of his *hof* ('temples' or 'houses'). As late as *c.* 1076, an informant described *Thor* to Adam of Bremen as one of three idols in a big temple at Uppsala, the others being *Wodan* ('Óðinn') and *Fricco* ('Freyr'): 'Thor, the most powerful of them, has a chair in the middle of their dining hall'.[53] The Æsir *hof oc hǫrf hátimbruðu* ('timbered high their (religious) courts and temples') in the beginning of their world in *Vsp* 7; and the settler Þórólfr of Mórstr is said to have dedicated a *hof* specifically to Þórr in *Eyrbyggja saga*, as is the Norwegian Dala-Guðbrandr in Snorri's *Óláfs saga helga*. In this light, it seems that Þjóðólfr now presents Þórr to us as he might have seen him physically on earth, as an idol sitting in a house of his own on a throne or even in a *reið* ('riding-chariot', cognate with *ríða*). Olce *hóg-* ('easy') is a common prefix, which, with *fœrr* ('capable'), in particular, denotes a 'light' or 'lively' horse. In conjunction with *reið* and *hafrar* in thus stanza, the *hóg*-prefix appears to emphasise the reckless speed at which Þórr travels.

15/7 *seðr gekk Svǫlnis ekkja sundr*] 'at the same time Svǫlnir's widow [Earth] split asunder'. Note how Þjóðólfr again illustrates the split metrically by placing *sundr* after the caesura (cf. 8/5). *Svǫlnir* (?'cooler') is apparently a by-name of Óðinn which is also found in the thirteenth-century earth-kenning *Svǫlnis beðja* ('Svǫlnir's bedmate', *Skj* B II, 439, 20). All in all, where the earth is

---

[52]'Den af den bekvemme vogn løftede = bårne guddom', cited in Marold, *Kenningkunst*, p. 170, n. 411.

[53]*Adam Bremensis Gesta*, ed. Schmeidler, p. 258 (IV.26): 'ita ut potentissimus eorum Thor in medio solium habeat triclinio'.

named through her marriage to Óðinn, Meissner (p. 87, § 1.a) lists seventeen surviving different kennings (in twenty instances), with basewords such as 'bride', 'wife', 'love', 'lady' and 'girlfriend'. Out of this number, Þjóðólfr's *Svǫlnis ekkja* is the only kenning in which the earth is known as Óðinn's 'widow' (a reference to Óðinn's death in Ragnarǫk). Þjóðólfr's reason for alluding to the earth with this rare if not unique kenning is probably to be found in the frequently ironic humour of this poem. With *grund* in 15/3, the earth is a phenomenon buffeted by hail; now in the kenning *Svǫlnis ekkja*, it is also a person identifiable through Óðinn, Þórr's father, as this young god's mother; that the earth is known as an *ekkja*, finally, reveals this mother for a moment, like Åse Gynt with her Peer, to be alone in the world in dealing with the wildness of a son. Þórr's race through the heavens is presented as exhilarating, but 'at the same time' (*seðr*) we see him setting fire to 'the sanctuaries of falcons' (*ginnunga vé*) as he speeds by, while with the hailstorm down below, by the personification of 'ground' (*grund*) into 'Óðinn's widow' (*Svǫlnis ekkja*), he brings his old mother out of doors. It is likely that Þjóðólfr invokes the earth's relationship with Þórr in this way in order to humanize the god whose idol he has probably shown us in *hofregin*, and whose natural power he showed us at the start of this stanza.

16. *Baldr's bosom-brother did not show mercy in that*
place (mountains shook and cliffs shattered, heaven
burned above) to the gorged mountain-foe of men; hugely,
I have learned, did he shrink back from the meeting, when
the witness for the whales of the dark-bone of Haki's land
knew his killer to be ready for war.

16/1 *Þyrmðit Baldrs of barmi*] 'Baldr's bosom-brother did not show mercy.' Þórr is named 'Baldr's brother' only here (Meissner, pp. 253–4, § 88.a). Why 'Baldr's bosom-brother' now? Although the number of Þórr-kennings is limited in which his family relationships are shown, it is reasonable to suppose that Þjóðólfr created this kenning for a contextual purpose. The answer seems to lie in the mythological background. Þórr's tie to Baldr is one reason why he cannot be trusted to show mercy to Hrungnir, not because he protects Baldr, but because he is partly responsible for his death. Snorri tells us in *Gylf*, ch. 49 (p. 45) that Frigg exacted oaths from all created things not to harm Baldr, and that once this general consent seemed assured, the Æsir tested Baldr's new immunity by pelting him with all kinds of missiles, until one of them, Loki's *mistilteinn*, accidentally proved fatal (cf. *Vsp* 31–2 and *Bdr* 9). If an older version of this tale was known to Þjóðólfr, Þórr can be assumed to be part of this disaster. Þórr's lack of subtlety is well known: with the giant-builder, the poet of *Vǫluspá* says that *Þórr einn þar vá*, Þórr alone of them there struck' (*Vsp* 26); and Loki, when he leaves Ægir's party in *Lokasenna*, tells Þórr that *ec veit at þú vegr*, 'I know that you strike' (*Lok* 64). The true implication of *Baldrs of barmi* in *Haustlǫng*

16/1 thus seems to emerge through its collocation with *þyrmðit* ('did not show mercy'): Þórr harms even a 'bosom-brother' whom he was protecting, and he has no reason to protect Hrungnir. There appears to be a similar irony in Bragi's use of *Erps of barmar* ('Erpr's bosom-brothers') as a kenning in *Ragnarsdrápa* 3 (*Skj* B I, 1) to indicate Hamðir and Sǫrli at the moment they try to kill Jǫrmunrekkr in revenge for their sister, for these loyal brothers, having killed Erpr on the way, now wish that he were there to help them. In *Haustlǫng*, Þjóðólfr's kenning *Baldrs of barmi* appears to be a unique formulation in the same slightly mocking vein as *Þórs of rúni* (8/5), *Loptr* (8/6), *hugreynandi Hœnis* (12/3), *sonr biðils Greipar* (13/3–4), *Svǫlnis ekkja* (15/7) and *heimþinguðr herju Vingnis* (19/1–2).

16/2–3 *berg hristusk bjǫrg ok brustu*] 'mountains shook and cliffs shattered.' The difficulty with this interpretation lies in the position of n. pl. *berg* ('mountains') relative to *hristusk bjǫrg ok brustu*, for n. sg. *berg* ('mountain-') seems to have a closer syntactical link with *solgnum þar dolgi* on 16/2. If *berg* is linked to *solgnum*, 16/1–4 could be read as three paratactic clauses, one in lines 1–2, the second in line 3 and the third in line 4. Kock reads 16/1–4 in this fluent fashion, although, because a new compound *bergsolginn* makes little sense in this context, he emends *bergsolgnum* to *bjargsolgnum* (*NN* § 141), then to *bergs solgnum* (ibid. § 2409) and finally to *bergfolgnum*, whereby he takes the line to mean 'Þórr's enemy hidden (covered) by stone' ('Tors av sten dolda (betäckta) fiende', *ibid.* § 2506 and *Ska*, p. 11). Kock thus reacts to Finnur, who fractures line 2 by putting a comma after *berg* and linking this word with *brustu* at the end of line 3, in order to read *bjǫrg hristusk ok berg brustu* (*Skj* B I, 17). Kiil, also rejecting Finnur's placing of *berg*, obviates Kock's problem with *bergsolgnum* by linking *berg* with *dolgi* in a tmesis (p. 88). Marold (p. 170, n. 413) rejects Kock's suggested *bergfolgnum* but does not put forward a solution of her own (although she does not link *berg* with *dolgi*). Kiil's solution is the one I have followed here, although it probably only goes part of the way towards explaining the relevance of *berg* in these lines. Finnur may yet be right in associating *berg* with *hristusk bjǫrg ok brustu*, even if not in placing this word before *brustu*. I suggest that Þjóðólfr's construction with *berg* resembles that which we have seen with *ár-Gefnar* in 2/6–8 (see note). Just as *ár-Gefnar* in these lines seems to go both with the following *mar* and with *birgi-Týr bjarga* on the next line, so it is possible that *berg* in 16/2 works both as a prefix to *dolgi* and as a component of the clause beginning with *hristusk* on 16/3. Here the easiest position for *berg* is before *hristusk*, in which case *ok* may be taken as an enclitic conjunction (perhaps similar to the use of *ok* in 10/7) and *bjarg* may be linked with *brustu*. Þjóðólfr's effect in postponing *ok* in this line, and thus in putting *bjarg* in an unusual position there, may be to illustrate the dislodging of rocks and stones metrically. Þórr's relentless drive to the giants' world was a poetic *topos*, as we see in *Þrymskviða*:

biǫrg brotnoðo, brann iǫrð loga,
óc Óðins sonr   í iǫtunheima.

(Þrym 21/5–8)[54]

16/2–4 *berg- solgnum -dolgi manna*] 'to the gorged mountain-foe of men', i.e.
to Hrungnir. The noun *berg* does not go with *manna* on line 4, for Hrungnir
cannot be a *solginn dolgr bergmanna* ('gorged foe of mountain-men', i.e. 'of
giants'). Thus he seems to be a *solginn bergdolgr manna* (see also previous
note). This kenning is quite unparalleled in the Scaldic corpus, as Meissner
shows (pp. 255–9, esp. 259, § 88.b), unless we compare it with *ballastan dolg
vallar* in *Haustlǫng* 6/6. With *solgnum* in 16/2 it is thus likely that Þjóðólfr
makes an unclichéd, thus individual, reference to an incident preceding the duel,
such as when Hrungnir drinks his fill in Ásgarðr and then threatens to take
Freyja and Sif with him back to the world of the giants (*Skáld*, ch. 17). A preliminary of this kind seems to be implied in Olce *solginn*, of which the literal
meaning is 'gorged' (from *svelgja*, 'to swallow') as only Kiil recognises (with
'forsluken', p. 88). Although *solginn* more commonly means 'ravenous' (so
Finnur, with 'glubsk', *Skj* B I, 17) or 'greedy' (so Marold, with 'gierig', p. 170),
neither of these meanings does more than refer generally to the nature of giants
in what is, after all, an unparalleled kenning. So with this kenning it is clear that
Þjóðólfr wishes to allude not to a general mythological *topos*, but to a specific
incident in a related story. Hrungnir is the 'foe of men' because he wishes to
steal Freyja, their source of harvest plenty, and thus to inflict hunger on mankind. With *solginn* in this kenning, just as with Þjazi's need for *ár-Gefnar marr*
('harvest-Gefn's horse', 2/6), *þrymseilar hvalr vára* ('the whale of the cracking-
rope of spring-times', 5/2–4) and *okbjǫrn* ('yoke-bear', 6/4), Þjóðólfr appears
to make a giant's fulfilment synonymous with human starvation. Hrungnir is
thus the enemy of men in this poem because he has already gorged himself on
their harvest. Since Hrungnir is made of rock, it is likely that the duel between
him and Þórr, as Þjóðólfr describes it in *Haustlǫng*, is intended (i.a.) to evoke
the image of clearing stony land for planting: or of breaking boulders into smaller
stones, and throwing them into a ravine, prior to ploughing a new field.[55]

16/5 *mjǫk frák móti hrøkkva*] 'hugely, I have learned, did he shrink back from
the meeting.' This is an acc. and inf. construction (lit. 'I heard [him] to shrink
back'), with the acc. subject understood within the subject of the following
subordinate clause. The adverb *mjǫk*, placed first, is emphatic: for example, in
Sonatorrek (*c.* 960), describing his own reaction to trauma (the drowning of his
son Bǫðvarr), Egill Skalla-Grímsson says in one stanza *mik hefr marr miklu
ræntan* ('me the Ocean has robbed of much', st. 10); yet in another, bringing the

[54]'cliffs smashed, the earth burned in flame, Óðinn's son was driving to the
world of the giants.'

[55]Cf. Williams, *Social Scandinavia in the Viking Age*, p. 165.

necessary adverb forward, he says *mjǫk hefr Rán ryskt um mik* ('hugely has Rán [the sea-goddess] shaken me', st. 8, *Skj* B I, 35–6). The use of *fregna* ('to hear') in *frák*, like that of *heyra* in *heyrðak* (12/1), implies that Þjóðólfr does not see an image of the accompanying scene painted on his shield. Since this scene concerns the imminent arrival of Þórr before he meets Hrungnir, it is likely that nothing of Þórr's journey in a goat-drawn chariot was represented on the shield and that Þjóðólfr composed st. 14–16 as a preamble to the only part of this story for which there was a painting or engraving, namely the duel. Here he appears to describe Hrungnir's dread at a 'meeting' (n. *mót*) as he sees Þórr approach. Finnur, however, takes his interpretation of the Hrungnir-kenning (see note below) to be the subject of this acc. and inf. construction: *frák [i.e. Hrungni] hrøkkva mjǫk móti*, 'I have heard that the giant took position for a powerful resistance' ('jeg har hørt, at jætten stillede sig til kraftig modstand', *Skj* B I, 17). Strictly, as Finnur shows, *móti*, the dat. of *mót*, is used as an adverb or preposition to indicate a position 'facing' or 'against'; just as *at fundi* ('for a meeting with', w. gen., 15/8) is a prepositional phrase made out of m. *fundr* ('discovery', 'meeting'). However, Finnur puts too much weight on the adverbial meaning of *móti* and thus strains the sense of *hrøkkva*. Given the brevity of Scaldic diction, instead, there is better reason to translate *móti* in 16/5 as 'from a meeting' after *hrøkkva* as 'shrink back' or 'recoil'. With 'meeting' in *mót*, Þjóðólfr prepares us for one of his conceits in the next *helmingr*, in which Hrungnir is a 'witness' (*váttr*) summoned to appear on behalf of the giants.

16/6–8 *myrkbeins Haka reinar vǫgna váttr*] 'witness for the whales of the dark-bone of Haki's land', i.e. Hrungnir. This is an extended kenning in which *Haka rein* appears to mean the sea, whose *myrkbein* ('dark-bone') is rock; the *vǫgnir* ('dolphins') of this rock are giants, whose *váttr* ('witness') on this occasion is Hrungnir. It is first necessary to consider which text to follow. Here the problem is that the W-text must be followed for 16/6, whereas the R-text is preferable in 16/8. First, in 16/6, R *myrk hreins baka reinar* is a group of words for which no interpretation seems possible; if we follow W *myrk beins* (T *meinþorns*) *haka reinar*, on the other hand, we arrive at an *ofljós* kenning for 'rock'. Second, in 16/8, WT *vatt* causes syntactical problems and must be rejected in favour of R *vátr*. Acc. *vátt* is preferred by Finnur (*Skj* B I, 17), Magnús (p. 350, n. 67) and Faulkes (*SSE*, p. 80), but this reading overloads the acc. and inf. construction after *frák* while leaving little room for the final subordinate clause after *þás* in st. 16/7–8. The form *vatt* may have been copied from *vat* with a diacritic *r* omitted in an earlier exemplar, and R *þatri* (for *þátti*) on the same line probably shows that the R-scribe did not invent the *r* in *vátr* but copied it from his exemplar twice. Thus it is necessary to keep R *vatr* while following the W-text in order to make the kenning *myrkbeins Haka reinar vǫgna váttr*. If we begin by looking at *Haka rein* ('Haki's land'), we find that this phrase is itself a kenning: since *Haki* (OE *Hoc*, ModE *Hook*) is listed as a sea-king in the *Þulur*, his 'land' is likely to be the sea. Meissner (pp. 92–3, § 5.c) lists forty-four surviving kennings of this type (in forty-five instances), including *Haka kleif* ('Haki's cliff', *Skj* B I, 291,

1), *Haka bláland* ('Haki's black land', *ibid.* B I, 78, 37), *Haka hlíð* ('Haki's hillside', *ibid.* B II, 71, 38) and *Haka vegr* ('Haki's road', *ibid.* B II, 82, 76). Next, it is likely that the sea's *myrkbein* ('dark-bone') is a larger kenning for rock. This compound is attested once elsewhere in an 'giant's bone' type of rock-kenning from the poet Vǫlu-Steinn (*c.* 1000, whom Nordal held to have composed *Vǫluspá*): *Hlǫðvinjar myrkbein* ('dark-boncs of Hlǫðyn', i.e. of the giantess', hence 'rocks', *Skj* B I, 93, 2). Our example of *myrkbein*, however, appears to be part of a different type of kenning which is contained in Þjóðólfr's *lagar bein* ('water's bone') in *Ynglingatal* 31 (*Skj* B I, 13; cf. Meissner, p. 90, § 3.c). There are only ten other kennings of this type, all shorter than *myrkbein Haka reinar*, but there is little doubt that this kenning means 'dark-bone of the sea', hence 'rock' (so Kiil, p. 89; and Marold, pp. 170–1). Kock, however, persistently reads *reinar myrkbeins Haki* as 'the Haki of the dark-bone of the land' (*NN* §§ 226 and 1813, 2505 and 3097 A). There are ten parallels for a giant-kenning of this type, including Þjóðólfr's *grjót-Níðuðr* in *Haustlǫng* 9/8 (cf. Meissner, p. 258, § 88.b). However, as Marold points out (p. 171, n. 415), *Haki* as the name of a sea-king is inappropriate as a synonym for the king of a land-domain; and Kock's interpretation disturbs the word-order of W *myrk beins haka reinar* in which one element leads naturally to the next: 'dark-bone of Haki's land', i.e. 'rock'. The next problem is what to do with *vǫgna váttr* in 16/7–8 (cf. note to 4/5). Reichardt (p. 102, followed by Marold, pp. 170–1), proposes to take *vǫgn* as 'dolphin' and renders *myrkbeins Haka reinar vǫgna váttr* as 'the close friend of the dolphins of the dark-bone of Haki's land', i.e. 'giant' ('der Vertraute der Delphine des Dunkelknochens des Rains des Haki', p. 102). An interpretation along these lines seems preferable (perhaps with 'whale' for 'dolphin' in this case), for otherwise it is difficult to integrate *vǫgna* into the giant-kenning. Finnur, who takes *vǫgna* as gen. pl. of *vagn* ('wagon'), ends up contorting the word-order more than Kock and places *vǫgna* next to *Haka*, taking these words as *Haka vagna reinar myrkbeins váttr*: 'the judge of the dark-bone of the land of Haki's wagons'(LP, p. 416), in which 'Haki's wagons' are ships, the ships' 'land' is the sea, the sea's 'dark-bone' is rock and the rock's 'judge', as it were, is Hrungnir. Magnús (p. 350) and Faulkes (*SSE*, p. 80) also take *Haka vagna* to refer to 'Haki's wagons', i.e. to ships. Kock, who stubbornly interprets *vǫgn* here and in 4/5 as a *heiti* for 'giant' (*NN* §§ 136, 1813 B and 2505), is obliged to treat this word (and *váttr*) separately and to propose 'not one lonely, long, unintelligibly contorted 'giant'-kenning with the last bits stuck in a completely different sentence (...) but two *individual, immediately understandable,* lucid expressions for the same idea, one in one sentence, and the other in the other!' (*ibid.* § 226).[56] Thus he takes his giant-kenning *Haka myrkbeins reinar* as part of the acc. and inf. construction after *frák* (with acc. *Haka*) and takes

---

[56]'Icke en ensam, lång, obegripligt tilltrasslad 'jätte'-kenning med sista biten instucken i en helt annan sats (...) utan två e n k l a, o m e d e l b a r t b e g r i - p l i g a, heljutna uttryck för samma begrepp, det ena i den ena satsen, det andra i den andra!'

vagna váttr to be the subject of the clause beginning with *þás*. Unfortunately, neither his giant-kenning with *Haki* as the baseword, nor his interpretation of *vǫgn* as 'giant' in its own right is strong enough to withstand Reichardt's interpretation. With *vagna* as the gen. pl. of 'whales' or 'dolphins', the kenning 'whales of the rock' is paralleled by *hraunhvalir* ('lava-whales', i.e. 'giants') in *Hym* 36. Thus the most likely word-order is *myrkbeins Haka reinar vǫgna váttr*: 'witness for the whales of the dark-bone of Haki's land', i.e. Hrungnir, who is the subject of the subordinate clause after *þás* in 16/7.

16/7–8 *þás vígligan sinn bana þátti*] 'when he knew his killer to be ready for war.' *Pace* Kock (*NN* § 226), the subordinating conjunction *þás* is clearly delayed until the start of 16/7 for metrical reasons. If we read nom. *váttr* after the R-text on the last line, the *ofljós* kenning for Hrungnir falls into place as the subject of *þátti* ('knew'), with the phrases *sinn bana* ('his killer') and *vígligan* ('warlike', i.e. 'ready for war') as respectively the subject and predicate of an elliptical acc. and inf. construction in which the infinitive *vera* ('to be') is left out. With two acc. and inf. constructions (and one ellipsis), this *helmingr* might be said to be overcrowded with verbal expressions. Accordingly, Finnur follows WT *vatt* and takes his Hrungnir-kenning (see note above) to be the subject (with acc. *vátt*) of the first (and in his view the only) acc. and inf. construction in this *helmingr*: *frák Haka vagna reinar myrkbeins vátt hrøkkva mjǫk móti, þás þátti sinn vígligan bana* (i.e. 'I heard that the judge of the dark-bone of the land of Haki's waggons took position for a powerful resistance, when he recognised his warlike killer'). This arrangement of words simplifies the subordinate clause, but at the expense of the main clause, in which the acc. and inf. construction after *frák* is overloaded with the Hrungnir-kenning which starts with Finnur's acc. *vátt*. It seems better, in this case, to treat nom. *váttr* ('witness') as the subject of *þátti* and thus to leave the rambling kenning for Hrungnir until the final clause of the whole stanza. Finally, why is this kenning so long? The answer to this question may lie in the word *váttr*, which in the Icelandic sagas is commonly used to denote a 'witness' in a court of law. Snorri says that *þóttusk jǫtnar hafa mikit í ábyrgð, hvárr sigr fengi* ('the giants thought they had much at stake in whichever won the victory', *SnE* I, 272). If n. *mót* in 16/5 is read at full strength as 'meeting', then with *váttr* it is possible that Þjóðólfr, for a moment, conceives of Hrungnir as a 'witness' testifying on behalf of the giants, Þórr as their legal challenger, and the kenning for Hrungnir in 16/6–8 ('witness for the whales of the dark-leg of Haki's land') as a sample of his longwinded discourse. Hrungnir does not speak in the poem, but in Snorri's account of the preliminary scenes Hrungnir speaks 'no lack of great words' (*skorti eigi stór orð*) and the wording of Hrungnir's challenge to Þórr is not brief:

> Hrungnir says that there will be little fame for Þórr of the Æsir in killing him unarmed; on the contrary, it will be a greater test of his courage if he dares to do battle with him on the borderland at Grjótúnagarðar: 'and it was a great act of folly,' he says, 'that I left my shield and whetstone behind at home; if I had my weapons

here, then we two should try a duel now, and I charge you otherwise with cowardice if you wish to kill me unarmed.'

Þórr's response is too obvious to be put into direct speech:

> There is no way that Þórr will fail to enter into single combat,
> once he has been challenged to a duel.

Nor does Þórr hesitate from a collision with Hrungnir when he arrives to
kill him, after three stanzas of blazing a trail from Ásgarðr to the world of the
giants (14–16). At the end of the sky-travel sequence in these stanzas, it is possible that Þjóðólfr makes a contrast between the bragging of Hrungnir understood earlier in the story and his speechless recoil now.

17. *Quickly the battle-pale ice of shield-rims flew (the
powers caused this) beneath the soles of the keeper of the
cliffs (the battle-spirits wanted it so); after that the eager
gallant of the rubble-field did not have to wait long for a
many-times-mutilating blow from the hard confidant of the
troll's snout.*

17/1 *bjarga gæti*] 'keeper of the cliffs', i.e. Hrungnir. This is not a typical kenning
for a giant. The baseword m. *gætir* ('keeper') is unparalleled in giant-kennings
and only *bergstjóri*, 'mountain governor', comes close (*Skj* B II, 111, 2; cf.
Meissner, pp. 255–9, esp. 256, § 88.b). Þjóðólfr in *Ynglingatal* 2 describes a
dwarf as *salvǫrðuðr Dúrnis niðja* ('hall-guardian of the kinsmen of Dúrnir
[dwarf]', *Skj* B I, 7), but that is because the dwarves of his mythology live in
caves underground. However, the noun *gætir* is common as a baseword for man-
kennings, with nine or ten different examples in which a man is defined as the
'keeper' of golden rings or ships or weapons (Meissner, p. 294, § 88.m). To this
extent, Hrungnir now seems to be presented as the chief of a cliff-dwelling
comitatus.

17/2 *bǫnd ollu því*] 'the powers caused this.' A heroic *topos* is represented here
(and in in *vildu svá (imun-) dísir*, 17/4) in which irrational deeds or unexplained
events may be attributed not to their perpetrators but to an external scapegoat
source. Óðinn makes use of this *topos* earlier in 3/3–4, when he says 'something
is the cause of this' (*hvat því valda*), failing thus to see the cause of his dying
fire in Þjazi, who sits nearby; here Óðinn also uses the verb *valda* of which *ollu*
is the 3rd pers. pl. preterite in 17/2. This *topos* is as old as the *Iliad*, in which
Agamemnon, for example, blames Zeus, his 'lot' and a savage Fury for having
stirred up a feud with Achilles (*Il.* XIX.88).[57] In Norway, in *c.* 985, Einarr

---

[57]Discussed in E. R. Dodds, *The Greeks and the Irrational* (Berkeley, 1951), pp.
13–18. See also North, *Pagan Words*, pp. 26–37.

skálaglamm appears to use this *topos* positively when he refers to the victories of his patron Hákon Jarl:

> Mart varð él áðr Ála   austrlǫnd *at mun banda*
> randa lauks af ríki   rœkilundr of tœki.
>
> (*Vellekla* 9/1–4)[58]

In this instance the words for the source of Hákon's spiritual guidance, *at mun banda*, contain the word *bǫnd* which appears in *bǫnd ollu því* in *Haustlǫng* 17/2. In *Hamðismál*, however, of which the original text may have been composed in Norway as early as the late ninth century, this *topos* is used negatively when the poet says that Hamðir and Sǫrli murder their half-brother Erpr *at mun flagði* ('at the joyous prompting of a hag-spirit', st. 15); later, when the brothers realise that Erpr could have helped them, had he lived, one of them says *hvǫttomc at dísir* ('the spirits incited me to it', st. 28) and *gǫrðomz at vígi* ('they brought about the killing', st. 28). Similarly, in the *Víkarsbálkr*, which was probably composed in the twelfth or thirteenth century and is preserved in a text of *Gautreks saga* (ch. 7), the anti-hero Starkaðr claims that he killed his friend and master Víkarr because *flǫgð ollu* ('the hag-spirits caused it', *Skj* B II, 347). By using this *topos* in *Haustlǫng* 17, Þjóðólfr casts Hrungnir in the heroic mould of the Niflungar in Eddic lays, with the added irony that Hrungnir's irrational act brings about his own rather than someone else's downfall. By the same token, it is evident that Þórr's servant Þjálfi cannot be part of this story as we know it from *Haustlǫng*, and it is likely that Þjóðólfr based this story on the image of only two humanoid figures painted on his shield, Þórr and Hrungnir.

17/2–4 *randa ímun-fǫlr íss (-dísir)*] 'battle-pale ice of shield-rims (battle-spirits)', i.e. the gleaming shield-boss. The word *ímun* appears to prefix not only *fǫlr* ('pale'), but also *dísir* ('ladies', 'spirits') which is placed at the end of 17/3–4. Finnur detaches *ímun* from *fǫlr* ('an impossible combination' – 'en umulig sammensætning') in order to join it to *dísir*, for want of another word, thus making *ímundísir*, which he renders as 'the battle-ladies' ('kampdiserne', *Skj* B I, 18).[59] Kock, who thinks that the parenthesis resulting from this arrangement would be unintelligible in an oral performance, keeps *ímunfǫlr* (*NN* § 142). I see every reason to keep both *ímun*-compounds, given that Þjóðólfr probably wishes to qualify the dull colour 'pale', in the first instance, while reinforcing his conceit of malign intervening powers in the second. In the first instance, OIce f. *ímun* is related to f. *íma* ('battle', *HHund* II, 53), describes a shield as *ímunborð* ('battle-board', *Skj* B I, 120, 17), a sword as *ímunlaukr* ('battle-leek', in Eyvindr's

---

[58]*Skj* B I, 118: 'many a storm of Áli [battle] took place before the shield-leek's [sword's] caretaking-tree seized by force the eastern lands of the kingdom *at the joyous prompting of divine powers*.'

[59]Finnur, 'Kenningers led-omstilling og tmesis', p. 10.

Háleygjatal 8, *c*. 985, *Skj* B I, 65), and here chiefly qualifies the collocation *fǫlr iss randa* ('pale ice of shield-rims'), which would have to mean 'sword' (as in ModE 'cold steel') if Þjóðólfr's kennings were typical of Scaldic poetry. Apart from Þjóðólfr's *iss randa*, Meissner (pp. 151–2, § 76.b) lists eighteen or nineteen sword-kennings (not all are certain) in which the baseword is either *iss* ('ice', eight examples) or *svell* ('ice-sheet', ten examples) or *jǫkull* ('glacier', one example). With the exception of *sikulgjarðar iss* ('ice of the sickle-dwelling', 'sword', in the *Knútsdrápa* of Hallvarðr háreksblesi (*c*. 1030), *Skj* B I, 293, 2), all sword-kennings with an *iss*-baseword are qualified by words for battle or valkyries (*Hlǫkk, gunn, álmdrós* and *hjaldr*) and blood or wounds (*sár* and *blóð*). So Þjóðólfr's kenning *randa iss* would be unusual even if it did mean 'sword'. *Hrungnis fóta stallr* ('foot-pedestal of Hrungnir', Skj B I, 73, 14), a shield-kenning which is attributed to the poet Kormákr but which is probably of the twelfth or thirteenth century, might be taken to refer to a sword, given that the prose-context of *Kormáks saga* (ch. 5), in which the relevant verse is contained, tells a story in which a sword is placed against a doorway to trap Kormákr, where the verse would lead us to expect a shield.[60] Meissner treats *randa iss* as a shield-kenning (pp. 161, § 76.c and 174, § 80.e), but draws attention to its oddity, interpreting *iss* in this case as a word related 'to the shield's iron mountings' ('auf die Eisenbeschläge des Schildes', p. 171, § 80.b). This supposition may be true, if this odd use of *iss* is related to the ambiguity of the word f. *spǫng*, which can mean both 'ice-floe' and a 'spangle' or 'mounting' on a shield: witness Einarr skálaglam's shield in *Egils saga*, on which 'spangles made of gold were mounted' (*váru lagðar yfir spengr af gulli*).[61] Snorri has no use for *iss* in Hrungnir's shield in *Skáld*, ch. 17 (*SnE* I, 274), when he refers to this shield as *steinn, víðr ok þjǫkkr* ('stone, wide and thick'). Yet if a spike or pointed boss was a feature of shields in his time, it is possible that with his kenning *iss randa* Þjóðólfr alludes to an iron shield-boss on Hrungnir's shield. What, then, does he mean with *imunfǫlr*? Marold (p. 172, n. 417) points out *fǫlr* refers to corpses and in one case to weapon-points (*fǫlvar oddar*, in *HHund* I, 53, where we find *ima* a few lines further on). Yet Kock, by suggesting that 'battle-pale' means 'battle-gleaming' in *Haustlǫng* 17/3 ('stridsglänsande', *NN* § 142), finds some purpose to *fǫlr* which would otherwise be lacking. There are more than one hundred surviving Norse sword-kennings of the type 'battle-fire' (cf. Meissner, pp. 150–1, § 76.b). This type of kenning is also found in OE *beadoleoma* ('battle-flash') in *Beo* 1523. As *imunfǫlr* ('battle-pale') probably describes a pointed shield-boss in *Haustlǫng* 17, it seems likely that this compound is a kenning for 'gleaming'. Þjóðólfr thus appears to have a very specific idea of Hrungnir's

---

[60]See Heather O'Donoghue, *The Genesis of a Saga Narrative: Verse and Prose in Kormaks Saga* (Oxford, 1991), pp. 43–4.

[61]*Egils saga*, ed. Sigurður, p. 272 (ch. 78).

shield as a board with a circular rim and gleaming pointed boss – did he illustrate Hrungnir's movements with his own shield when he publicly recited *Haustlǫng*?

17/6–8 *hraundrengr tíðr*] 'the eager gallant of the rubble-field', i.e. Hrungnir. In Iceland, *hraun* refers to the rubble of cold lava-fields. The other three extant giant-kennings with *hraun* are probably all Icelandic: *hraunbúi* ('lava-dweller', *Hym* 38); *hraunhvalr* ('lava-whale', *ibid.* 36); *hraun-Atli* ('lava-Atli [prince]', in the twelfth-century *Íslendingadrápa* of Haukr Valdísarson, *Skj* B I, 540, 5; this is also Kock's parallel for his interpretation of the giant-kenning in *Haustlǫng* 16/6); and the thirteenth-century *hraunskjǫldungar* ('lava-Scyldings', *Skj* B II, 328). Yet *hraun* was a Norwegian word before it arrived in Iceland.[62] OIce *drengr* occurs twice in Eddic poems: as a term for Gunnarr and Hǫgni as they escort their sister to her arranged marriage with Atli (*Guð* II, 35); and as a term for two of Atli's younger brothers whom Guðrún slaughters in the brawl that follows her brothers' arrival later in the same story, when this marriage is over (in *Am* 50). Besides *hraundrengr*, there are eleven other giant-kennings of the 'heroic' type (Meissner, p. 258, § 88.b), including *moldrekr* ('earth-nobleman', *Skj* B I, 294, 7), *fjarðleggjar fyrðar* ('troops of the fjord-leg', *ibid.* B I, 117, 1) and *hǫrga hǫlðr* ('cairn-hero', *ibid.* II, 228, 6). The implication of *drengr*, however, is not that of a ruthless fighting man: in later Icelandic prose *drengskapr* denotes 'courage' or 'nobility of character' and Snorri defines *drengir* as:

> young men without estate, while they win wealth for themselves and reputation; those men who travel from land to land are called 'faring *drengir*'; those men who serve rulers are 'king's *drengir*'; they who serve rich men and landowners are also *drengir*; *drengir* are known to be valiant and up-and-coming men. (*Skáld*, ch. 65)[63]

In Modern Icelandic the old-fashioned word *drengur* approximates to 'knight' or 'chivalrous young man'; in Modern Danish, *dreng* is the standard word for a young 'boy'. This general connotation of honest and unmarried youthfulness, if present in *drengr* in *Haustlǫng* 17/6, probably reinforces the meaning of *tíðr*, the adjective which qualifies this noun. Finnur emends *tíðr* (all MSS) to *tíðs*,

[62]It is possible that a Norwegian word *raun* may be found in the place-name Raundalen a little to the east of Voss (Vors) below the northern border of Hǫrðaland: see Berg and Berg, *NAF Veibok*, p. 22, C1. However, this element may mean 'rowan-tree'.

[63]*SnE* I, 530: 'ungir menn búlausir, meðan þeir afla sér fjár eða orðstír; þeir fardrengir, er milli landa fara; þeir konungs drengir, er hǫfðingjum þjóna; þeir ok drengir, er þjóna ríkum mǫnnum eða bóndum; drengir heita ok vaskir menn ok batnandi.'

probably because its meanings (such as 'pleasant', 'customary', 'prompt', 'smart', 'eager') do not appear to fit Hrungnir and because *tíðs* goes better with *hǫggs* as 'a quick blow' in 17/5 ('et hurtigt hug', *Skj* B I, 18). Finnur's emendation is accepted by Magnús (p. 350, n. 68) and by Faulkes (*SSE*, p. 80). But there are semantic reasons for keeping *tíðr*, apart from the obvious palaeographical one (cf. Marold, p. 173). When Freyr, in *Skírnismál*, says that he has seen *mér tíða mey* ('a girl just right for me', st. 6/2–3), he means a girl whose eagerness to have sex with him is not in her mind, but in his. In the next stanza, Freyr says *mær er mér tíðari enn manni hveim* ('the girl is more right for me than for any man'). Olce *tíðr* thus refers to a person who 'seems eager'. If we return to Hrungnir with his shield slipped under him in *Haustlǫng* 17/8, we see that from Þórr's point of view Hrungnir makes an irresistible target — as if Hrungnir, in the words of the axe-happy Icelander Þorgeirr Hávarsson (who strikes dead an innocent shepherd in the *Hauksbók*-recension of *Fóstrbrœðra saga*), 'stood just right for the blow' (*stóð svá vel til hǫggsins*, ch. 8).[64] Þórr's point of view is that of Þjóðólfr in the second *helmingr* of *Haustlǫng* 17, for the sardonic implication of his words *varðat tíðr lengi bíða* is that Hrungnir waits for his death-blow like a young *drengr* waiting eagerly for his bride. It may be no coincidence that Hrungnir's desire was fixed on Freyja and Sif in Snorri's account of his story before the duel. My interpretation of the following kenning lends some support to this idea of a 'wedding-night' conceit.

17/5–8 *hǫggs frá hǫrðu[m] trjónu trolls of rúna fjǫllama*] 'a many-times-mutilating blow from the hard confidant of the troll's snout', i.e. from Mjǫllnir. Marold provides a clear discussion of these words and of the difficulties in putting them into a coherent order (pp. 172–3). So far, the sentence runs *varðat hraundrengr þaðan lengi tíðr at bíða* ('after that the eager gallant of the rubble-field [Hrungnir] did not have to wait long'). Since the infinitive *at bíða* ('to wait') in 17/8 looks back to *hǫggs* ('for a blow'), the remaining part of the sentence leads off from *frá hǫrðu[m]* ('from the hard'). The next problem is the form and meaning of RT *fiollama* W *fiǫll lama*. Lindquist treats this compound as *fjǫr-lama*, as a *nomen agentis* meaning 'life-lamer' ('livförlamare', pp. 88–9). Marold sympathises with the reading of *fjǫr* ('life') in this compound, but does not commit herself and translates *fjǫllama* as 'life-' or 'much-laming' ('"lebens-" oder viellähmend', p. 175). Finnur stays with *fjǫllama* as an adjective of the type 'much-shattering' ('brusende', *Skj* B I, 18); as does Magnús, with 'who thrashes many' ('sem lemur marga', p. 350, n. 68); and then Faulkes, with 'multitude-smashing' (*SSE*, p. 80). There is no doubt that the weak adjective *lami* on this occasion will have to mean 'laming' rather than 'lame', its usual sense. The related verb *lemja* ('to lam', 'mutilate', 'destroy') occurs with Þórr in *Þrym* 31, in which he *ætt iǫtuns alla lamði* ('destroyed the whole giant's

[64] *Vestfirðinga sǫgur*, ed. Björn K. Þórólfsson and Guðni Jónsson, ÍF 6 (Reykjavík, 1943), 157.

family'); and when, in particular, Snorri says that Þórr killed Hrungnir *ok lamði hausinn í smá mola* ('and shattered his skull into little fragments', *SnE* I, 274–6). Kock, who emends *tíðr fjǫllama* to *tíðr fjall-Ámu*, 'dear to mountain-Áma' [a giantess] (*NN* § 227), goes his own way; as does Kiil (pp. 92–3), who wants *fjǫllama* (dat. sg. of *fjǫllami*) to be an allusion to Mǫkkurkálfi as 'the completely useless one' ('den heilt ubrukelige') to whom Hrungnir, as *tíðr*, 'was dear' ('lå på hjerte'). Some suggestions are thus more far-fetched than others. I shall follow in Marold's path and read 'many-times-mutilating', so as to emphasise the elements of *fjǫl-lama*; I also follow Marold in taking this compound to be separate from *tíðr* and instead as a gen. sg. adjective in agreement with *hǫggs* near the beginning of this *helmingr*: thus 'the eager gallant of the rubble-field [Hrungnir] did not have to wait long for *a many-times-mutilating blow*'. The other elements of the sentence, in the word-order of this *helmingr*, are *frá hǫrðu[m] trjónu trolls of rúna*. Marold (p. 173) says that there is a scholarly agreement in taking *trjóna* ('snout') to be a part of Þórr's hammer (probably through *fyr skǫrpum hamri* in 18/6), thus as a synonym for the hammer itself. She then appears to treat *troll* as (an unspecified) part of the *trjóna*, now the 'hammer'; and so translates *of rúni trolls trjónu* as 'the confidant of the troll of the hammer', friend of Mjǫllnir, i.e. Þórr ('der Vertraute des Trolls des Hammers'). This procedure, which is based on dubious parallels (*hamartroll* and *fetils troll*, both appearing to mean 'hammer'), seems unnecessarily complicated. Having established that *fjǫllama* is not a noun, it seems easier to leave Þórr out of this kenning and to translate *trjónu trolls of rúni* as 'confidant of the troll's snout', i.e. as an epithet of Mjǫllnir at the moment it impacts on Hrungnir's face. This is the bridal kiss that the young man was waiting for (see previous note), a parodic inversion of Hrungnir's lust for goddesses. Þjóðólfr's imagery in this stanza is focussed not on Þórr, but on Hrungnir at the moment Þórr's hammer smashes his skull. It is reasonable to suppose that the shield-painting on which Þjóðólfr bases his story in st. 14–20 consisted of Hrungnir on his shield, Þórr, and a smaller symbol for Þórr's hammer adjacent to Hrungnir's head.

18. *The life-spoiler of Beli's horrific troop let fall the bear of the hide-out of high sea-swells on the island of his shield; there sank the king of the bottom of ravines before the sharp hammer, and the breaker of the Agðir-men of mountains pushed against the titanic boar.*

18/1–3 *fjǫrspillir bǫlverðungar Belja*] 'life-spoiler of Beli's horrific troop', giant-killer, i.e. Þórr. The tale to which this kenning refers is unknown. Elsewhere Beli's name appears in the epithets *Belja dólgr* ('Beli's foe'), in Eyvindr's *Háleygjatal* 5 (*Skj* B I, 60), and *bani Belia* ('Beli's killer') in *Vsp* 53, *Kálfsvísa* (*SnE* I, 482) and *Gylf*, ch. 37 (p. 31, in which Snorri identifies Beli's killer with

Freyr). *Beli* is presumably a giant, but in that his name seems to mean 'bellower', it is equally possible that he represents a bull or an ox in the now lost legend with Freyr to which the poetic sources refer. Þórr kills an ox for fish-bait just before he sets out with Hymir on his world-serpent fishing-trip in *Hym* 18–19; Þórr also eats two of Hymir's oxen in *Hym* 15 and one of Þrymr's in *Þrym* 24: in this sense, too, Þórr could be known as the destroyer of oxen, if Beli was the name of an ox. In short, it is not known who Beli is or what his 'troop' could be. At the same time, there is also a heroic dimension to this mysterious kenning for Þórr. The word f. *verðung* refers to a 'troop' or 'retinue' in *HHund* I, 9, *Sigsk* 42, *Helreið* 11 and possibly in *Hynd* 2. Elsewhere Olce *spillir*, the *nomen agentis* of *spilla* ('to spoil', 'destroy'), is found in six instances, always denoting 'king': three with *bauga* ('of rings'), in *Fáf* 32, *Skj* B II, 26, 13 and 43, 93; one with *baugs* ('of the ring'), in *Skj* B II, 580, 45; and two with *odda* ('of spear-points'), in *Skj* B II, 574, 18 and 577, 34 (Meissner, p. 302). It is possible, therefore, that in addition to the primary sense of 'destroyer' in *fjǫrspillir* (only here), there is an ironic connotation of 'ring-smashing' in this kenning in which Þórr, as if a king redistributing rings to a *verðung*, returns the lives of Beli's people to them in broken pieces. Kiil reads *bǫl-Belja* by tmesis, 'damage-Beli' ('mein-Bele', p. 94), because in his view the heroic context of *verðung* cannot support the *bǫl*-prefix.

18/2–4 fjalfrs ólágra gjalfra bolm] 'the bear of the hide-out of the high sea-swells', i.e. Hrungnir. Olce *fjalfr* appears to be related to *fela* ('to hide', 'conceal') and to mean 'hide-out' or 'refuge'. Elsewhere this noun occurs only *c.* 985 in a giant-kenning in *Þórsdrápa* 20, in which Eilífr appears to describe giants as *kalfar undirfjalfrs bliku alfheims* ('calves of the underground refuge of the elf-realm's gleam', *Skj* B I, 144). Eilífr presents Þórr in his poem as the *hneitir* ('slayer') of these 'gold-cavern calves', i.e. giants. Þjóðólfr's kenning nearly a century earlier appears to refer to Hrungnir as a bear of a cliff-cave which traps water from the high tide. His extraordinary image of this giant in shoreline surroundings is unparalleled, but is extended into a conceit by his kenning in the note below.

18/4 á randar holmi] 'on the island of his shield', i.e. on his shield-boss. Here the noun f. *rǫnd* must denote the 'rim' of the shield, otherwise we have no shield-kenning on this line. That being so, forty shield-kennings survive in which the baseword is 'land' or a similar term (Meissner, p. 169, § 80.b). Only two of these kennings have 'island' as their baseword: Þorbjǫrn Brúnason's *hjalm-Fenris holmr* ('island of the helmet-Fenrir', hence 'warrior's shield' (*c.* 1015), *Skj* B I, 199, 3); and Sigvatr Þórðarson's *ógnar sker* ('menace-skerry', in his *Erfidrápa Óláfs helga* 20 (*c.* 1040), *Skj* B I, 243). Þjóðólfr's kenning is thus untypical, but also extends the metaphor of *fjalfr gjalfra* into a conceit in which Þórr duels with a monstrous cave-bear on an island near the sea: an idiomatic use of *hólmr*, as in f. *hólmganga* ('island-going', 'duel') and *skora e-m á hólm* ('challenge s-one to a duel', lit. 'to an island'), also appears to be intended in *lét falla á randar holmi*.

18/5 *hné*] 'sank.' Kock (*NN* §§ 2504 and 3033) emends all MSS *hne* to *fell* ('fell'), in order to make an *aðalhending* rhyme with *gilja*. As Kiil points out (p. 96), however, *fell* in this line repeats *falla* in 18/1. Finnur keeps *hné* (*Skj* B I, 18), which is in any case closely paralleled in *Skí* 25 (*hnígr sá inn aldni iǫtunn*, 'that old giant will fall') and in *Hárbarðsljóð*:

> Hins viltu nú geta,   er við Hrungnir deildom,
> sá inn stórúðgi iǫtunn,   er ór steini var hǫfuðit á;
> þó lét ec hann falla   oc fyrir *hníga*.
>
> (*Hárb* 15)[65]

The last line, in particular, presents *lét falla* and *hníga* in sequence, as if the poet of *Hárbarðsljóð* was imitating the words *lét falla* and *hné* in *Haustlǫng* 18. These two poems may not be connected in the way that this simple vocabulary suggests, but nonetheless, *Hárb* 15 may show that *hné* rather than *fell* is the genuine form to follow in *Haustlǫng* 18/5, despite the resulting lack of *skothending* on this line.

18/5–6 *grundar gilja gramr*] 'the king of the bottom of ravines', i.e. Hrungnir. This 'rock-dweller' type of giant-kenning is common, with about seventy examples (Meissner, pp. 256–7, § 88.b). Þjóðólfr's kenning not only points to Hrungnir as a preeminent giant, but since Hrungnir is identical with stone, the words *gilja grundar gramr* are also a proleptic indication of his state at the bottom of the ravine after Þórr has shattered him with Mjǫllnir.

18/7 *bǿgði við*] 'pushed against.' All MSS have *bagdi*, which must be emended to make sense, to *bǿgði* (from *bǿgja*, 'to push', 'make one give way'). Finnur renders this verb as 'to overcome' ('overvinde', *Skj* B I, 18), but elsewhere it is used of pushing a ship out from her moorings in *bǿgja skipi ór lægi*. In *Haustlǫng* 18 it is likely that *bǿgja við* alludes to the final part of the story in which Hrungnir collapsed across Þórr's body, with his leg over Þórr's neck. In Snorri's prose version of Þórr's duel with Hrungnir, Þórr cannot lift Hrungnir's leg himself and he and the Æsir, who are now gathered at the scene, must wait until his little son, Magni, arrives; Magni lifts the leg off, proves his strength as Þórr's son and gets Hrungnir's horse as a prize, much to the chagrin of Óðinn, his

---

[65]'Now you want to bring that up, when I contended with Hrungnir, that giant of great courage who had a head of stone on him; and yet I made him drop, I made him *fall* on account of me.'

grandfather. It is uncertain how much of this epilogue is the subject of this part of *Haustlǫng* or how much of it was known to Þjóðólfr even though he did not include its details. In this stanza it seems that Þórr lifts the leg off himself. No other help is implied in *Haustlǫng* and once again, the limited evidence implies that the relevant picture on Þjóðólfr's shield contained no more than the figures of Þórr and Hrungnir, each with his distinguishing symbol: in Þórr's case, his hammer Mjǫllnir; and in Hrungnir's, perhaps the whetstone to which Þjóðólfr alludes in st. 19–20.

18/7–8 berg-Egða brjótr] 'the breaker of the Agðir-men of mountains', i.e. Þórr. Here I read *berg-Egða* for all MSS *berg-Dana*. According to Meissner (pp. 330–1, § 88.r), the baseword *brjótr* is usually applied to rings or weapons in warrior-kennings (cf. *spillir* in note 18/1), but there is one parallel for its use with giants in *moldreks orðbrjótr* ('breaker of the earth-warrior's word', *Skj* B I, 294, 7). Kock (*NN* § 3203) is probably right to emend *berg-Dana* to *berg-Agða*, in order to secure a *skothending* rhyme with *bægði* on the same line. The use of Norwegian regional names in giant-kennings is common, and especially in *Þórsdrápa*, in which, according to a suggestion made by Daphne Davidson, Eilífr intended a political allegory, the giants being the internal and external enemies of Hákon Jarl.[66] With *berg-Agðir* in *Haustlǫng*, therefore, it is reasonable to suppose that Þjóðólfr of Hvinir (Kvinesdal) makes a self-deprecating allusion to the men of Agðir, his own province in the south-west of Norway. The substitution of *Dana* for *Agða* or *Egða* (a better variant) would have come about when a reference to 'Agðir' no longer had any meaning; when, thus, the poem *Haustlǫng* was circulated outside its local context in Norway (probably to Iceland in the tenth century) and when both Icelanders and Norwegians may have regarded 'Danes' as a more appropriate butt of satire. This emendation has thus more to recommend it than any of the others suggested by Kock. Although the form *berg-Dana* is contained in all MSS, a giant-kenning *berg-Agðir* it is enough to point out what is likely to have been Þjóðólfr's form in *Haustlǫng* at the first stage of this poem's development, when it was composed, probably in Þorleifr's province of Hǫrðaland at the end of the ninth century.

18/8 við jǫrmunþrjóti] 'the titanic boor', i.e. Hrungnir. Given that m. *þrjótr* seems to mean 'defiance' or 'obstinacy', Kiil is probably right to take this kenning as an allusion to the colossal weight of Hrungnir when his dead body lies over Þórr, and thus to translate *jǫrmunþrjótr* as 'the big defier' ('den stortrasseren', p. 97). Since Eilífr uses this word metonymously of a giant in the Þórr-kenning *urðar þrjóts støkkvir* ('flight-inciter of the scree-boor') in *Þórsdrápa* 5 (*Skj* B I,

[66]Davidson, 'Earl Hákon and his Poets', pp. 25–30.

140), it is probably correct to treat *jǫrmunþrjótr* as a reference to Hrungnir himself. The *jǫrmun*-prefix derives from an ancient word connoting immense size (and antiquity): other examples are *iǫrmungandr* ('colossal ?magic', a euphemism for the world-serpent in *Vsp* 50); and *iǫrmungrund* ('colossal earth', *Grím* 20). Other Germanic cognates also survive only as prefixes: OS *irmin* (in *Irminsul*, a Saxon pillar by the river Weser which Charlemagne destroyed in 772); and OE *eormen*, which occurs in a number of compounds, such as *eormencyn* ('immense kin', i.e. 'mankind', in *Beo* 1957), *eormenlaf* ('immense legacy', a word for the treasure in the dragon's barrow in *Beo* 2234) and *eormengrund* ('colossal earth', in *Beo* 859, *Juliana* 10 and *Christ* 481). I have translated this prefix as 'titanic' in *Haustlǫng* 18 in order to suggest both the immense size and antiquity of Hrungnir as Þórr begins to shift him off.

19. *And the hard-broken hone of the home-caller of*
Vingnir's warrior-woman whizzed into the ridge of the
brains of Ground's lad, so that there to this day, rigid in
the skull of Óðinn's boy, the pumice-stone of steel blades
has been standing soaked in the blood of Einriði,

19/1 *harðbrotin*] 'hard-broken.' As RWT have *harð brotin*, Kock reads these words as *harðbrotin* (i.e. 'hard-broken hone', *Ska*, p. 12). Given the slight metrical awkwardness of this compound, with the stress on *brotin* much reduced, Finnur emends *harð* to *hǫrð* to make two separate adjectives *hǫrð* and *brotin* both qualifying f. *hein* in 19/4 (*Skj* B I, 18). However, as Kiil points out (p. 98), Hrungnir casts his whetstone as soon as Þórr hurls his hammer and the whetstone breaks when it collides with the hammer in mid air. Thus the greater hardness of Mjǫllnir, which Þjóðólfr appears to describe as *harðr* in 17/5, may be seen in the compound adjective *harðbrotin* which qualifies *hein* in 19/1.

19/1–2 *herju heimþingaðar Vingnis*] 'the home-caller of Vingnir's warrior-woman', i.e. Hrungnir. *Vingnir* is a name for a giant in the *Þulur* (*SnE* I, 550) and Finnur (*Skj* B I, 18), Magnús (p. 351, n. 70) and Faulkes (*SSE*, p. 81) all take Vingnir to be a *heiti* for 'giant'. Yet *Vingnir* also refers to Óðinn (*SnE* II, 472) and Þórr is known as *fóstri Vingnis* ('Vingnir's foster-son', *ibid.* I, 252). Kiil, however, identifies Vingnir in *Haustlǫng* 19 with Þórr (pp. 98–9). In older texts, in both *Vaf* 51 as Snorri quotes this stanza in *Gylfaginning* (ch. 53, p. 54) and in variant readings of *Vaf* 53, *Vingnir* is given as the name of the father of Móði and Magni, whom we know to be Þórr from *Hárb* 9. *Vingþórr* is Þórr's name, furthermore, in *Þrym* 1. If Vingnir is Þórr, as the earliest references thus suggest, then his *herja* ('warrior-woman') may be *Þrúðr* and Þjóðólfr's kenning may allude to Hrungnir as a would-be seducer of Þrúðr, Þórr's girlfriend. Eilífr alludes rather insolently to Þrúðr (while Þórr duels with Geirrøðr) as one of two women other than Sif in Þórr's life:

Svát hraðskyndir handa   hrapmunnum svalg gunnar
lyptisylg á lopti   langvinr síu Þrǫngvar,
þás ǫrþrasis eisa   ós Hrímnis fló drósar
til þrámóðnis Þrúðar   þjóst af greipar brjósti.

(Þórsdrápa 17)[67]

It is not known who Þrǫng (only here) might be. If not identical with Sif, the
long-established wife of Þórr in a number of sources (cf. Eysteinn Valdason, *Skj*
B I, 131, 1 (*c.* 1000); *Hym* 3, 15 and 34; *Þrym* 24; and in the thirteenth- or
fourteenth-century *Ævikviða*, attributed to Grettir Ásmundarson, *Skj* B I, 288,
7), Þrǫng may be considered as a name for Freyja; or even as synonymous with
Þrúðr, whom Eilífr's kenning *þrámóðnir Þrúðar* ('eager and persistent yearner
after Þrúðr') implies to be Þórr's lover. Although Eysteinn above refers to Þórr
as Þrúðr's father, and Snorri again in *SnE* I, 252–4, it is worth noting that in
Grím 36 (a verse which Snorri quotes in *Gylf*, ch. 36 (p. 30) Þrúðr is described
as a valkyrie. This description makes Þrúðr the most likely referent of the unique
herja ('warrior-woman') in *Haustlǫng* 19. If we put these ninth- and tenth-century scraps of information together, it appears that 'Vingnir's warrior-woman'
(Kiil reads *Vingnis hetja*, 'Vingnir's hero (-woman)') is a kenning for Þrúðr, a
valkyrie whom Hrungnir has visited in her home while her lover Þórr was out.
The word *heimþinguðr* at first implies nothing but 'one who initiates a meeting
at home': this word is found in *hanga heimþinguðr* ('hanged man's home-caller'),
an emended kenning for Óðinn in a verse attributed to the tenth-century skald
Þorbjǫrn Brúnason (*Skj* A I, 209, 3; B I, 199, 3); and there are two man-kennings
with *þinguðr* (cf. Meissner, p. 324, § 88.o). Yet OIce n. *þing* has an erotic meaning when applied to a female subject: Óðinn boasts to Þórr that he 'played with
the linen-white woman and arranged a secret meeting' (*léc ec við ina línhvíto
oc launþing háðac*) in *Hárb* 30; and Skírnir implies a sexual encounter when he
asks Gerðr 'when it is that you will appoint a meeting with the vigorous son of
Njǫrðr' (*nær þú á þingi munt inom þrosca nenna Niarðar syni*) in *Ski* 38. So the
word *heimþinguðr* in Þjóðólfr's kenning may imply Hrungnir's sexual interest in
the *herja* Þrúðr while her lover Vingnir, apparently a name for Þórr, was out.
Snorri says that Hrungnir threatened to destroy Ásgarð *en drepa goð ǫll nema
Freyju ok Sif vill hann heim fœra með sér* ('and kill all the gods except that
Freyja and Sif he will take *home* with him', *SnE* I, 278). Snorri thus seems to
know a version of this story in which Hrungnir threatened to steal Þórr's wife,

[67]*Skj* B I, 143: 'in such a way that the swift-hastener of battle [Þórr], the long-
term friend of Þrǫng, swallowed with his hands' quick mouths the lifted draught
of a molten ember in the air, when the wild sparking flame flew from the grip's
breast [hand] of the passionate coveter of Hrímnir's lady [giantess-lover, Geirrøðr]
towards Þrúðr's eager and persistent yearner'. I am grateful, as ever, to Jon
Grove for allowing me to consult his translation of this difficult poem.

plus another goddess. In this way, when Þórr arrives in the hall, Snorri succeeds in presenting him as both a valiant protector of the Æsir and a respectably married man (as if he were Hector of Troy: cf. the epilogue to *Gylf*, ch. 54, *SnE* I, 206). It is possible that both Eysteinn's and Snorri's references to Þrúðr as Þórr's daughter were intended to stabilize the image of this god as a middle-aged figure at the heart of a family which also consisted of father and mother (Óðinn and Earth), sons (Magni and Móði), a step-son (Ullr), a mistress (Járnsaxa) and a loving wife (Sif, cf. *Skáld*, ch. 4). But it does not follow that Þjóðólfr had the same idea of Þórr in the late ninth century as Eysteinn did in the late tenth or Snorri in the early thirteenth. In Þjóðólfr's poem Þórr appears, on the contrary, to be youthful, hot-headed and now apparently infuriated that Hrungnir has made advances to Þrúðr while he was out. Something of this image of Þórr may survive in a story preserved in one text of *Gautreks saga* (ch. 7) in which Þórr curses Starkaðr, his father's protégé, because Starkaðr's grandmother had once rejected Þórr in favour of a giant.[68] Þórr as an angry lover is an image which brings Þjóðólfr's tradition a step closer to the (otherwise dissimilar) story contained c. 850 in Bragi's kenning *Þrúðar þjófs ilja blað* ('leaf of the foot-soles of the thief of Þrúðr', Hrungnir's shield, i.e. shield) in *Ragnarsdrápa* 1 (*Skj* B I, 1). Þjóðólfr thus shows why Þórr dispatches Hrungnir so quickly even while he describes a sherd from the whetstone hurtling back towards Þórr. At the same time, there is a dismissive humour in Hrungnir's role as *heimþinguðr herju Vingnis*, for what is a giant with a whetstone but a travelling knife-grinder when he calls on an unattended valkyrie in her home? This mockery of Hrungnir may be compared with Þjóðólfr's allusion to Þjazi in *Haustlǫng* 13 as *sonr biðils Greipar* ('the son of Greip's suitor'), whereby Þjazi's chances of survival are compared unfavourably with those of his father in the house of Geirrøðr (see note to 13/3–4).

19/3 *í hjarna mæni*] 'into the ridge of the brains', i.e. into the brow, or into the skull generally. The gen. pl. *hjarna* must be emended from RT *hinka* and W *hina*. Only *hinna* might make some sense, as Marold points out (p. 174), if this form were read as the gen. pl. of *hinna* ('of membranes', from f. *hinna*), thus as 'into the ridge of membranes'. But *í hjarna mæni* seems less strained, especially since Þjóðólfr uses m. *hjarni* ('brain') in his description of King Aðils' death in *Ynglingatal* 22, where Aðils falls from the saddle, hits his head on a stone *ok við aur ægir hjarna bragnings burs of blandin varð* ('and with the mud the sea of the king's son's brains was blended'). The head-kenning *hjarna mænir* is furthermore parelleled by *hjarna háturn* ('brains' high-tower', *Háttalykill*, *Skj* B I, 496–7, 20b), *hjarna byggð* ('brains' settlement', *ibid*. B II, 17, 35),

[68]*Fornaldarsögur Norðurlanda*, ed Guðni Jónsson and Bjarni Vilhjálmsson, 3 vols. (Reykjavik, 1944) III, 12–29.

hjarna kleif ('brains' cliff', *ibid*. B I, 650, 7) and *hjarna klettr* ('brains' crag', *ibid*. B II, 79, 64; cf. Meissner, p. 127, § 45.b).

19/4 *at Grundar sveini*] 'of Ground's lad', i.e. of Þórr. The use of *at* as a possessive preposition is paralleled with *åt* in Norwegian dialects to this day, although rare in Modern Icelandic (*móðir at barni*, 'the mother of the child'), unless after a partitive verb such as *nema* ('to take', 'learn'). The closest extant analogue of the Þórr-kenning *Grundar sveinn* is Þjóðólfr's own *Jarðar sunr* in *Haustlǫng* 14, at the beginning of this narrative sequence; *iarðar burr* in *Þrym* 1 and (probably) *Lok* 58 are also similar; the other allusions to Þórr through his mother the earth, *Hlǫðyniar mǫgr* and *Fiǫrgyniar burr* both in *Vsp* 56, are more elaborate. Þjóðólfr thus takes his leave of Þórr (whether for a while, or for good in this poem, it is not clear).

19/5 *eðr*] 'to this day.' Snorri repeats this important adverb with his own *enn*, before appearing to instructs his readers to throw a (new) whetstone across the floor in order to dislodge the hone in Þórr's head: *ok stendr enn í hǫfði Þór; ok er þat boðit til varnanar at kasta hein of gólf þvert, því at þá hrœrisk heinin í hǫfði Þór* (*SnE* I, 278). Þjóðólfr, however, makes no such point out of the whetstone in Þórr's head, although an aetiology of sorts is implicit in his statement that the sherd stays there 'to this day'.

19/7 *stála vikr*] 'the pumice-stone of steel blades.' Þjóðólfr's close attention to the whetstone here and in the rest of this stanza suggests that it was an object represented on his shield whereby he could identify Þórr's opponent as Hrungnir.

19/8 *Einriða*] 'of Einriði', i.e. of Þórr. This rare name is unknown in the Eddic corpus, but is found as a *heiti* for Þórr in the Prologue to *Gylfaginning* (*Gylf*, p. 5: probably not entirely by Snorri) and in the *Þulur* (*SnE* I, 553). Also spelt *Eindriði*, with a medial *d*, this name apparently belonged in the tenth century to Eindriði Styrkársson of Gimsar, whom Snorri cites in *Haralds saga gráfeldar* (ch. 14) and in *Óláfs saga Tryggvasonar* (ch. 101).[69] Given that this name appears to mean 'single-rider' (*einn-riði*, cf. *ball-riði*, 'bold-rider', Freyr's epithet in *Lok* 37), it may be right for Þórr, to whose chariot-riding Þjóðólfr alludes with *hógreið* in *Haustlǫng* 15/6 and *reiði-Týr* later in st. 20/3.

---

[69]*Heimskringla I*, ed. Bjarni, pp. 218 and 353.

20. *until such time as a nursing-Gefjun of the wounds of*
the chariot-Týr might chant the red horror of rust's boast-
ing out of his hair's sloping hillsides. I behold these
expeditions clearly on the fortress of Geitir. I have received
the coloured cliff of the shield-rim, painted with tales, from
Þórleifr.

20/1–2 *ór hneigihlíðum hárs*] 'out of his hair's sloping hillsides.' This kenning
for Þórr's head is a particularly vivid example of a 'hair's land' type of head-
kenning of which there are fifteen other examples, in sixteen instances, including *skarar háfjall* ('hairlock's high-fell', *Hym* 23), *skarar haugr* ('hairlock's
mound', *Skj* B I 63, 5) and *svarðar strǫnd* ('hair-sward's beach', *ibid.* B I, 495,
16; cf. Meissner, p. 127, § 45.b). Kock puts this kenning with gen. pl. *sára* in 20/2,
in order to show Þórr's 'sores' in this case (*NN* § 1918 A), but it is more straightforward to link *sára* with *ǫl-Gefjun* in the following.

20/2–3 *ǫl-Gefjun sára*] 'a nursing-Gefjun of wounds'. This kenning may allude
to Gróa, whose chants to remove the whetstone-sherd from Þórr's head come to
nothing when he interrupts her with a prematurely grateful tale concerning her
husband Aurvandill. Þjóðólfr has already used both *ár-Gefn* ('plenty-Gefn')
and *ǫl-Gefn* ('nursing-Gefn') as kennings for Iðunn in the earlier surviving part
of *Haustlǫng* (st. 2/6 and 11/2 respectively; cf. notes). The name *Gefn* denotes
the 'giving' for which Iðunn, as an aspect of Freyja, is invaluable; in 2/6 this
name appears to be synonymous with *Gefjun*, to whom Þjóðólfr alludes here in
an equally specific way. Although neither Freyja nor Gefjun seems to be intended as the subject of this kenning, Þjóðólfr here probably alludes to the story
in which Gefjun's ploughteam drags enough land out of Sweden for a new island in the Øresund. As Bragi says in *Ragnarsdrápa* 13, 'Gefjun drew, gleaming, from Gylfi the deep-sea sun [jewel] of his estates, to the increase of Denmark' (*Gefjun dró frá Gylfa glǫð djúprǫðul óðla, Danmarkar auka*, in *Skj* B I,
3). The implication in *ǫl-Gefjun sára* of an extraction on this gigantic scale
builds on Þjóðólfr's conceit of Þórr's supernatural size in *hneigihlíð hárs* in
20/1–2.

20/3 *reiði-Týs*] 'of the chariot-Týr', i.e. of Þórr. Kock emends RWT *reiþi* to
reiðar to make *reiðar-Týr*, 'the chariot-god' ('vagnguden', *NN* § 1918 B), because Snorri defines Þórr with this form in the *Bragarœður* (*svá ok at kalla
Reiðartý*, in *SnE* I, 230); but his meaning is the same as that supported by *reið* in
hógreið in st. 15/6. Finnur (*Skj* B I, 18), Magnús (p. 352, n. 71) and Faulkes
(*SSE*, p. 81) all take *sára* with *reiði-Týs*, to translate these words along the lines
of 'god who inflicts injuries', i.e. as a more militant kenning for Þórr than
simply 'chariot-god'. Þórr's role has certainly been violent in the poem up to
now; however, since *reiði-Týr* works well enough on its own whereas *ǫl-Gefjun*
does not, it seems better to leave *sára* with the latter kenning for the sorceress
Gróa.

20/3–4 *et rauða ryðs hælibǫl*] 'the red horror of rust's boasting', i.e. the whet-stone-sherd. The minute detail of this kenning for Hrungnir's hone, a variant of *stála vikr* in 19/7, again emphasises the likelihood that Þjóðólfr saw it painted on his shield as an object that along with Mjǫllnir (see note to 17/5–8) helped to distinguish Hrungnir from Þórr.

20/5–6 *á Geitis garði*] 'on the fortress of Geitir', i.e. on the shield. This shield-kenning is one of eighteen surviving examples of the type '(sea-)king's wall', including Vigfúss Víga-Glúmsson's *Geitis hurð* ('Geitir's door', in a poem about Hákon Jarl (*c.* 985), *Skj* B I, 115, 1), Bragi's *Hjarranda hurð* ('Hjarrandi's door', in *Ragnarsdrápa* 11, *Skj* B I, 3) and Einarr Skúlason's *Reifnis rann* ('Reifnir's house', in *Geisli* (1153), *Skj* B I, 441, 54; cf. Meissner, p. 172, § 80.c). On analogy with his proleptic shield-kenning *Finns ilja brú* ('bridge of the Lapp's foot-sole') in 13/6, one reason why Þjóðólfr chooses this type of shield-kenning above others in 20/6 may be to anticipate the story of a sea-battle (as in Bragi's story of Hǫgni and Heðinn) in a part of *Haustlǫng* which is no longer extant.

20/6 *ferðir*] 'expeditions.' Holtsmark emends all MSS *farðir* to *ferðir*, on the grounds that the form **fǫrð*, which would be required as the singular of *farðir*, is never found as a variant of OIce *ferð* ('journey'): '*a* came in because the scribe expected *aðalhending*' ('*a* er kommet inn fordi skriveren ventet adalhending', p. 9). In the absence of a recorded *o*-stem variant of *ferð* in any Germanic language, this argument has much to recommend it. Kiil, however, reconstructs a noun f. **farð*, which he translates as 'colour' ('farge') on the basis of a Nynorsk noun of that meaning, f. *fard*; Þjóðólfr's line would thus mean 'clearly I see these coloured-in figures on the fence of Geitir ('tydelig ser jeg disse fargelagte figurene på Geites gjerde', p. 104).[70]

20/7–8 see note to 13/7–8.

[70]Cf. Aasen, *Norsk Ordbog*, p. 144. Also according to Aasen (*ibid.*, p. 145), the Nynorsk f. noun *farde* means 'a kind of thin mould (mucor) on liquid, especially on milk' ('et Slags tynd Skimmel (mucor) paa Væedske, især paa Mælk'). Kiil uses also *farde* in support of his reading *farðir* in *Haustlǫng* 20/6.

III

Glossary

Only poetic instances are instanced.

1st	first person	num.	number
2nd	second person	P	in the prose
3rd	third person	pcl.	particle
a.	adjective	pl.	plural
acc.	accusative	poss.	possessive
adv.	adverb	pp.	past participle
art.	article	pref.	prefix
card.	cardinal	prep.	preposition
conj.	conjunction	pres.	present
dat.	dative	pret.	preterite
def.	definite	pron.	pronoun
f.	feminine	refl.	reflexive
gen.	genitive	rel.	relative
impers.	impersonal	sg.	singular
indef.	indefinite	subj.	subjunctive
inf.	infinitive	sup.	supine
instr.	instrumental	superl.	superlative
intrans.	intransitive	sv.	strong verb
m.	masculine	tr.	transitive
n.	neuter	v.	verb
neg.	negative	w.	with
nom.	nominative	wv.	weak verb

á, prep. (w acc.) on, onto, to (2/8; P); (w. dat.) on (1/7, 13/5, 14/3, 18/4, 20/6; P), in (*á Baldri*, in Baldr P), into (*upp á himin*, up into the sky P)

á, see *eiga*

ábyrgð, f. responsibility, something at stake (P)

áðr, adv. before (6/5, P), until (20/1), previously (P)

af, prep. (w. dat.) off (6/3), from (3/8, 4/3, 5/5, P), from among (*af Ásum*, from among the Æsir P), with (*af ǫllu afli*, with all his strength P); adv. of (him) (P), off (P)

afl, n. strength (P)

aka, sv. drive (3rd sg. pret. *ók* 14/5)

ákafliga, adv. mightily, with great speed (P)

ákveðinn, pp. appointed (P)

aldri, adv. never (P)

allfrægr, a. very famous (P)

allhræddr, a. very scared (P)

allr, a. all (f. nom. pl. *allar* 10/5, n. nom. pl. *ǫll* 7/3, 15/1; P)

allreiðr, a. very angry, enraged (P)

allþarfliga, adv. very urgently, in dire need (P)

annarr, ǫnnur, annat, a. other (P)
aptr, adv. back, back here (11/8)
ár-Gefn, f. harvest-Gefn (gen. sg. 2/6; see note)
armr, m. arm (gen. pl. 7/2)
arnarhamr, m. eagle's shape (P)
arnarins, see *ǫrn*
arnsúgr, m. eagle-soughing, eagle's wingdraft (acc. sg. 12/8; P)
Ása-Þórr, m. Þórr of the Æsir (P)
ásǫl, n. ale of the Æsir (P)
Ásgarðr, m. home of the Æsir (P)
Ásgrind, f. the Æsir's gate (P)
ásmóðr, m. a god's fury (P)
áss, m. a god, a member of the Æsir (nom. pl. *æsir* 2/5, gen. pl. *ása* 5/7, 9/3, 12/2; P)
at, prep. (w. acc.) after (*at þat* 5/6, 10/2); (w. dat.) at, in (1/1, 10/6, P; *at ákveðinni stundu*, at an appointed time P), for (*at sinni*, for the time being P), by (*at fótum*, by his feet P), from (1/4, 13/8, 20/8), of (19/4), right onto (12/7), towards (14/5), to meet (*at fundi* 15/8, *at móti*, 2/2); to (w. inf. *at bíða* 17/8)
at, conj. that (*þat* 12/1; P), so that (P)
át, see *eta*
átt, átti, áttu, see *eiga*
átt, f. kin-group, kin (nom. pl. 10/5)
áttrunnr, m. kin-branch, family member (nom. sg. 9/4)
auga, n. eye (P)
aukinn, a. increased, strengthened (m. nom. sg. 12/4)
Aurvandill, m. friend of Þórr (P)
Aurvandilstá, f. Aurvandill's toe, possibly a star (P)
Austrvegar, m. pl. regions in the east (P)

bað, see *biðja*
báðir, báðar, bæði, a. both (P)
bak, n. back (*á baki sér* P)
Baldr, m. a dying god (gen. 16/1; P)
ballr, a. bold (m. acc. sg. superl. 6/6)
band, n. bond (dat. pl. 7/4); (pl.) the gods (nom. *bǫnd* 17/2)
bani, m. bane, killer (acc. sg. 16/8; P)
bára, f. wave, surf (gen. sg. 3/6)
barmi, m. bosom-brother (nom. sg. 16/1)

barn, n. bairn, child (dat. sg. 12/7)
báru, bǫru, see *bera*
batt, see *binda*
bauð, see *bjóða*
baugr, m. ring (dat. sg. 14/4), shield-rim (gen. sg. 13/7, 20/7)
beið, see *bíða*
bein, n. leg, bone (gen. pl. 3/2)
bekkr, m. beck, brook; bench (gen. sg. 9/5; see note)
Beli, m. 'bellower', a giant (gen. *Belja* 18/3)
bera, sv. bear, carry (P; 3rd pl. pret. *bǫru* 2/6, *báru* P; pp. *borit* P)
berg, n. mountain (nom. pl. 16/2)
berg-Agðir, m. pl. Agðir-men of mountains (gen. 18/7; see note)
berg-dolgr, m. mountain-foe (dat. sg. 16/2; see note)
berja (barða), wv. beat (P); (refl.) fight (P).
bíða, sv. (w. gen.) bide, wait for (inf. 17/8; 3rd sg. pret. *beið* P)
biðill, m. wooer, suitor (gen. sg. 13/3)
biðja, sv. (acc. person, gen. thing) bid, ask (P; 3rd sg. pret. *bað* 4/1, 5/1, 9/1), beg (inf. 8/8)
bif, n. tale; image (dat. pl. 13/7, see note; 20/7)
bifkleif, f. coloured cliff (acc. sg. 13/8, 20/8)
bila (að), wv. fail, hesitate (P)
binda, sv. bind (3rd pl. pret. *bundu* 11/4); (w. um) tie around (3rd sg. pret. *batt um* P)
bjarg, n. rock, cliff (nom. pl. *bjǫrg* 16/3; gen. pl. 2/7, 17/1)
bjartr, a. bright (gen. pl. 10/1; see note)
bjóð, n. (earth-) table (dat. sg. 5/5; cf. *Burs synir bjóðum um yppo*, 'Burr's sons lifted up tables of earth', *Vsp* 4)
bjóða, sv. offer, challenge (3rd sg. pret. *bauð* P, 3rd pl. pret. *buðu* P), recommend (sup. *boðit* P)
bjǫrg, see *bjarg*
blása, sv. blow (inf. 4/4)
bleyði, f. cowardice (dat. 2/8)
blóð, n. blood (dat. sg. 19/8)
blóði, m. blood-kinsman (poss. dat. sg. 14/7)
boð, n. invitation, challenge (P)

boðit, see *bjóða*
bógr, m. (animal's) shoulder (P)
bolmr, m. bear (acc. sg. 18/4)
borð, n. table, margin, mountain-top (gen. pl. 10/1; see note)
borg, f. fortress, citadell (P)
borgarveggr, m. fortress-wall (P)
borit, see *bera*
brá, see *bregða*
bragðvíss, a. prank-wise (m. nom. sg. 5/6)
Bragi, m. a minor member of the Æsir (P)
brann, see *brinna*
brast, see *bresta*
brátt, adv. quickly (17/1, P)
braut, adv. away, off
braut, see *brjóta*
bregða, sv. (w. dat.) turn, change (3rd sg. pret. *brá* P); (refl.) start, move (3rd sg. pres. *bregzk* P)
breiðr, a. broad (n. dat. sg. 5/5, P)
bresta, sv. burst, shatter (3rd sg. pret. *brast* P; 3rd pl. pret. *brustu* 16/3)
brinna, sv. burn (inf. 13/2, 15/4; 3rd sg. pret. *brann* 16/4)
Brísingr, m. unknown figure associated with Freyja's necklace (gen. sg. 9/6; see note)
brjóta, sv. break, (w. *af*) break off (3rd sg. pret. *braut af* P)
brjótr, m. breaker (nom. sg. 18/8)
bróðir, m. brother (P; see also note to 14/7)
brotna (að), wv. intr. break (P)
brú, f. bridge (acc. sg. 1/2; dat. sg. 13/6)
brunnakr, m. well-spring's cornfield (gen. sg. 9/5; see note)
brustu, see *bresta*
brynja, f. coat of mail (P)
bú, n. house, dwelling (P)
buðu, see *bjóða*
bundu, see *binda*
burr, m. boy (gen. sg. 19/6)
byggvendr, m. pl. dwellers, those who dwell (nom. 10/2)
byrðr, f. load (P)
byrgi-Týr, m. the Týr who would imprison (nom. 2/7; see note)
bægja (ð), wv. make give way, push (3rd sg. pret. w. *við*, off 18/7; see note)

bǫlverðung, f. horrific troop (gen. sg. 18/3)
bǫnd, see *band*
bǫrr, m. tree (acc. sg. 14/3)

dagr, m. day (P)
dalr, m. dale, valley (P)
deila (d), wv. deal out, distribute (inf. 4/2, 5/4)
dís, f. (divine) lady (dat. sg. 9/6; nom. pl. 17/4, see note)
djúphugaðr, a. deep-minded, deep-counselled (m. nom. sg. 6/5)
dolgr, m. enemy, foe (acc. sg. 6/6; dat. sg. 16/2, see *berg-dolgr*)
dóttir, f. daughter (P)
draga, sv. draw (3rd pl. pret. *drógu* 15/6), move with (3rd sg. pret. *dró* P)
drápu, see *drepa*
drekka, sv. drink (P)
drepa, sv. beat, strike (3rd sg. pret. subj. *dræpi* 6/5), kill (inf. P, 3rd pl. pret. *drápu* P)
dró, drógu, see *draga*
dróttinn, m. lord (nom. sg. 5/1)
drukkinn, pp. drunk (P)
drykkja, f. drink (P)
dræpi, see *drepa*
dynja (dunða), wv. din, clatter (3rd sg. pret. 14/6)
dæligr, a. pleasant to look at (P)
dœmi, n. example, instance (P)

eða, conj. or, and (P)
eðr (= *enn*), conj. and yet (14/1), to this day (19/5)
ef, conj. if (P)
eiga, pret. pres. v. have, own (3rd sg. pres. *á* P, 3rd sg. pret. *átti* P, 3rd pl. pret. *áttu* P, pp. *átt* P)
eigi, adv. not (P)
eik, f. oak (P)
eikirót, f. oak-tree's root (dat. pl. 6/3)
einn, ein, eitt, a. one (P)
Einriði, m. a name for Þórr (gen. 19/8)
einvígi, n. single combat, duel (P)
ek, 1st pron. I (13/7, P; dat. sg. *mér* P)
ekki, adv. nothing (P)
ekkja, f. widow (nom. sg. 15/7)
elding, f. fiery body, star (P)
eldr, m. fire, flames (P)

Élivágar, m. pl. 'snowstorm waves', cosmic rivers (P; see *Gylf*, pp. 9–10 and 165)

ellilyf, n. old-age medicine (acc. sg. 9/3, P)

en, conj. and, and yet (5/5, 7/7, 13/3, 18/7, P), while (13/1, 14/6, 15/1)

endi, m. end (acc. sg. 7/8, P)

endilágr, a. down below (f. nom. sg. 15/2)

engi, engi, ekki, a. pron. no-one (P)

enn, adv. still, yet (P)

epli, n. apple (P)

ept, adv. back (12/2)

eptir, prep. (w. dat.) after, behind (P), in accordance with (*eptir þeirri sǫgu* P); adv. behind, afterwards (P)

er (= *es*), rel. ptcl. and conj. who, which, that (P); when (P); where (P)

er, eru, see *vera*

ern, a. vigorous (m. acc. sg. 12/7)

erninum, see *ǫrn*

es, rel. ptcl. and conj. where (14/1)

et (= *it*), the (n. def. art. acc. 20/3)

eta, sv. eat (3rd sg. pret. *át*)

eyðimǫrk, f. desert, wilderness (P)

eygja (ð), wv. eye, glare at (3rd pl. pres. 7/3)

fá, sv. get, obtain (inf. P, 3rd sg. pres. *fær* P, 3rd pl. pret. *fengu* P, 3rd sg. pret. subj. *fengi* P)

faðir, m. father (nom. sg. 6/4, 8/4, 12/8, P)

fáðr, a. painted (f. acc. sg. 13/7, 20/7; n. nom. sg. 13/5)

fagna (að), wv. rejoice at, welcome (P)

fagr, a. fair, beautiful (P)

falla, sv. fall (inf. 18/1, 3rd sg. pres. *fellr* P); (refl.) fall (P)

fangsæll, a. happy in his booty (m. nom. sg. 8/2)

fann, see *finna*

fár, a. few, little (P)

far, n. passage, track, destiny (acc. sg. 1/6)

fara, sv. go, travel, come (3rd sg. pres. *ferr* P, 3rd sg. pret. *fór* P, 3rd pl. pret. *fóru* P, m. nom. sg. pp. *farinn* P, pl. pp. *farnir* 4/8)

Fárbauti, m. Loki's father, probably a giant (gen. 5/2)

farðir, see *ferð*

farmr, m. cargo (nom. sg. 7/2)

farnir, see *fara*

fastr, a. set fast (m. nom. sg. 7/1; f. nom. sg. *fǫst* P)

feginn, a. glad (P)

fellr, see *falla*

fengi, fengu, see *fá*

ferð, f. journey, expedition (P; emended acc. pl. *ferðir* 20/6; see note)

ferr, see *fara*

fet-Meili, m. stepping-Meili (acc. sg. 4/2; see note)

fiðri, n. feathers (P)

finna, sv. find, meet (3rd pl. pret. *fundu* 11/2, sup. *fundit* P); (w. *fyrir*), notice (P)

Finnr, m. a Lapp (gen. sg. 13/6)

fjalfr, n. hiding-place, hide-out (gen. sg. 18/2)

fjall, n. fell, mountain (P; gen. pl. 13/5)

fjallgylðir, m. wolf of the fells (nom. sg. 4/1)

fjórir, card. num. four (acc. pl. 5/8)

fjǫðr, f. feather (gen. sg. *fjaðrar* 12/6)

fjǫllami, a. many-times-mutilating (m. gen. sg. 17/8; see note)

fjǫrspillir, m. life-spoiler (nom. sg. 18/1)

flaug, see *fljúga*

fleiri, a. more, further (P)

fljótt, adv. swiftly (5/1)

fljúga, sv. fly (3rd sg. pres. *flýgr* P, 3rd sg. pret. *fló* 2/1, 8/1, 17/1, *flaug* P)

fló, see *fljúga*

flokkr, m. herd (P)

flugbjalfi, m. flying-fur (instr. dat. sg. 12/4)

flugr, m. flight (P)

flýgr, see *fljúga*

fold, f. earth, the land (gen. sg. 5/1)

fólskuverk, n. act of folly (P)

fór, fóru, see *fara*

forkunnar, adv. exceptionally (P)

forn, a. ancient (m. dat. sg. 3/8)

fóstri, m. foster-father (acc. sg. 7/1)

fótr, m. foot (nom. acc. pl. *fœtr* P)

frá, prep. (w. dat.) from (17/5, P)

frák, see *fregna*

fram, adv. forward (15/6; *fram at, fram yfir* P)

frami, m. fame, glory (P)

frásǫgn, f. report, story (P)

fregna, sv. hear of, learn (1st sg. pret. *frák* 16/5)

Freyja, f. goddess of the Vanir (P)

friðr, m. (peace-) contract, deal (gen. sg. 8/8, P)

fróðugr, a. experienced, wise now (m. dat. sg. 8/1)

frægr, a. famous (P)

frœkinn, a. valiant (P)

frørinn, pp. frozen (P)

fundi, see *at* (prep.)

fundit, fundu, see *finna*

furðu, adv. amazingly (P)

fylli, f. (one's) fill (gen. sg. 4/1, P)

fyr (= *fyrir*), prep. (w. dat.) for (*fyrir* P), before (*fyr* 18/6), of (*fyrir sér*, of oneself P), because of, thanks to (*fyr* 15/2; *fyrir því at*, conj. because P), ago (w. *ó- fyr -skǫmmu* 2/4; w. *lǫngu* 6/2); (w. acc.) *fyrir innan*, on the inside of (P); adv. before (*fyrir* P), in exchange (*fyrir* P)

fyrr, comp. adv. before (P); as conj. *fyrr en,* before, earlier than (P)

fyrstr, a. superl. first (P)

fær, see *fá*

fœra (ð), wv. bring, take (inf. 9/2, P)

fǫr, f. journey (acc. or dat. sg. 13/4, P)

fǫst, see *fastr*

gaf, see *gefa*

gala, sv. chant (3rd sg. pret. *gól* P, subj. *gæli* 20/4)

galdr, m. spell, charm (P)

gamall, a. old, worn-out (m. dat. sg. 2/3; f. nom. pl. 10/8; P)

ganga, sv. go (P; 3rd sg. pret. *gekk* w. *sundr,* split asunder 15/7, 3rd pl. pret. *gengu* P)

garðr, m. dwelling, courtyard (dat. sg. 20/7; acc. pl. 9/7)

gat, see *geta*

gefa, sv. give (3rd sg. pret. *gaf* P)

gegna (d), wv. (w. dat.) mean (P)

geirr, m. spear (dat. sg. 11/4; see note)

geit, f. (she-) goat (P)

Geitir, m. a sea-king (gen. 20/5)

gekk, see *ganga*

gemlir, m. vulture (gen. sg. 2/3)

gengu, see *ganga*

gera, wv. do, make (P); (refl.) become (P)

geta, sv. (w. pp.) be able to (3rd sg. pret. *gat* P)

gil, n. gill, ravine (gen. pl. *gilja* 18/5)

gildi, n. feast, banquet (P)

ginnregin, n. pl. enticer-gods (nom. 13/2)

ginnungr, m. falcon (gen. pl. 15/4; see note)

girðiþjófr, m. girdle-thief (nom. sg. 9/7; see note)

gjald, n. payment (dat. pl. 1/1)

gjalfr, n. sea-swell (gen. pl. 18/2)

gjǫrr, pp. made (P)

glamm, n. din, crash, clatter (gen. pl. 2/4; see note)

goð, n. a god (P; gen. pl. 4/8, 9/6)

góðr, a. good (P; m. gen. sg. 1/1)

gól, see *gala*

gólf, n. floor (P)

gramr, m. prince, king (nom. sg. 18/6)

gráp, n. hail (dat. sg. 15/3)

Greip, f. 'clutch', a giantess (gen. 13/4; see note)

greip, see *grípa*

grið, n. quarter, sanctuary (P)

grípa, sv. grip, seize (3rd sg. pret. *greip* P)

gripr, m. precious thing (P)

grjót, n. stone (P)

grjót-Níðuðr, m. rock-Níðuðr (gen. - *Níðaðar* 9/8; see note)

Grjótúnagarðar, m. pl. realm of Grjótúnir (a proper noun P)

grjót[t]ún, f. stone-enclosure (gen. pl. 14/4; see note)

Gróa, f. 'grove', Aurvandill's wife and Þórr's nurse (P)

grund, f. ground (nom. sg. 15/3), bottom (gen. sg. 18/5), Ground (= Þórr's mother, gen. 19/4)

Gullfaxi, m. 'gold-mane', Hrungnir's horse (P)

gullhjálmr, m. golden helmet (P)

gunnveggr, m. battle-wall, shield (gen. sg. 1/2)

gýgjarsonr, m. giantess' son (P)
gæta (tt), wv. watch over; (refl.) deliberate (10/5; see note)
gætandi, m. f. she who keeps (P)
gætir, m. keeper (dat. sg. 17/1)
gœli, see *gala*
gǫrla, adv. clearly (20/5)

hafa (ð), wv. have (P)
hafr, m. buck, billy-goat (nom. pl. 15/5)
Haki, m. 'hook', a sea-king (gen. 16/6)
hallardyrr, f. pl. hall-doors (P)
háls, m. neck (P)
hamarr, m. hammer (dat. sg. 18/6)
hamljótr, a. ugly of shape, looking ugly
(n. nom. pl. 10/8)
hamr, m. skin, shape (dat. sg. 2/3)
hann, hon, þat, pron. he, she, it (P; m.
dat. sg. *hǫnum* 3/7, 14/8)
hapta, see *hǫpt*
hár, a. high (P)
hár, n. hair (P; gen. sg. 20/2)
harðbrotinn, a. hard-broken (f. nom. sg.
19/1)
harðr, a. hard (m. dat. sg. *hǫrðu[m]* 17/5)
harmr, m. harm, sorrow (P)
hárr, a. grey-haired (m. nom. pl. P; f.
nom. pl. 10/7)
haugr, m. grave-mound (gen. sg. 14/4)
haukr, m. hawk (gen. sg. 12/4)
hauss, m. skull (P; dat. sg. 19/6)
Haustlǫng, f. 'autumn-long [poem]',
Þjóðólfr's poem (P)
hefja, sv. begin (3rd sg. pret. *hóf*, pl. *hófu*
P), start to (3rd pl. pret. *hófu* 13/1)
hefna (d), wv. (w. gen.) avenge (P)
heilagr, a. holy (m. dat. sg. *helgum* 4/3)
heimr, m. home (P; adv. *heim*, home P,
heima, at home P, *heiman*, from home
P)
heimþinguðr, m. home-caller (gen. sg.
19/2)
hein, f. hone, whetstone (nom. sg. 19/4,
P)
heinberg, n. quarry for whetstones (P)
heita, sv. be called (3rd sg. pret. *hét* P);
(impers. w. dat.) promise (P)
hel, f. hell; *í hel*, dead to death (P)
heldr, adv. rather (10/7)
helgum, see *heilagr*
hellir, m. cavern (gen. sg. 14/3)

hendr, see *hǫnd*
hér, adv. here (P)
herðar, f. pl. shoulders (gen. 6/7)
herfang, n. war-booty (gen. sg. 6/8)
herja, f. warrior-woman (gen. sg. 19/1)
hervápn, n. weapons of war (P)
hestr, m. horse, stallion (P)
hét, see *heita*
heyra (ð), wv. hear (P; 1st sg. pret.
heyrðak 12/1)
Hildr, f. a valkyrie (gen. 1/8)
himinn, m. heaven, the sky (P)
hinn, hin, hit(t), art. and pron. the, this,
that (n. pl. *hin*, these ones P)
hirði-Týr, m. Týr who was watching over
(nom. 6/7)
hjalmfaldinn, a. encased in a helmet (m.
nom. sg. 3/4)
hjálmr, m. helmet (P)
hjarni, m. brain (gen. pl. 19/3; see note)
hjarta, n. heart (P)
hlaupa, sv. leap (3rd sg. pres. *hleypr* P)
hlaut, see *hljóta*
hleypa (t), wv. make to leap, gallop (P)
hleypr, see *hlaupa*
hlið, f. side (P)
hljóta, sv. obtain by lot, get as one's portion (3rd sg. pret. *hlaut* 4/3)
hló, see *hlæja*
hlutr, m. part (P)
hlýr, n. cheek (dat. sg. 1/7)
hlæja, sv. laugh (P; 3rd sg. pret. *hló* P)
hné, see *hníga*
hnefi, m. fist (P)
hneigihlíð, f. sloping hillside (dat. pl. 20/
1)
hníga, sv. sink, fall (3rd sg. pret. *hné* 18/5)
hnot, f. nut (P)
hóf, hófu, see *hefja*
hofreginn, m. temple-deity (acc. sg. 15/
5; see note)
hógreið, f. easy-riding-chariot (gen. sg.
15/6)
hollr, a. loyal, gracious (m. nom. sg. 3/8,
m. gen. sg. 7/7)
hólmganga, f. (island-) duel (P)
holmr, m. island (P; dat. sg. 18/4)
hólmstefna, f. summons to a duel (P)
horn, n. corner (P)
Hœnir, m. 'cockerel', a god (P; gen. sg.
3/7, 7/7, 12/3)

hrafnáss, m. raven-god (gen. sg. 4/4)
hraundrengr, m. gallant of the rubble-
    field (nom. sg. 17/6)
hreðjar, f. pl. testicles (P)
hreingǫrr, a. polished finely-wrought (n.
    dat. sg. 1/7)
hrista (t), wv. shake (3rd pl. pret. refl.
    hristusk 16/3)
Hrungnir, m. a giant (P; gen. 15/8)
Hrungnishjarta, n. 'Hrungnir's heart',
    name of a runic character (P)
hryggr, a. downcast (m. nom. pl. 10/2)
hrynsær, m. falling sea (gen. sg. 11/1;
    see note)
hræ, n. corpse (gen. pl. 11/1)
hræddr, a. scared (P)
hrœra (ð), wv. stir; (refl.) stir oneself,
    move (P)
hrœrir, m. stirrer, rouser (acc. sg. 9/1)
hrøkkva, sv. intr. shrink back (inf. 16/5)
hrundinn, a. kicked (f. nom. sg. 15/3)
hugraun, f. test of courage (P)
hugreynandi, m. he who puts courage
    to the test (nom. sg. 12/3)
hundr, m. hound (acc. sg. 11/2)
hundvíss, m. dog-clever, very wise (P)
hvalr, m. whale (acc. sg. 5/4)
hvar, adv. where (P)
hvarf, n. loss, disappearance (P)
hvárr, hvár, hvárt, pron. each of two (P)
hvártveggja, a. pron. gen. pl. from both
    of them (P)
hvat, n. pron. something (acc. 3/3);
    interrog. pron. what (P; dat. sg. *hví*,
    why, for what reason P)
hvats (= *hvat es*), rel. n. pron. whatever
    (8/7)
hvé, adv. how (1/1)
hvein, see *hvína*
hvergi, adv. nowhere (P), by no means
    (*gat hvergi valdit*, could not lift it by
    any means P)
hvernig, interrog. adv. how (P)
hverr, hver, hvert, pron. each (of more
    than two) (P); interrog. pron. who,
    which (P)
hví, see *hvat*
hvína, sv. whine, whizz (3rd sg. pret.
    hvein 19/3)
hvinverski, a. 'from Hvinir (in Norway)',
    epithet of Þjóðólfr (P; see introduction)

hyggja (hugða), wv. think, intend (P)
Hymir, m. a giant (gen. 9/4)
hyrr, m. fire (gen. sg. *hyrjar* 14/3)
hœlibǫl, n. horror of boasting (acc. sg.
    20/4)
hǫfuð, n. head (P)
hǫgg, n. blow (P; gen. sg. 17/5)
hǫll, f. hall (P)
hǫnd, f. hand (nom. pl. *hendr* 7/8)
hǫpt, n. pl. fetters, gods, divine powers
    (gen. pl. *hapta* 3/3, [supplied] 11/8)
í, prep. (w. acc.) into (9/7, 19/3, P), in
    (13/4); (w. dat.) in (2/3, 7/4, 19/5, P);
    adv. in (it, them) (P)
Ið-, see *unnr*
iðrask (að), wv. (w. gen.) regret (P)
Iðunn, f. goddess of the apples (of eter-
    nal youth) (P)
il, f. foot-sole (acc. pl. *iljar* 17/3; gen.
    pl. *ilja* 13/6)
illa, adv. badly (*urðu illa við hvarf
    Iðunnar*, took Iðunn's disappearance
    badly P)
illr, a. bad, evil (*ills ván*, no good to be
    expected P)
ímunfǫlr, a. battle-pale (m. nom. sg. 17/
    2; see note)
Ing[v]i-freyr, m. a god, the leading male
    Van (gen. 10/6; see note)
inn, adv. in, inside (P); (w. acc.) *inn um*,
    into (P)
inn, in, it, def. art. the (P)
innan, fyrir i. (w. acc.), inside, into (P)
ísarnleikr, m. iron-play, play of iron (dat.
    sg. 14/5)
íss, m. ice (nom. sg. 17/4)

jafngóðr, a. equally good, as good (P)
Jarðar, see *jǫrð*
Járnsaxa, f. 'iron-knife', Þórr's giantess-
    mistress, mother of Magni (P)
jartegn, n. token (*þat til jartegna*, in to-
    ken of that P)
játa (að/tt), wv. (w. dat.), say yes to, agree
    to (P)
jǫrð, f. the earth (P; gen. *Jarðar*, of Þórr's
    mother 14/6)
jǫrmunþrjótr, m. titanic boor (dat. sg. 18/
    8)
jǫtunmóðr, m. giant's fury (P)

jǫtunn, m. giant (P; gen. pl. 14/1; dat. pl. 10/3)

kalla (að), wv. call (P)
kasta (að), wv. (w. dat.) cast, throw (P)
kemr, see *koma*
kenna (d), wv. refer to (P)
kenning, f. kenning, periphrasis (P)
kjósa, sv. choose (P; 1st sg. pres. *kýs* P)
kló, f. claw, talon (P)
kná (tt), pres. pret. v. can, do (3rd pl. pret. *knǫttu* 15/1)
kné, n. knee (P)
koma, sv. come (3rd sg. pres. *kemr* P); (w. dat.) bring, get (3rd sg. pret. *kom* 9/5, P)
kona, f. wife (P)
kostr, m. choice, option (*at ǫðrum kosti*, otherwise, as a second choice P)
kroppr, m. body (P)
kunna (kunna), pres. pret. v. know (3rd sg. pret. *kunni* 9/4)
kvað, kvazk, see *kveða*
kveða, sv. say (3rd sg. pret. *kvað* 3/3, see note; refl. *kvazk*, said P)
kýs, see *kjósa*

lá, see *liggja*
lagsmaðr, m. companion (P)
landamæri, n. boundary, border (P)
langr, a. long (P; m. acc. sg. 8/2); *fyr lǫngu*, adv. long ago (6/2)
láta, sv. let, allow (3rd sg. pres. *lætr* P, pret. *lét* 4/5, 14/2, 18/1, P), leave s-thing behind (3rd pl. pret. *létu þau ýmsi eptir*, each left the other behind in turn P); (refl.) say, declare (3rd sg. pret. *lézk* P), perish (3rd sg. pret. subj. *létisk* P)
launa (að), wv. (w. dat.) reward (P)
laust, see *ljósta*
leggja (lagða), wv. lay (3rd sg. pret. w. *at*, right onto 12/5), lay up (*leggr upp it fyrsta lær*, lays up for himself the first thigh-bone P), build (inf. 1/2), serve up (w. *upp*, 5/6–8), charge (*legg ek þér við níðingskap*, I charge you with cowardice P)
leið, f. road (P)
leiða (dd), wv. lead (2nd sg. pres. subj. 11/6)

leiðask (dd), wv. refl. impers. (w. dat.) get tired of (3rd sg. pret. *Ásum leiddisk hans ofrefli*, the Æsir got tired of his bragging P)
leiðiþírr, m. leading servant, the servant who had led (acc. sg. 11/3; see note)
leika, f. playmate (acc. sg. 12/2; see note)
leikblað, n. swinging leafblade (gen. sg. 12/6)
leir, n. mud, clay (P)
leirjǫtunn, m. clay-giant (P)
leiti, n. hill, rise (P)
leiti, see *annarr*
lemja (lamða), wv. lame, shatter, mutilate (3rd sg. pret. P)
lengi, adv. long, for a long time (17/6)
lesta, sv. injure; (*í hel*) strike dead (sup. *lostit* P)
lét, létisk, létu, lézk, see *láta*
liðinn, pp. passed (P)
liggja, sv. lie (3rd sg. pret. *lá* P)
líki, n. form, likeness (P)
líta, sv. look upon, behold (1st sg. pres. *lítk* 20/5, 3rd pl. pret. *litu* P)
lítill, var. *lítinn*, a. little, small (P)
ljá (ð), wv. (w. dat. pers. and gen. thing) lend (P)
ljósta, sv. strike (3rd sg. pret. impers. *laust þá eldinum í fiðri arnarins*, then the flames struck the eagle's feathers P)
ljótr, m. ugly
loða (dd), wv. stick to (w. *við*, 3rd sg. pret. 7/5)
lokarspænir, m. pl. planed shavings (acc. pl. *lokarspánu*, dat. *lokarspánum* P)
Loki, m. god of mischief (nom. 11/8; P)
lómhugaðr, a. loon-minded; deception-minded (m. nom. sg. 12/5; see note)
Loptr, m. 'air', 'sky', hence 'Lofty', a name for Loki (nom. 8/6)
loptr, m. air, sky (*lopt ok lǫg*, sky and sea P)
losna (að), wv. intr. loosen, come loose (P)
lostit, see *lesta*
lundr, m. tree (gen. sg. 11/4; see note)
læ, n. poison, venom (gen. pl. 11/3)
lækning, f. treatment, cure (P)
lær, n. thigh-bone (P)
lætr, see *láta*
lǫgr, m. sea (*lopt ok lǫg*, sky and sea P)

maðr, m. man (P; gen. pl. *manna* 16/4)

Magni, m. Þórr's son by Járnsaxa (P)

mágr, father-in-law (dat. sg. 15/2)

mál, n. talking (P)

mǫlunautr, m. meal-companion (acc. sg. 8/7)

Máni, m. the moon (gen. 14/8)

mǫr, m. seagull (nom. sg. 3/6)

margspakr, a. much-wise, much-prophetic (m. nom. sg. 3/5)

marr, m. stallion, horse (acc. sg. 2/6)

matr, m. food, meat (P; see also note to 2/6)

mátti, see *mega*

með, prep. (w. dat.) with (8/1), among (5/3, 10/3); adv. with (it) (P)

meðal, prep. (w. gen.) among (3/2), between (6/7)

mega (mátta), pres. pret. v. can, be able to (3rd sg. pret. 8/7)

meig, see *míga*

Meili, m. a kinsman of Þórr (gen. 14/7; see note)

meiri, a. comp. greater, more (P)

meiss, m. basket (P)

mér, see *ek*

merr, f. mare (P)

mest, adv. superl. most (*sem mest*, flat out P)

mey, see *mær*

miðjungr, m. giant (gen. sg. 8/8; see note)

miðr, a. mid, middle of (P)

míga, sv. piss, urinate (3rd sg. pret. *meig* P)

mikill, var. mikinn, a. much (P)

milli, á m., prep. (w. gen.) between (P)

minn, mín, mitt, poss. a. my (P; f. dat. sg. *minni* 13/6; see note)

minni, n. memorial (nom. sg. 13/6; see note)

missa (t), wv. (w. gen.) miss (P)

mjǫk, adv. hugely (16/5)

móðr, m. mood, passion (nom. 14/7)

moli, m. fragment, cube (P)

mót, í m., adv. against (him) (P)

móti, at m., prep. (w. dat.) towards, to meet (2/2)

móti, noun and adv. facing, from the meeting (16/5)

munr, m. difference (*fyrir engan mun*, by no means P)

munstœrandi, a. joy-increasing (f. acc. sg. 11/7)

muna (munda), pres. pret. v. remember (P)

munu (munda), pres. pret. v. shall, will, be ready to (P; 3rd sg. pret. *mundi* 8/4, pret. inf. *mundu verða mikinn fyrir sér*, would make himself a great man P)

myrkbein, n. dark-bone (gen. sg. 16/6)

mæla (t), wv. speak (P; inf. 3/5; 3rd sg. pret. 11/6)

mær, f. maid, girl (acc. sg. *mey* 9/2, 11/8)

mærr, a. glorious (f. acc. sg. 11/7)

mœnir, m. ridge (acc. sg. 19/3)

mœta (tt), wv. (w. dat.) meet (P)

mǫgr, m. son, boy (acc. sg. 5/2)

Mǫkkurkálfi, m. 'muck-calf', a clay-giant made to assist Hrungnir (P)

Mǫrn, f. a giantess, ?a Norwegian river (gen. sg. *Mǫrna[r]* 6/4, see note; 12/8)

ná (ð), wv. get (P)

naddkleif, f. rivet-cliff, shield (nom./acc.? 1/4)

nagr, m. a bird, ?woodpecker (nom. sg. 8/3; see note)

nam, see *nema*

neðan, adv. from down below (P)

neðra, it n., adv. beneath, down under (P)

nefna (d), wv. name, appoint (P)

nema, adv. unless (11/5, P)

nema, sv. take; (w. inf.) begin to (3rd sg. pret. *nam* 3/5)

níðingskapr, m. villainy, cowardice (P)

niðr, adv. down (P)

níu, card. num. nine (P)

Njǫrðr, m. eldest of the Vanir, father of Freyr and Freyja (P)

Nóatúnir, f. pl. 'ships' enclosures (= ocean)', Njǫrðr's home (P)

norðan, adv. from the north (P)

norðr, adv. north, northwards (P)

nú, adv. now (P)

nýkominn, a. newly arrived (f. nom. sg. 10/4)

nær, comp. adv. near, close by (P)

næst, superl. adv. nearest (*því næst*, the next moment P)

nǫkkurr, nǫkkur, nǫkkurt, a. certain, some (P)

ó-, neg. pref. un-, not (w. *fyr -skǫmmu* 2/ 4)

Óðinn, m. father-figure of the Æsir (P; gen. 19/5)

of (= *um*), pcl. (1/6, 3/5, 8/5, 8/6, 9/5, 13/ 5, 14/1, 14/2, 16/1, 17/7, 19/7, 20/8)

of (= *um*), prep. (w. acc.) over (8/2, P), across (*of (...) þvert* P), around (*batt um skegg* P)

ofan, adv. from above, down (4/6, 6/8, P)

ofrefli, n. bragging, excess (P)

ofrmæli, n. big words (P)

ok, conj. and (1/8, 6/1, 10/7, 11/3, 12/5, 16/3, 19/1, P), again (*ok var ekki soðit* P), especially as (*ok þat at* P)

ók, see *aka*

okbjǫrn, m. yoke-bear (acc. sg. 6/4)

ólágr, a. 'unlow', high (gen. pl. 18/2)

ólauss, a. 'unloose', rigid (f. nom. sg. 19/ 6)

ollu, see *valda*

ór, prep. (w. dat.) out of (20/1, P)

orð, n. word (P)

orðinn, see *verða*

orðstírr, m. renown (P)

ort, see *yrkja*

ósvífrandi, m. disobliger (nom. sg. 5/7; see note)

ótti, m. fear, dread (nom. sg. 14/2)

óvarliga, adv. carelessly, unawares (P)

oxans, oxanum, øxna, see *uxi*

písl, f. torture (P)

rǫ́, f. sailyard (nom. sg. 7/5)

ráða, sv. (w. dat.) decide (P; 3rd sg. pres. *ræðr* P)

rammr, a. strong, mighty (m. acc. sg. 7/ 5)

randar, randa, see *rǫnd*

ránfengr, m. robbed haul (P)

rangr, a. wrong (P)

rann, see *renna*

rasta, see *rǫst*

rauðr, a. red (n. indef. acc. sg. 20/3)

raufa (að), wv. break up, put out (*raufa seyðinn* P)

regin, n. pl. the gods, divine rulers (nom. 7/3, 10/8)

reginn, m. ruler-deity (nom. sg. 12/6)

reið, see *ríða*

reiða (dd), wv. lift, swing (P)

reiði-Týr, m. chariot-Týr (gen. 20/3; see note)

reiðr, a. wroth, angry (P; m. nom. sg. *[v]reiðr* 11/6)

reimuðr, m. ghost, spectre (acc. sg. 7/6)

rein, f. strip of land, land (gen. sg. 16/6)

reka, sv. tr. drive (P)

renna, sv. run (3rd sg. pret. *rann* P)

reyna (d), wv. test, try (P)

ríða, sv. ride (3rd sg. pret. *reið* P)

ristubragð, n. runic character (P)

ritaðr, pp. written (P)

róa, sv. row (pp. m. nom. sg. *róinn* P)

rúni, m. intimate friend, confidant (nom. sg. 8/5; dat. sg. 17/7, see note)

ryð, n. rust (gen. sg. 20/4)

ræðr, see *ráða*

rǫgnir, m. prince (nom. sg. 4/5)

rǫnd, f. shield-rim (gen. sg. *randar* 18/4, gen. pl. *randa* 17/2)

rǫst, f. four miles (gen. pl. *rasta* P)

sá, see *sjá*

sá, sú, þat, pron. this (P)

saga, f. story (P)

sagna, see *sǫgn*

sakna, wv. (w. gen.) miss, feel the loss of (P)

saman, adv. together (P)

sár, n. wound (gen. pl. 20/2)

sás (= *sá es*), rel. pron. (he) whom (7/3)

sat, see *sitja*

seðr (= *senn*), adv. at the same time (15/ 7)

segja (sagða), wv. say, tell (P; pres. part. dat. pl. *segjǫndum* 2/1; pp. n. nom. pl. *sǫgð* P)

sék, see *sjá*

selja (d), wv. give (P)

sem, adv. as (P)

sér (14/1), see *sjá*

sér, dat. refl. pron. to him (4/2, 9/1, P)

sét, see *sjá*

setja (tt), wv. set, put (refl. 3rd sg. pres. *sezk* P, pret. *settisk*, settled down 2/5)

seyðir, m. cooking fire (P; acc. sg. 2/8)

síð, adv. late (P)

síðan, adv. then (6/1, P), later (9/8), afterwards (12/1)

síðarst, adv. superl. last, latest (P)

Sif, f. 'family-cohesion', Þórr's wife (P)

síga, sv. sink, fall (refl. inf. *sígask* 4/6, P)

sigr, m. victory (P)

Sigyn, f. Loki's wife (gen. 7/2)

sik, refl. pron. acc. himself, herself, itself, themselves (P)

sinn, n. time, occasion (P)

sinn, sín, sitt, poss. a. his, her, its, their (m. acc. sg. 16/8)

sitja, sv. sit (3rd sg. pret. *sat* P)

sjá, sv. see (1st sg. pres. 1/5; 3rd sg. pres. 14/1; 3rd sg. pret. *sá* P, sup. *sét* P)

sjóða, sv. boil, cook (sup. *soðit* P)

Skaði, f. 'Scandinavia', daughter of Þjazi and divorced wife of Njǫrðr (P)

skafa, sv. shave (3rd pl. pret. *skófu* 13/1)

skál, f. drinking bowl (P)

skammr, a. short (*fyr óskǫmmu*, adv. not a short time ago 2/4)

skapt, n. shaft (nom. pl. *skǫpt* 13/2)

skarpr, a. sharp (m. dat. sg. 18/6)

skaut, see *skjóta*

skegg, n. beard (P)

skenkja (Mod Ger, Du *schenken*), wv. serve, pour (P)

skildinum, see *skjǫldr*

skjǫldr, m. shield (P; dat. sg. def. *skildinum* P)

skjóta, sv. shoot, whip (3rd sg. pret. *skaut* P)

skjótt, adv. quickly (13/1)

skófu, see *skafa*

skógr, m. wood (P)

skora (að), wv. challenge (P)

skorta (t), wv. impers. (w. dat. pers. and gen. thing) be lacking (P)

skrækja (t), wv. screech (3rd sg. pret. impers. *skrækti*, there was screeching P)

skulu (skylda), pres. pret. v. shall (1st sg. pres. *skalk* 1/1; 2nd sg. pres. *skalt* 11/5)

skutill, m. plate, trencher; harpoon (dat. sg. 4/4)

slá, sv. strike (3rd pl. pret. *slógu* P)

Sleipnir, m. Óðinn (P)

slíðrliga, adv. ferociously (6/1)

slitna (að), wv. tear (P; intrans. w. *sundr*, tear asunder 8/3)

slógu, see *slá*

smár, a. small (P)

snerta (t), wv. quaff quickly (P)

snót, f. gentlewoman (gen. sg. 2/2)

snúa (ð), wv. prepare (*til seyðis*, for the cooking-fire P)

snytrir, m. wisdom-teacher (nom. sg. 3/3)

soðit, see *sjóða*

soðna (að), wv. intr. become boiled (P)

solginn, a. having swallowed; gorged (m. dat. sg. 16/2)

sonr, see *sunr*

sorgœrr, a. mad with pain (m. acc. sg. 9/2; see note)

sóttan, sótti, see *sœkja*

sprunginn, a. bursting, near dead with exhaustion (m. nom. sg. 8/6; see note)

spyrja (spurða), wv. (w. acc. pers. and gen. thing) ask, find out (3rd pl. pret *spurðu* P)

stál, n. steel, steel blade (gen. pl. 19/7)

standa, sv. stand (3rd sg. pres. *stendr* P, pret. *stóð* 19/8, P), stick up (sup. *staðit* P)

stefnulag, n. appointment (P)

steinn, m. stone (P)

stendr, see *standa*

sterkr, m. strong (P)

stjarna, f. star (P)

stóð, see *standa*

stokkinn, a. soaked (f. nom. sg. 19/7)

stórfetaðr, pp. long-striding (P)

stórr, a. big, great (P)

stund, f. time, hour (P)

stǫðugr, a. steady, stable (P)

stǫðva (að), wv. stop (P)

stǫng, f. staff, pole (P; gen. sg. 7/8, dat. sg. 6/8)

sundr, adv. asunder, apart (8/4, 15/8, P)

sunnan, adv. from the south (10/4)

sunr, m. son (nom. sg. 14/6; *sonr* 13/3, P)

svá, adv. so, thus (11/6, 12/1, 17/4, P), just as (w. *sem* P)

svall, see *svella*

svangr, a. hungry (m. nom. sg. 6/2, 8/5)

svara, wv. answer (P)

svardagi, m. oath, promise (P)

svát (= *svá at*), adv. so (...) that (19/5; *of veg langan...svát*, over such a long way that 8/2–3; *svá þat* 12/1) sveik, see *svíkja*

sveinn, m. swain, lad (poss. dat. 19/4)

sveipr, m. fold, commotion, flurry (nom. sg. 13/4)

sveiti, m. blood (gen. sg. 8/3)

svella, sv. swell (3rd sg. pret. *svall* 14/7)

sviðna (að), wv. intr. singe (3rd sg. pres. 13/3)

svíkja, sv. deceive, betray (3rd sg. pret. *sveik* 12/2)

Svǫlnir, m. a name for Óðinn (gen. sg. 15/7; see note)

sær, m. sea (P)

sætt, f. agreement, terms (P)

sættargjǫrð, f. peace-agreement (P)

sœkja (sótta), wv. seek (3rd sg. pret. P), look for (*eptir* w. dat. P), visit (P; *lét sóttan*, paid a call on 14/2)

sœma (sómða), wv. impers. (w. dat.) be fitting, suitable for (3rd sg. pret. P)

sǫgð, see *segja*

sǫgn, f. speech, tale; band of men (gen. pl. 2/1, 9/1)

søkkva (t), wv. (w. dat.) make to sink, destroy (P)

tá, f. toe (P)

ta[ð]lhreinn, m. dung-reindeer, ox (nom. sg. 3/2; see note)

taka, sv. take (3rd sg. pres. *tekr* P, 3rd sg. pret. *tók* P, pl. *tóku* P, pp. m. nom. sg. *tekinn* P, fem. nom. pl. *teknar* P); (w. *af*), stop (*tók þá af fluginn*, his flight then came to a standstill P); (w. *upp*), lift up (P)

tekinn, teknar, tekr, see *taka*

teygja (ð), wv. entice (P)

tíðindi, n. pl. tidings, news (P)

tíðr, a. eager (m. nom. sg. 17/8)

til, prep. (w. gen.) to (*til Ásgarðs, bús, Iðunnar*, P), for (*illt til matar*, not good for food P), for the purpose of (*til seyðis* P), in (*til yfirbóta* P), as (*til varnanar* P); adv. to him (*gengu til* P), of it (*dœmi til* P), up (*litu til* P); conj. until (*til þess er, þar til er* P)

tindóttr, a. pointed, spiked (P)

tíva, tívi, see *týr*

tók, tóku, see *taka*

tormiðlaðr, a. divided with difficulty (m. nom. sg. 3/1)

tré, n. tree (P)

trjóna, f. snout (gen. sg. 17/7)

troll, n. troll (gen. sg. 17/7; var. *trǫll* P)

trygglauss, a. unsure, unsafe (n. acc. sg. 1/6)

trǫll, see *troll*

tveir, tvær, tvau, card. num. two (P)

tvíhenda (d), wv. hurl with both hands (P)

týframr, a. divinely prominent (gen. pl. 1/5)

týr, m. a god, formerly the proper noun *Týr* (dat. sg. *tívi* 8/1; gen. pl. *tíva* 1/5; dat. pl. *tívum* 3/1; cf. also *birgi-Týr, hirði-Týr* and *reiði-Týr*)

ulfr, m. wolf (nom. sg. 2/2, gen. sg. 8/4)

Ullr, m. 'brilliance', a god (gen. 15/1)

um, prep., see *of*

und, prep. under, beneath (w. acc. 17/3; w. dat. 14/8)

undir, prep. (w. acc.) under (P), below (*undir Ásgarð* P); *undir hǫnd*, across the chest (P)

unnr, f. wave 10/3 (gen. sg. *unnar ið[u]*, of the wave of the eddy 10/3–4; see note)

unz, adv. until (11/1)

upp, adv. up (5/8, P)

upphiminn, m. heaven above (nom. 16/ 4)

uppi, adv. up (P)

urð, f. scree (P)

urðu, urðut, see *verða*

út, adv. out (P)

uxi, m. ox (gen. sg. def. *oxans* P, dat. sg. def. *oxanum* P, gen. pl. *øxna* P)

vá, see *vega*

vaða, sv. wade (sup. *vaðit* P)

valda, sv. (w. dat.) wield, lift (sup. *valdit* P), cause (inf. 3/4; 3rd pl. pret. *ollu* 17/2)

Valhǫll, f. 'hall of the slain' or 'choice hall', feasting hall of Óðinn's dead warriors (P)

valkǫstr, m. slaughter-heap (gen. sg. 3/ 6)

vallar, see *vǫll*

valr, m. falcon (P)

valshamr, m. falcon's shape (P)

ván, f. expectation (*ills ván*, no good to be expected P)

vanr, a. accustomed (P)

vápn, n. weapon (P)

vápnlauss, a. unarmed, without weapons (P)

var, see *vera*

vár, n. spring, spring-time (gen. pl. 5/2; see note)

varð, varðat, see *verða*

varnan, f. precaution (P)

varnendr, m. pl. defenders (nom. 4/8)

váru, vǫru, see *vera*

vas, vasa, vasat, see *vera*

váttr, m. witness (nom. sg. 16/8)

vé, n. sanctuary (nom. pl. 15/4)

veðja (dd), wv. bet, pledge (P)

vega, sv. fight; *vega at* (w. dat.), attack (3rd sg. pret. *vá at* P)

vegr, m. way (nom. sg. 14/8; acc. sg. 8/2)

veita (tt), wv. grant, propose (P)

vel, adv. well, heartily (P)

vél, f. trick, trickery (dat. pl. 11/5)

vélsparr, a. trick-sparing (m. nom. pl. 4/7)

véltr, pp. tricked, tricked out of one's mind (m. nom. sg. 11/5; see note)

vera, sv. be (3rd sg. pres. *er* P; 3rd sg. pret. *vas* 3/1, 6/2, 8/6, 10/3, 15/3; neg. *vasa* 2/7, *vasat* 3/7; sup. *verit* P); (as auxiliary v.) have (3rd pl. pret. *vǫru* 4/7, 10/7)

verða, sv. become, be (3rd sg. pret. *varð* 7/1, 13/4; 3rd pl. pret. *urðu* P, neg. *urðut* 10/1; pp. *orðinn* P), make (*verða mikinn fyrir sér*, make a great man of himself P); (w. infin.) have to, be obliged to (3rd sg. pret. 8/5, neg. *varðat* 17/5)

vett, n. lid, drum (gen. sg. 1/8: see note)

við, prep. (w. acc.) with (*við hana* P), (close) to (w. acc. 7/1, 7/5, 7/8; *við kroppinn, annan enda* P), by (*við borgarvegginn* P), at (*við hǫggit, hvarf* P); (w. dat.) off (18/8); adv. at it (*skrækti við* P)

víðr, a. wide (P)

viðr, m. tree, forest (acc. pl. *viðu* P)

víg, n. killing (P)

vígfrekr, a. combat-fierce (m. nom. sg. 4/6)

vígligr, a. warlike, ready for war (m. acc. sg. 16/7)

víkr, f. pumice-stone (nom. sg. 19/7)

vilja (vilda), pres. pret. v. will, want (P; 3rd pl. pret. *vildu* 17/4)

vinarauga, n. friendly eye (P)

ving-, pref. wind- (w. *vagna* 4/5; see note)

Vingnir, m. possibly a name for Þórr (gen. 19/2)

ving-rǫgnir, see *rǫgnir*

vinr, m. friend (nom. sg. 3/7, 4/4; gen. sg. 7/7)

vit, dual 1st pl. pron. we two, the two of us (P)

vita (vissa), pres. pret. v. know; (w. *til*) know of (3rd sg. pret. subj. P)

vreiðr, see *reiðr*

vændr (from *væna*, wv. think, judge), a. accused (w. dat. 2/8)

vǫgn, f. whale, dolphin (gen. pl. 4/5, 16/7; see notes)

vǫll, f. terrain, (battle-) field (gen. sg. 6/6)

vǫlva, f. sorceress, witch (P)

yfir, prep. (w. acc.) over (*yfir sik, yfir Þór* P), across (*fram yfir Þór* P), through (*yfir Élivága* P)

yfirbœtr, f. pl. atonement, compensation (P)

yrkja (orta), wv. compose (3rd sg. pret. *orti*, sup. *ort* P)

ýmsi, n. pl. in turn (P)

þá, adv. then (7/1, P), this was when (10/3); rel. conj. when (*þá er* P)

þá (13/7), **þák** (20/7), see *þiggja*

þaðan, adv. thence, after that (17/6)

þannig, adv. there, to that place (P)

þar, adv. there (18/5, 19/5, P), in that place (16/2, P); conj. *þar til er*, until (P); rel. conj. *þar er*, where (P)

þars (= *þar es*), adv. where (2/5, 4/7)

þás (= *þá es*), adv. when (15/5, 16/7)

þás (= *þá es*), rel. pron. f. acc. sg. (her) who (9/3)

þat, n. pron. that, this (5/6, 6/2, 10/2, P; dat. sg. *því* 3/4, 17/2, P)

þats (= *þat es*), that is (13/5)

þátti, see *þekkja*

þau, see *þeir*

þegar, adv. straightaway, immediately (P)

þegn, m. thegn (dat. pl. 5/3)

þeir, þær, þau, pl. pron. they, these (P; f. *þær* 20/6)

þekkiligr, a. graceful, handsome (m. nom. sg. 5/3)

þekkja (þátta), wv. know (3rd sg. pret. *þátti* 16/8)

þenna, see *þessi*

þér, 2nd pl. pron. you (P)

þessi, þessi, þetta, pron. this (m. acc. sg. *þenna* P)

þiggja, sv. receive (1st sg. pret. *þá* 13/7, *þák* 20/7)

þing, n. meeting, assembly (P; dat. sg. 10/6)

Þjálfi, m. Þórr's servant, a man (P)

Þjazi, m. a giant (P; gen. sg. 1/8)

þjórhlutr, m. bull-portion (acc. pl. 5/8)

þjǫkkr, a. thick (P)

þollr, fir-tree, tree (dat. sg. 3/8)

þora (ð), wv. dare (P)

Þorleifr, m. the poet's benefactor (dat. 1/4, 13/8, 20/8)

Þórr, m. god of thunder (P; gen. sg. 8/5)

þótti, þóttusk, see *þykkja*

þrévetr, a. three winters old (P)

þriggja, see *þrír*

þrimr, see *þrír*

þrír, þrjár, þrjú, card. num. three (gen. *þriggja* 1/6, P, dat. *þrimr* P)

Þrúðvangar, m. pl. 'strength-plains',

Þórr's residence (P)

þruma, f. peal of thunder (P)

Þrymheimr, m. Hrungnir's abode (P)

þrymseil, f. cracking rope, whip (gen. sg. 5/4; see note)

þú, 2nd sg. pron. thou, you (11/5, P)

þungr, a. heavy (m. nom. sg. 8/6)

þvert, of (...) þ., prep. (w. acc.) athwart, across (P)

því, see *þat*

þykkja (þótta), wv. seem (3rd sg. pret. *þótti* P); (refl.) think (3rd pl. pret. *þóttusk* P)

þyrma (ð), wv. (w. dat.) show mercy to (3rd sg. pret. neg. *þyrmðit* 16/1)

þær, see *þeir*

Ægir, m. a god of the sea, Bragi's interlocutor (P)

æsir, see *áss*

ǫglir, m. bird of prey (gen. sg. 12/7)

ǫl-Gefjun, f. nursing-Gefjun (nom. 20/2; see note)

ǫl-Gefn, f. nourishing-Gefn, probably Iðunn (gen. 11/2)

ǫndurgoð, n. ski-god, ski-goddess (gen. sg. 7/4)

ǫrn, m. eagle (nom. sg. 2/5; P, dat. sg. def. *erninum* P, gen. sg. def. *arnarins* P)

ǫxl, f. shoulder (P)

Select Bibliography

Aasen, Ivar, *Norsk Ordbog med dansk Forklaring*, 4th ed. (Christiania [Oslo], 1918)

Bately, Janet, ed., *The Old English Orosius*, Early English Texts Society, s.s. 6 (1980)

Berg, Mette Tellander and Gunnar Berg, eds., *NAF Veibok*, Norges Automobil-Forbund (Oslo, 1985)

Bjarni Aðalbjarnarson, ed., *Heimskringla I*, 3rd edition, ÍF 26 (Reykjavík, 1979)

Bjarni Einarsson, ed., *Ágrip af Nóregskonunga Sǫgum. Fagrskinna – Nóregs Konunga Tal*, ÍF 29 (Reykjavík, 1985)

Clunies Ross, Margaret, *Prolonged Echoes: Old Norse Myths in Medieval Northern Society*, Studies in Northern Civilization 7 (Odense, 1994)

Davidson, Daphne, 'Earl Hákon and his Poets' (unpublished D. Phil. dissertation, Oxford University, 1983)

Faulkes, Anthony, 'Descent from the Gods', *MScan* 11 (1982), 92–125

———, ed., *Snorri Sturluson: Edda: Prologue and Gylfaginning* (Oxford, 1982)

———, ed., *Codex Trajectinus: the Utrecht Manuscript of the Prose Edda*, Early Icelandic Manuscripts in Facsimile, 15 (Copenhagen, 1985)

———, trans., *Snorri Sturluson: Edda* (London, 1987)

Finnur Jónsson, ed., *Den norsk-islandske Skjaldedigtning*, A I, II, B I, II (Copenhagen, 1912–15)

———, ed., *Edda Snorra Sturlusonar* (Copenhagen, 1931)

———, 'Kenningers led-omstilling og tmesis', *ANF* 49 (1933), 1–23

Fritzner, Johannes, *Ordbog over det gamle norske Sprog*, 3 vols. (Christiania [Oslo], 1860–8)

Gutenbrunner, Siegfried, *Die germanischen Götternamen der antiken Inschriften*, Rheinische Beiträge und Hülfsbücher zur germanischen Philologie und Volkskunde 24 (Halle a. S., 1936)

Hastrup, Kirsten, *Culture and History in Medieval Iceland: an Anthropological Analysis of Structure and Change* (Oxford, 1985)

Hollander, Lee M., *The Skalds: A Selection of Their Poems with Introduction and Notes* (Princeton, 1945)

Holtsmark, Anne, 'Myten om *Idun og Tjatse* i Tjodolvs *Haustlǫng*', *ANF* 64 (1949), 1–73

Jakob Benediktsson, ed., *Íslendingabók. Landnámabók*, ÍF 1[.1–2] (Reykjavík, 1986)

Jón Jóhannesson, *Gerðir Landnámabókar* (Reykjavík, 1941)

Jón Sigurðsson, ed. *et al.*, *Edda Snorra Sturlusonar*, Sumptibus Legati Arnamagnaeani, 3 vols. (Copenhagen, 1848–87)

Jónas Kristjánsson, *Eddas and Sagas: Iceland's Medieval Literature*, trans. P. Foote (Reykjavík, 1992)

Kiil, Vilhelm, 'Tjodolfs Haustlǫng', *ANF* 74 (1959), 1–104

Kock, E.A., *Notationes Norrœnæ*, 2 vols. (Lund, 1923–41)

——, ed., *Den norsk-isländska skaldediktningen*, 2 vols. [printed in 1 vol.] (Lund, 1946–9)

Kuhn, Hans, *Das Dróttkvætt* (Heidelberg, 1982)

Magnús Finnbogason, ed. *Edda Snorra Sturlusonar* (Reykjavík, 1952)

Marold, Edith, *Kenningkunst. Ein Beitrag zu einer Poetik der Skaldendichtung*, Quellen und Forschungen zur Sprach- und Kulturgeschichte der germanischen Völker, n.s. 80 (Berlin and New York, 1983)

North, Richard, *Pagan Words and Christian Meanings*, Costerus, n.s. 81 (Amsterdam and Atlanta GA, 1991)

Olrik, Axel, and Hans Ellekilde, *Nordens Gudeverden*, 2 vols. [numbered consecutively] (Copenhagen, 1926–51)

Olsen, B. M., 'Om ordet seyðir', *Aarbøger for Nordisk Oldkyndighed og Historie* (1909), 317–331

Reichardt, Konstantin, *Studien zu den Skalden des 9. und 10. Jahrhunderts* (Leipzig, 1928)

Schmeidler, B., ed., *Magistri Adam Bremensis Gesta Hammaburgensis Ecclesiae Pontificum*, Monumenta Germaniae Historica, Scriptores Rerum Germanicarum 2, 3rd edition (Hanover and Leipzig, 1917)

Sigurður Nordal, ed., *Codex Wormianus (The Younger Edda): MS No. 242 fol. in the Arnemagnean Collection in the University Library of Copenhagen*, Corpus Codicum Islandicorum Medii Aevi, 2 (Copenhagen, 1931)

————, ed., *Egils saga Skalla-Grímssonar*, ÍF 2 (Reykjavík, 1933)

————, *Snorri Sturluson*, 2nd ed. (Reykjavík, 1973)

Simpson, Jacqueline, w. drawings by Eva Wilson, *Everyday Life in the Viking Age* (London, 1967)

Turville-Petre, [E.O.]G., *Origins of Icelandic Literature* (Oxford, 1953, repr. w. corrections, 1967)

————, *Scaldic Poetry* (Oxford, 1976)

Unger, C.R., ed., *Flateyjarbók*, 3 vols. (Christiania [Oslo], 1860–8)

de Vries, Jan, *Altgermanische Religionsgeschichte*, 2nd ed., 2 vols. (Berlin, 1956–7)

Wessén, Elias, ed., *Codex Regius of the Younger Edda: MS No. 2367 4to in the old Royal Collection in the Royal Library of Copenhagen*, Corpus Codicum Islandicorum Medii Aevi, 15 (Copenhagen, 1940)

Whaley, Diana, *Heimskringla:An Introduction*, Viking Society for Northern Research, Text Series 8 (London, 1991)

Williams, Mary Wilhelmine, *Social Scandinavia in the Viking Age* (New York, 1920, repr. 1971)

Åkerblom, Axel, 'Bidrag till tolkningen af skaldekvad', *ANF* 15 (1899), 269–74.